Silvio Borner

Internationalization of Industry

An Assessment in the Light of a Small Open Economy (Switzerland)

With 17 Figures and 45 Tables

Springer-Verlag
Berlin Heidelberg New York
London Paris Tokyo

Professor Dr. Silvio Borner
Institut für Angewandte Wirtschaftsforschung
Universität Basel
Leonhardsgraben 3, CH-4051 Basel
Switzerland

ISBN-13: 978-3-642-71424-5 e-ISBN-13: 978-3-642-71422-1
DOI: 10.1007/978-3-642-71422-1

Library of Congress Cataloging-in-Publication Data. Borner, Silvio. Internationalization of industry. Bibliography: p.
1. International economic relations. 2. Investments, Foreign. 3. Switzerland-Foreign economic relations. 4. Switzerland-Industries. I. Title.
HF1411.B6679 1986 338.09494 86-15618

Softcover reprint of the hardcover 1st edition 1986

Typesetting, printing and bookbinding: Appl, Wemding
2142/3140-543210

"(T)he interests of scientific economics would be better served by a more modest approach. (T)he true functions of analytical economics are best described informally: to organize our necessarily incomplete perceptions about the economy, to see connections that the untutored eye would miss, to tell plausible - sometimes even convincing - causal stories with the help of a few central principles, and to make rough quantitative judgements about the consequences of economic policy and other exogenous events. (T)he end product of economic analysis is likely to be a collection of models contingent on society's circumstances (...) and not a single monolithic model for all seasons ...".

ROBERT SOLOW (1985)

Preface

About 10 years ago, the first very small steps towards this book were taken. The starting point was marked by the deep and sudden slump of the Swiss economy in the mid-seventies: a crisis wiping out about 10 percentage points of GNP and employment within just two years. To this writer, it was clear from the beginning that neither the exogenous shocks nor the structural changes were in fact exogenous or structural. They were given and shaped by global forces. They were part and parcel of capitalist development.

There is no other highly developed country in the world which is so extremely and integrally exposed to world-wide currents of financial and economic changes as Switzerland. The degree and dimensions of openness of the Swiss economy led to the formulation of our research approach for studying the internationalization of the economy, a topic theoretically and politically developed in this book. Empirical evidence relates to our study of Swiss experience.

A well-known Swiss-American economist offered the following comment on our previous work on the internationalization of industry: "You are very good in raising interesting questions ..." What was undoubtedly meant as a criticism was received as a compliment. Too much talent and too many research efforts are, in my opinion, wasted by research programs which place technique over substance. This unfortunate development in our profession has already greatly reduced the social utility of economists. What good is it to answer with technical brilliance questions which no one outside the ivory tower ever even asked! And what damage is done to the science and practice of economics when impeccable, formally logical - yet wholly irrelevant - models are carelessly applied to real world issues?

Many people have contributed to this latest research project and to this report. Dr. Barbara Stuckey has again lent me her amazing editing talent. Without her, loose ends and bad English could trap the reader almost anywhere. My personal research assistants Rolf Bürgin, Kuno Hämisegger, and Carlo Knöpfel carried out most of the empirical work. My friend and colleague, Prof. Cuno Pümpin shared with me the task of interviewing Swiss business leaders and advised our research team in his capacity as a specialist of business strategies.

The project on New Forms of Internationalization was mainly financed by the Swiss Science Foundation (grant 4.6899.0.83.09), partly by the Swiss Federal Trade Office (BAWI) and the "Stiftung zur Förderung der rechtlichen und wirtschaftlichen Forschung an der Universität Basel".

Last but not least, I thank my long-term secretary, Ms. Esther Weyermann who suffered gracefully through the successive versions of the manuscript and patiently assembled bits and pieces to produce the finished product.

A last thank you goes to those business leaders who gave us the opportunity of discussing many aspects of entrepreneurial strategy in personal and lengthy interviews, to those who collaborated in our written survey, and finally to those who consented to our using their firms as case studies.

The usual disclaimer about the exclusive responsibility of the author for all errors of omission and/or commission fully applies.

Basle, April 1986 SILVIO BORNER

Table of Contents

Abreviations

DCs	Developing Countries
FDI	Foreign Direct Investment
GDP	Gross Domestic Product
LDCs	Low Developed Countries
MNEs	Multi National Enterprises
NFI	New Forms of Internationalization
NFII	New Forms of International Investment
NFEF	New Forms of Export Financing
NICs	Newly Industrializing Countries
OMAs	Orderly Marketing Argreements
R&D	Research and Development
SMEs	Small and Medium Enterprises
VERs	Voluntary Export Restraints

Part I

Interdependency Through Internationalization in an Historical and Global Perspective

Chapter 1

The "International Disorder": Some Historical Digressions on the Structure of Global Interdependencies

The highly visible political phenomenon which motivated the author of this book to undertake, structure, and carry out this study was the "growth of protectionism" in the global economy. We want to emphasize at the outset, however, that this investigation is not a study about protectionism in the traditional sense. While the general aim of our work was to examine the circumstances surrounding government policies which are aimed at protecting domestic economic activities from foreign competition, the specific goal was to study entrepreneurial response to these policies. Thus the particular object of our detailed research is New Forms of International Investment (NFII) and New Forms of Export Financing (NFEF), what is referred to jointly as New Forms of Internationalization (NFI). The rise and utilization of these new forms cannot be understood without reference to the current employment of protectionist policies by national governments in both the industrialized and the developing countries. At the same time our approach (moving from protectionism to new forms of entrepreneurial behaviour) enables us to situate political conflicts within a long-term historical context. Thereby we are able to identify dogmatic, ideological, and out-dated theories for what they really are and thus to identify patterns of inconsistency between domestic policies and global realities.

Beginning with Adam SMITH, economists of all political shadings (and even shady economists!) have argued that the expansion of international trade is a - if not the - principle source of the accumulation of material wealth. The economic argument is in fact rather trivial. Expanding markets allow increased production to be sold, which in turn induces specialization. This is followed by rationalization and mechanization. Taken together, these various steps of the economic growth process lead to expanded productivity of the single worker. In and of itself, this argument has no geographical dimension, that is, it has no relationship to nation states or to political borders. It is, however, related to the size of the market, i.e. the quantity of demand. Markets can be expanded by increasing the total level of per-capita consumption of commodities, by population increase, by commercializing more and more spheres of human life, and/or by expanding the geographical borders of the market area. International trade is thus one of four possible motors of growth in the capitalist market economy. Hence the importance of colonialism in the past and the importance of trade agreements and common markets in the present.

Economists begin to argue among themselves, however, when it comes to the evaluation of who benefits from an increase in the quantity of consumable commodities: the producer or the consumer, the employee or the employer, the rural or the urban area, the more developed or the less developed country? One group insists that the theory of comparative advantage is sufficient proof that areas - regions or nations – with different levels of development can both benefit from free trade relations. Others recognize the cosmopolitan nature of this argument: the global economy grows but the question "who benefits?" is not necessarily answered by the theory of free trade. Such economists have postulated that the internationalization of domestic markets in a country with a relatively low level of economic development can lead to "a blockage of the creative function of competition". (SENGHAAS 1979:60, authors' translation). Local entrepreneurs are not able to keep up with the pace of competition.

The study of economic history indeed reveals that free trade has traditionally been the argument of the stronger economic actors and that the weaker actors have argued against free trade, defended their borders, and/or worked implicitly against the full implementation of policies of trade liberalization. The most progressive, the most dynamic, and the most innovative entrepreneurs, firms, sectors, regions, and nations have been the most vehement defenders of free trade, their absolute advantages and profits being greater. The decisive issues become political: the struggle for and against free trade and the means by which a competitive economic environment is institutionalized. In the realm of international trade each participating state must "voluntarily" give up constituent elements of its national sovereignty – either to an international institution or simply to the principle and the consequences of a free market economy. Capitalist institutions, that is, the private, decentralized, market-oriented, competitive way of organizing and carrying out economic life must be accepted.

There are three situations in which a government can be induced to give up part of its sovereignty in favor of the benefits of free trade:

- The global economy is characterized by protectionism and stagnation. Interested countries forge a trade liberalization agreement in order to take advantage of the situation: enlightened self-interest – the ideal of the free trade theoretician (cf. KRUEGER 1985).
- The global economy is clearly in a growth phase and with the liberalization of trade receives additional growth impulses. With a minimum of risk a country can "climb aboard a fast moving train".
- A country is forced to open its borders to trade.

The first case is perhaps logically possible but not really politically probable since most sectors of any national economy would also be suffering from stagnation, over-capacity, etc. Under such circumstances few governments would be politically able to open their borders to foreign competition. We share YOFFIE's conviction that international trade has – under all circumstances – a strong political component: "Because international trade relations are political, the theory and practice of world commerce usually diverge. The problem with traditional approaches to international trade is that they have lacked perspective on politics. Trade barriers are erected for political reasons, and they operate in a political environment. This means that who gets what, when, and how is a function not only of the market but also of bargaining, implementation, coercion, and the use of symbols." (YOFFIE 1983:18 and 14). To talk about a "politicization of the economy" is historically naive. The framework and nature of the market economy is inherently political. The following short sketch of the "old economic order" and the transition to the current "new economic disorder" is included as an illustration of this crucial

Table 1-1. Average Growth of GNP for 16 OECD Countries 1870–1979

	1870–1950	1950–1973	1973–1979
Average yearly growth	2.3	4.9	2.5

Source: MADDISON (1982:126)

point. Interestingly, the public choice approach to political economy has "rediscovered" international economics. Contrary to normative and/or axiomatic theories of trade, this approach tries to explain positively why tariffs, quotas, and other protectionist measures are a highly likely result of political markets.[1]

The epitaph "Pax Americana", written on the tomb of the 25 years of post-war prosperity, refers to a political framework within which economic activity flourished. Pax Romana and Pax Britannica shared this characteristic: a politically guaranteed peace by a world power in whose realm long-distance trade and inter-regional economic relations could come into existence and blossom. The dominance of the USA in the post-war era has not been only economic, it has been political and technological as well. At the end of World War II, the USA stood in the shoes Great Britain had worn a century earlier. It was the economy with the momentary upper hand – it could only gain from "free trade". Before the Second World War the great depression hit the central nerve of the American economy and then that of the world economy. After the war the Americans dedicated themselves to the task of preventing another such catastrophe among the Western industrialized countries. To that end the USA sought to construct an open market economy which, however, was to be controlled by an American-led order of monetary and financial stability. A principle condition for staging this vision was the reconstruction of productive capacity in Western Europe. In a euphoria of enlightened self-interest the pro-reconstruction Europeans were given a big push onto a path of growth which was to last a quarter of a century.

Hence the European road to post-war recovery was in fact a combination of scenarios two and three characterized above. It was not difficult for the Western Europeans to agree to give up part of their sovereignty in exchange for the Marshall plan, coffee, and cigarettes. The result was the "painless" creation of a North Atlantic division of labor. The cumulative effects resulted indeed in unprecedented growth. Consequently, MADDISON calls Pax Americana "The Golden Age".

In the period 1950–1973 exports of OECD countries increased by a factor of 6.7 (MADDISON 1982:128). Table 1-2 presents MADDISON's World Export Index:

"The Golden Age" was based on a particular global division of labor. The North Atlantic countries grew through intra-industry specialization and intra-industrial trade to become a compact, mutually dependent industrial landscape. The developing countries – within the framework of an inter-sectoral division of labour – provided the raw materials. In exchange, they purchased consumer goods from the North. Under the rubric "development" they also functioned as consumers of investment goods. The Soviet Union stood in the wings while this new economic drama was being staged. If the Soviet Union could be said to be standing in the wings, a

[1] FREY (1984a) or SCHNEIDER/FREY (1985), FREY (1984b).

Table 1-2. World Export Volume 1870–1970

	MADDISON Index
1870	25.0
1913	100.0
1950	151.5
1970	588.1

Source: MADDISON (1982:254)

few other countries - notably Japan and a few of its Eastern neighbors - could be said to have been lurking in the wings, props ready - waiting for their cue: their props - low wage levels in labor intensive branches of industry; their cue - post-war liberal trade policy. And indeed they took their cues and came on stage in grand style - so that by the 1950s American textile and garment producers were in Washington demanding protectionist policies. And they got it: first the VERs (voluntary export restraints) and later OMAs (orderly marketing agreements). The textile and garment sectors were the first and the largest group to be protected, but they were certainly not the only one. A whole slew of other small industries demanded help: from umbrellas to wood-screws. Moreover, they were successful.[2] It is obvious that these subsequently protected branches are characterized by labor intensive production and that this is where developing countries first gained a comparative advantage. Thus, the beginnings of the new protectionism must be seen as protection from imports from developing countries.

Although the USA - as the hegemonic post-war power - identified its interests with those of the world economic order (ZYSMAN/TYSON 1983), the USA was not ready to support consequently and thoroughly a policy of free trade. The dichotomy between American policy and ideology was, in fact, embarassingly obvious. In all modern branches of industry the USA held an absolute advantage. Here the USA was prepared to work within the context of a division of labor among the North Atlantic countries. In sectors where technological progress was negligible, however, the USA was not willing to put up with the necessary pain of restructuring. This dichotomy (cf. e.g. WEHRLE 1984c) led to a partial loosening of the American-led world economic order during the 1970s,[3] a world order which depended on regulatory intervention and on import tolerance on the part of the USA (cf. ARRIGHI 1982:57). For MADDISON (1982:128), the "Golden Age" was the era of "managed liberalism": "Managed liberalism added greatly to the buoyancy and resilience of the Western economies. These policies of enlightened self-interest and mutual support were due not only to intelligent digestion of the lessons of the 1930s, but to the urgency of cold war pressures and to the overwhelming power of the USA to enforce its views."

[2] YOFFIE (1983:238). He draws his information from BHAGWATI (1977:166–168).

[3] Note the contradiction between the developing countries as a market for investment goods vs. the barriers to imports of industrial goods from the developing countries.

Since 1973, the global rate of growth (cf. Table 1-1) has again approached the "natural" rate of growth. (We refer to the debate about the level at which growth can be sustained in the long run.) A full explanation of why the boom petered out must take account of the following factors: the reduction of innovative activity - existing innovation potential had been used up - and the growing number of markets which showed signs of saturation. Standardized processes for standardized products were scattered all over the globe. Japan established itself as one of the major industrial powers, while other developing countries used their comparative advantages to compete with the industrial countries. The latent contradictions between North and South became economically explosive. The global economic dynamic was no longer the monopoly of the Northern Atlantic states; the technical and scientific monopoly of the North began to show significant cracks. Nevertheless, the North continued to represent for all intents and purposes global demand - if no longer global supply.

The result was a "division" of the family of nations into four groups, each group having a specific function within the international division of labor:

(1) Nation states which grew-up, culturally and historically with the principle of capitalism as a private, decentralized, market-oriented, competitive economic system: the Western industrial countries.
(2) Countries which opposed the principles of capitalism - at least ideologically - but which nonetheless participated in the global system: the Eastern block countries and various religious states.
(3) Countries which were not culturally and historically closely allied with the development of capitalism, but which have been highly successful participants in the international division of labor: Japan and some of the Newly Industrializing Countries (NICs).
(4) Nation states which do not historically and culturally identify with the traditions of capitalism but which are more or less voluntarily participating in the global system: the developing countries.

Despite frequent proclamations concerning the efficiency of uncontrolled capitalism, the market mechanism, and decentralized decision-making, government intervention is part and parcel of the global system. Traditionally, intervention was explained as the result of an ill-informed political process. The experience of the NICs speaks against this hypothesis perhaps more radically even than the history of the older industrial countries. In the following pages we present three theoretical answers to questions concerning government intervention in the form of protectionism and so-called neo-mercantilism.

The first explanation originates with institutional economists. "From the instrumental standard, one can easily understand the frustration of conventional economic thinking on economic policy. People attempt to protect the continuity of their lives against the disruptive strains of the unregulated exchange economy." (STANFIELD 1984:26/27). From this point of view people are simply not willing - especially in times of crisis - to let a set of theoretically based axioms decide their fate, whether or not historical evidence and theoretical proofs "guarantee" success in the long-run. More precisely, this means that people are willing to use their time and energies to remove themselves to the greatest extent possible from being subject to market forces if they feel these forces could alter their life style adversely. This is not only true in times of crisis but also true in periods when the speed of socio-economic change is too rapid for human comfort.

The second explanation associates economic behavior with the conception of economic development as a conscious national effort, thus implying the existence of an integrated political strategy. Albert HIRSCHMANN (1968: 5) refers to "a strategy that calls forth and enlists for development purposes resources and abilities that are hidden, scattered, or badly utilized". Note, however, that this emphasis on a national strategy is not identical with an inward-looking or even a de-linking strategy. As the recent history of Japan and the NICs demonstrates, the combination of strong national policies with an orientation to the world market can be most successful. A national economic plan results from conscious reflection which is dedicated to the realization of a collective aim. The idea of an "invisible hand", "laisser faire", or "laisser passer" can hardly be realistically thought of as a principle of national economic development. In this sense protectionism is one of many measures which can be used by an economically aware political regime.

The third explanation is that of neo-classical economics. Neoclassical theoreticians focus on the market mechanism in its operation for ready-made goods (ROBINSON 1979: 12), in other words, study is limited to the problems of the circulation of goods and forms of payment (SOMBART 1927: 914). This approach to the problem is not adequate to deal with the globally internationalized system of capitalist production. Market forces are only one aspect. "Market economy" is itself a misleading term because the aspect of planning is left out, whether that planning is carried out at the entrepreneurial, the governmental, or the consumer level (cf. CANTWELL 1984: 24). For our purposes, we investigated the relationship between planning and marketing. On the one hand firms interact with buyers and sellers on the market. But on the other hand the very functioning of the market is a hindrance to their internal planning processes. The situation of nations facing global markets is analogous. It follows that firms' organizational structures are an essential element of study because entrepreneurial organization is aimed at consolidating, maintaining, and increasing the power of individual firms on the market. Firms must remain competitive but the marketplace is only one field of competitive action (cf. BORNER/WEHRLE 1984b). Moreover, successful market activity can lead to the elimination of competitors and to the establishment of monopoly.

Our conclusion is that interventions are inherent in and inseparable from the functioning of the capitalist economic system. What varies over time is the intensity and the nature of the interventions, but above all the character of the actors who intervene (cf. CODDINGTON 1974: 435–436). Some periods of capitalist economic history are characterized by a dominance of public actors, others by private actors. Our example of the USA shows that a country can redeploy the effects of competition to the weaker partner and that public action can support private needs. Hence, free trade must be seen as a function of the competitive strategies of the Western countries – and not as a permanent characteristic of capitalist, market-oriented national economies. Since American firms suffered more and more from increased competition in all traditional branches of industry,[4] it is not surprising that the GATT con-

[4] We refer to the so-called NEWTONian industries, that is, to industrial branches where production processes are based on NEWTON's theories of mechanics and physics.

ventions were ignored, changed, or eliminated. We find ourselves in a period of economic history in which protectionism dominates practically and free trade dominates rhetorically.

Many observers - economists, political scientists, sociologists, etc. - contend that an emancipation of certain developing countries from the industrial countries is taking place. Their evidence is the increased technical, organizational, and legal competence of these countries. Emancipation in this sense means better adaptation to the dominant foreign culture. And it is certainly true that it has become easier for firms and citizens of the world's many nations to do business with each other. At the same time, however, protectionism blossoms.

Pax Americana has been characterized much less than Pax Britannica by free trade. "The world system established under US hegemony was not even free-tradist, as was that established under British hegemony in the nineteenth century. Though the United States actively promoted the liberalization of trade, it did so through bilateral and multilateral negotiations rather than through unilateral measures, as Britain did in the 1940s when it repealed the Corn Laws and Navigation Acts.

Moreover, it is significant that immediately after the war (World War II) the United States gave priority to the liberalization of intra-European trade rather than to the liberalization of its own trade with European countries.

As a matter of fact, the main objective of US imperial domination seems to have been to guarantee an "open door" - not primarily to trade but to capitalist enterprise, particularly to threats of nationalization. It is in this sense that I speak of a free enterprise system rather than a free trade system." (ARRIGHI 1982:58).

Why the USA should have "preferred" foreign investment to free trade is partially explained by theories about multinational corporations. Up until the middle of this century the dominant motive for foreign investment was to secure a steady supply of raw materials and agricultural products. This sheds light on the high stock of foreign investment in the developing countries in the early 1950s - 50% of world's direct investments (WEHRLE 1983b:48). Moreover, the history of direct investments in this century is primarily the history of direct foreign investment by American firms (WEHRLE 1983b:38). Until the 1950s, US firms were "content" to satisfy domestic demand. During the 1950s and 1960s, they ventured to satisfy global demand by local production, commencing on the newly unified Western European continent. All in all, the American firms were first concerned with global sourcing and only later with global marketing. "Direct investment rather than trade had become the main weapon of US (...) capital in international competition and, from this point of view, some measure of protectionism could enhance its competitive edge." (ARRIGHI 1982:58).

We would like to stress the fact that the Americans were intensely interested in Europe (HARRIS 1983 and ARRIGHI 1982). They were interested "to once and for all pry open Europe and its empires to American exports." (HARRIS 1983:36). But "US efforts to secure American markets in Europe (could not) work, unless Europe (was allowed) also to enter into an exchange with the United States, by finding markets in America. That was something Washington steadfastly opposed." (HARRIS 1983: 37). Consequently, European trade with North America has up until recently always shown a deficit (cf. GATT: various volumes). Additionally, the volume of trade has not all been significant (cf. HAGER 1982). This, of course, is not to deny that in

Table 1-3. Average Annual Number of Newly Established Subsidiaries of American and British Firms, (in Percent)

	1914–19	1920–29	1930–38	1939–45	1946–52	1953–55	1956–58	1959–64	1965–67	1968–70
US Firms										
Canada	45	28	22	23	22	22	14	10	11	
Latin America	17	13	21	48	31	32	38	21	25	
Europe	14	31	25	9	20	22	21	35	34	
UK	7	16	17	7	11	7	8	9	9	
Africa	2	2	4	3	4	4	5	8	4	
Asia/Pacific	15	10	11	11	12	13	14	17	17	
	100	100	100	100	100	100	100	100	100	
UK Firms										
US+Canada	11	15	9	2	9	19	41	13	10	16
Latin America	16	12	7	9	3	14	8	7	4	4
Europe	22	39	42	16	13	12	11	29	28	30
Africa	11	14	9	22	40	24	14	21	25	23
Asia/Pacific	40	20	33	51	35	31	26	30	33	25
	100	100	100	100	100	100	100	100	100	100

Source: BUCKLEY/CASSON (1976:3)[5]

[5] Cf. VAUPEL/CURHAN (1974)

an historical sense there has been phenomenal growth of intra-industrial trade. But it took place largely within the Western European "family"! In fact, it seems that the free trade rhetoric of the USA has been accompanied by a potent economic nationalism (cf. YOFFIE 1983).

The military and political power of the USA secured the framework in which transnationalization of American business could take place. "You may find some irony that it is entirely legitimate for a country to discriminate between foreign and domestic goods, that is, laying tariff duties on the former which are not applied to the latter, while binding themselves not to discriminate between foreign and domestic enterprise. Such is the practice, however, and this country (the USA, authors' note) has benefited greatly from it over the years" (KINDLEBERGER 1984: 190).

Table 1-3 shows that since the end of the Second World War Europe has experienced a steady increase in American direct investment. Using the establishment of subsidiaries per year as an indicator, Table 1-3 shows the take-off of American and British investment. The take-off of transatlantic investment and trade can be said to have occurred between about 1958 and 1963, that is, at the time when the Bretton Woods-GATT monetary and trade system had finally become operational and the liberalization of capital flows had been solidified under the aegis of the OECD (cf. HAGER 1982, HARRIS 1983, UNCTC 1983).

In the meantime the concept of "export led growth" has virtually become a school room slogan. As indicated by the figures in Table 1-4, however, we could just as accurately speak of "direct investment led growth" – especially in the 1960s.

The "Golden Age" was characterized not only by "free-trade" but also by an investment based interpenetration of the European and American economies. We identified the early 1960s as the take-off date for this boom in direct foreign investment. Indeed, 1961 was the year in which both the Code of Liberalization of Capital Movements and the Code of Liberalization of Current Invisible Transactions was agreed to by the OECD countries (UNCTC 1983: 77). These codes contributed significantly to the ease with which direct investments could be carried out.

As in the case of free trade, the liberalization of investment is based on an agreement among nations. "In harmonization there is a considerable loss of national sovereignty since national regulations can be changed only by agreement." (KINDLEBERGER 1984: 233). This observation by KINDLEBERGER suggests that there are numerous similarities in the problems associated with liberalization of trade and liberalization of investment regulations. In fact, most countries practice investment

Table 1-4. Growth Rates of GNP, Trade, and Investment in Industrial Countries 1960–1980 (Real Prices)

	1960–1970	1970–1980
GNP	8.9	14.0
Gross Capital Accumulation	9.7	14.0
Imports	10.9	19.6
Exports	10.9	18.7
Capital Inflow	11.7	14.6
Capital Outflow	11.5	15.6

Source: UNCTC (1983: 18)

protectionism to a certain degree. Switzerland, West Germany, the Netherlands, as well as the USA, all maintain certain restrictions on foreign investment.

"Even in the United States, which advocates a generally open international system and where foreign-controlled companies are estimated to account for not more than about 5 per cent of all domestic sales, the growing foreign investment in the United States (...) is raising some concern. A two-year study of foreign investment in the country by the Commerce, Consumer, and Monetary Affairs Subcommittee of the House of Representatives calls for a basic reassessment of American policy toward foreign investment, which it terms 'indiscriminate neutrality', and for establishing one central authority for registering and monitoring incoming foreign investment, so that harmful investments could be barred and the 'dangerous vulnerability' of the country arising from foreign investment could be minimized." (UNCTC 1983: 79).

This suggests that the USA might become interested in unbundling direct investment packages. At any rate it can no longer be assumed that just the developing countries are concerned with distilling only the useful components of foreign investments from the entire package. In the near future we might expect that foreign investment and capital movements will come under a growing array of national restrictions (cf. KINDLEBERGER 1984, UNCTC 1983). In this sense, the seeds of the present period of trade and investment protectionism - and with them New Forms of Internationalization (NFI) - were laid already in the 1950s. It seems appropriate to use SCHUMPETER's term "creative destruction" to characterize the entire spectrum of entrepreneurial activity and not just the rather narrow field of productive activities. "Capitalism is by nature a form or method of economic change, (it) incessantly revolutionizes the economic structure from within, incessantly destroying the old one, incessantly creating a new one. This process of creative destruction is the essential fact about capitalism." (SCHUMPETER 1962:82-83).

It seems obvious that national governments and various nationally oriented interest groups will have their influence on these changes. New regulations will result in a new pattern of trade and investment. If we observe today at the macro-economic level, that both trade and investment are going through a period of national protectionism, we must not overlook that at the micro-level the financial and contractual security for firms doing business abroad has increased significantly. As we shall see in this report, entrepreneurs have already found and begun to use NFI - forms which are appropriate and successful in the current situation.

Chapter 2

Dimensions and Perspectives of Interdependence: Exports, Multinationals, and New Forms of Internationalization

2.1 Introduction

In the first chapter we demonstrated how the intensity and the nature of international interdependence has undergone radical and partly cyclical changes. This stands in sharp contrast to the basic tenets of the theory of "comparative advantage" as developed by RICARDO some 150 years ago. This paradigm is still not fundamentally questioned by main-stream economists - despite the following trends, which obviously fly in the face of its main assumptions:

- The replacement or supersession of spot transactions at arm's length by transactions within hierarchically structured international organizations and/or by contracts with mutual influence on the behavior of the "transactors" cum "partners".
- The replacement or supersession of international transactions with final goods and primary inputs such as raw materials, foodstuffs, energy, etc. by intermediate inputs (parts, semifinished goods, information, technical know-how, etc.) on the one hand and assets or rights to assets on the other (patents, licenses, capital equipment with embodied know-how, human and financial capital).
- Fundamental changes in the political environment and thus the climate of national policy-making (dramatic increase in the number of trading partners, new industrial competitors from the NICs and the LDCs, the rise of protectionism and neomercantilism, etc.), as well as in the behavior of interest groups affected by international forces within different types of countries.

From the vantage point of our study, these three dimensions of historical change - in the political environment, in the nature of international transactions, and in the type of relationship between transactors - have not only increased the extent of global interdependence. Even more significantly, they have intensified the qualitative nature of interdependence. The result is that the organizational forms of international transactions have begun to determine the structure of international economic relations. In other words, the institutional or organizational modes in which international transactions are planned, arranged, executed, and evaluated become of cardinal interest. Seen in this light, we can also understand that, given the political constraints, the strategic priorities, the nature of firm-specific competitive advantage, and other characteristics of the transactors involved (size of firms), these different modes are only very imperfect substitutes. Except in special situations, trade, FDI by MNEs, or so-called "New Forms of Internationalization" are not alternatives for carrying out a particular transaction. This is because in general there is no specific transaction which is independent of the political environment, the contents of the transaction, or the type of exchange or cooperation arrangement. In our view, these questions are best analyzed in the framework of a strategic entrepreneurial perspective.

In the following paragraphs we try to explain this transformation of the traditional "trade paradigm" into the "internationalization paradigm" on the conceptual level. This will serve as a backgroud for the taxonomy (Part II), the theoretical re-interpretation of interdependence (Part III), and, finally, its empirical testing (Part IV).

One basic point should be clarified at the outset. Theoretical controversies in the social and political spheres are not basically of the KUHNian type, i. e. one paradigm destroying and then replacing the other. Paradigms within the social sciences (including economics) are tied to developments - in historical conditions, human nature, and human behavior - in ways which do not allow us as positivists to distinguish between true and false. Rather, we distinguish between adequate, fruitful - and inadequate, unfruitful. From this we should expect that economic paradigms are extremely flexible, adaptable, or dialectical in nature. What we see, however, is the contrary. The criteria of internal consistency (equilibrium) and ideological attachment (free trade) mislead most theoreticians into defending and extending the existing paradigms within the narrow boundaries of academic tradition. Consequently the empirical i. e. historical realities are disregarded.[1]

We try to proceed in a different way. Starting from the global trends which are shaping international interdependence, we point out what we consider to be the main issues. Questions, which arise then have to be mirrored by a "perspective" or "vision" before they can be answered (hopefully) by theoretical and/or empirical analysis. Our goal is not so much to discredit certain perspectives and to favor others. Rather, by observing human behavior, we try to develop a "richer world view" of interdependencies. This "richer world view" can then serve as a basis for synthesizing various strands of theory and observation. At the heart of such a "world view" must be the recognition that interdependence implies a world-wide division of labor which is governed by the aims of a multitude of private and public actors on the one hand and the rules and regulations governing the means of international transactions on the other.

2.2 The Trade View: Exports and Imports

From an historical as well as from a theoretical point of view, the trade view is our point of departure. According to the classical school, interdependence was, in fact and theory, basically international trade. What do we mean by that?

The trade view can be characterized in the following manner:

- Traders are independent economic agents located in different nation states.
- Their relationship is based on an exchange transaction which takes place on a spot market, i. e. the traders deal at arm's length, exchanging goods for (international) money in the framework of a supra-national trading and monetary system.
- The real side of this exchange transaction consists mainly of final goods and/or raw materials of all sorts, produced/extracted by national firms.

---

[1] Cf. BORNER (1984a, b) or MARRIS (1984).

- The technologies of production and extraction are quasi-free goods and thus known to all specialized producers in all regions of all nations.
- Competitive advantages originate from country-specific assets which are non-tradable and which, therefore, remain geographically immobile. This is straightforward in the case of agriculture, primary raw materials, energy sources, etc. For industrially produced final goods this assumption is much less evident, but can be defended by stressing national assets (goods) of a quasi-collective type, such as economic policies (infrastructure, incentives), the socio-political environment (political system), or technological competence (R&D, schooling, etc.).

Schematically we may present this model as follows:

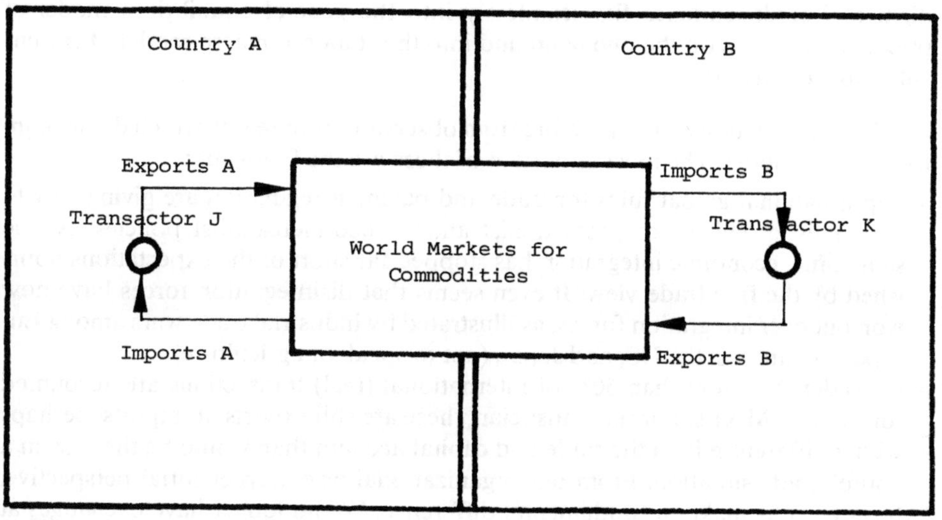

Fig. 2-1. Diagram of the Trade View

It is quite obvious that the usual exchange paradigm is only slightly altered by extending it to include classical elements of international trade. The pre-conditions and welfare consequences of an exchange transaction remain exactly the same. All that is needed are international rules for the trading and payment system. The principle of comparative advantage merely adds one more "welfare dimension": the national level. Just as any transaction between J and K can benefit both parties, any transaction between J and K of different nations can benefit both nations by achieving a better exploitation of the given (nationally immobile) resources.

This macro-economic dimension of international interdependence through mutually advantageous or (free) trade fits furthermore very nicely into the accounting framework of the national economy (balance of payments). This is even more true when the model is extended to include capital movements and global financial markets. As long as interdependence is viewed as a mere macrophenomenon of exchange through trade, the problem of structural adjustment seems to be completely analogous to purely domestic adjustments i.e., adjustments to the changing competitiveness of sectors, industries, regions, branches, or individual enterprises. All that is different is that there are additional aggregate real income effects (efficiency gains) due to the extension of the division of labour, i.e. the optimal allocation of resources in a larger trading area. Both free trade agreements (such as EFTA) or regional integration (such as the Common Market) are completely congenial with this perspective.

So, what is wrong with it? Really nothing, as long as it is an appropriate descriptive framework for what is actually happening in the realm of international interdependence. With regard to mining activities, trade in oil or other raw materials, the exchange of tropical agricultural products, etc. – all parts of the economy where characteristics (i) through (v) apply – this perspective is indeed appropriate. Nor is the problem one of inconsistency. On the contrary, consistency of the trade paradigm of interdependence fits seamlessly into the general equilibrium model of prices and markets on the one hand and into the standard macro-model of the circular flow on the other.

Critical objections arise therefore from observations of reality which do not conform to this model. The most important of these are the following:

- Supra-national global rules for trade and payment regulation are giving way to nationalistic revivals of protectionist and/or neo-mercantilist policies. At the same time, economic integration has stopped far short of the expectations nourished by the free trade view. It even seems that disintegration forces have now won out over integration forces, as illustrated by industrial trade wars among European countries, the US, and Japan (not to speak of agriculture).
- Considerably more than 50% of international (real) transactions are accounted for by large MNEs. For the statistician, these are still exports or imports, perhaps with a different mix in the trade and capital account than would be the case in a "pure" trade situation. From our organizational or entrepreneurial perspective, however, this makes a fundamental difference. We no longer have exchanges at arm's length on spot markets between completely independent traders. Instead, we have to deal with transnational hierarchies with their central management, common property, and permanent ties between units located in different nations. More and more we also notice longer term contractual, cooperative agreements between firms of different nation states.
- If we look further at the object of international transactions, we observe a great and constantly changing variety of "what is traded". One-dimensional goods (be they final or raw materials) no longer dominate. Intermediate products embodying know-how, information, complex assets or even rights to exploit certain productive resources are in the forefront. Parallel to this, pure financial flows to pay for imports are being superseded by multi-dimensional bundles of money, technical know-how, hardware, and services of all kinds. Or in other words, most firms are multi-product firms and exchange complex bundles of capital, goods, and services.
- Defenders of the principle of comparative advantage are hard pressed to explain competitiveness in the industrial sector. This has two aspects. One is the question of attributing MNEs to individual countries. What is so Swiss about Nestlé or so Dutch about Phillips? The second is the point stressed already 150 years ago by

LIST that industrialization is not decisively restrained by natural (immobile) resources, but rather by social, political, and cultural conditions.

The success stories of Japan and the NICs and the decline of Great Britain prove beyond any doubt how right LIST was. LINDBECK (1981:395) confirms LIST's observation: "Success stories in a specific country can occur in practically any branch of manufacturing, services and marketing."

This is also very true for the opposite case, namely rapidly deteriorating industries in certain countries (watches in Switzerland). There is nothing "natural" in the sphere of national endowments to explain why the Swiss are strong in large ship engines, the Swedes in telephone equipment, the British in jet engines, etc. "There is no doubt that the traditional H-O-theoretic framework, characterized by (...) no firm-specific organizational and technological differentiation is inadequate as a model to explain international trade in modern manufacturing not to speak of FDI." (KOJIMA/OZAWA, 1984:2).

2.3 The Perspective of Foreign Direct Investment

These criticisms lead us to ask the following questions: Why do MNEs come into existence? Why are their activities growing faster than "trade"? How shall we interpret this? Let us characterize the MNE-FDI perspective in the same manner in which we characterized the trade view:

- International actors are centralized, strategically operating firms. The various units located in different nation states are common property.
- The transactions are governed by hierarchical channels of a quasi-permanent nature. Centralized hierarchical structures replace decentralized exchanges at arm's length. Organization supersedes the market.
- MNEs are multi-procuct, multi-purpose institutions. Consequently, the contents of their transactions mirror this situation. What is transferred over national frontiers remains within the confines of the corporation. It is, therefore, rarely a substitute for traded goods and/or capital. MNEs "exchange" complex and varied bundles of financial, material, intellectual, and organizational goods and services. These activities range from supplying complete production units to sending experts abroad to solve special problems.
- In the broadest sense technology is not considered a free good but rather an intermediate product resulting from R&D activities. This makes know-how appropriable and therefore mobile, at least within the boundaries of the MNE. Together with the mobility of financial capital, as well as high-grade human capital, comparative advantages are primarily attributable to corporations - instead of countries.

Thus interdependence intensifies in a different way - and for different reasons. The more risky (costly) international market transactions become (due to government interference, imitation strategies of competitors, or progress in information technologies), the more international interdependence will shift towards FDI. The basic driving forces are then no longer global and static market conditions and/or given (national) endowments of productive resources (allocation problem). Rather, the driving forces are the dynamic strategies of growing business enterprises with global plans and centralized management.

The FDI model is illustrated in the following diagram:

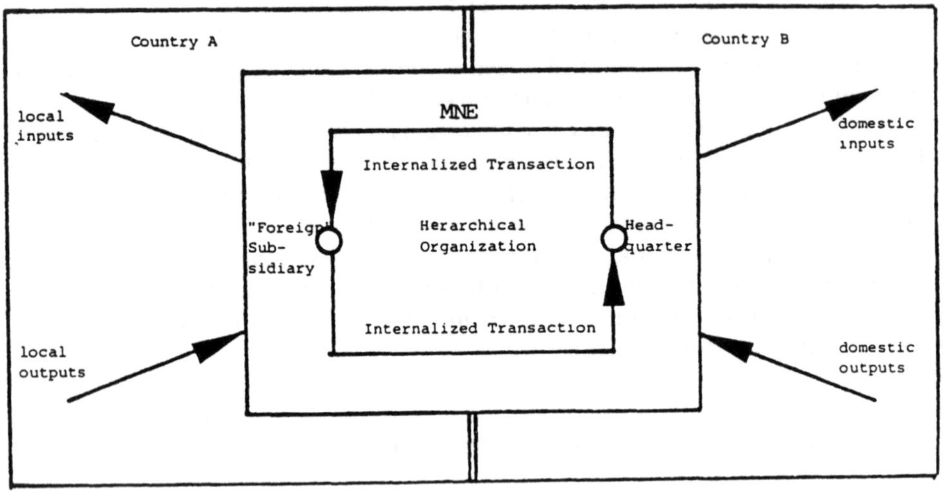

Fig. 2-2. Diagram of the MNE and FDI Perspective

MNE-transactions crossing national borders differ fundamentally from international transactions in world markets for two reasons: (1) The replacement of an exchange at arm's length implies the replacement of a sales contract by a semi-permanent, hierarchical relationship. This alters the meaning of "prices". Instead of "transaction prices" (spot market prices), we get "transfer prices", which must be seen in terms of long-term management goals of the corporation-center. This hotly debated point is, however, actually less important than the second (2). The arrows between units in different nations belonging to the same corporation imply qualitatively quite different flows of goods, capital, services, etc. than would occur in spot market transactions. This eases the transaction price controversy, because what is exchanged is not the same thing. At the same time, it makes an evaluation of the FDI operations of MNEs extremely difficult because the trade paradigm can no longer be considered as the benchmark for assessing efficiency and welfare.

Both the concepts of parallel markets (for the legal evaluation of transfer prices) and the free trade paradigm of global efficiency only serve as useful measuring rods where MNE transactions represent "arbitrage activities". We shall return to this issue in Part III, thereby explaining more convincingly why most MNE transactions are not substitutes for open market exchanges.

What is wrong with this MNE-FDI paradigm? Again, we conclude that it is relevant and consistent - as far as it goes. At this point, the reader should also notice that the trade and MNE-FDI paradigms are not mutually exclusive. The relevant questions pertain to the circumstances rendering one or the other the more powerful framework, the richer concept, so to speak.

But why and where does this paradigm fall short? Again we have to realize that the reality of international interdependence is more complex than this polar contrast of spot exchange and permanent property ties in centralized hierarchies suggests. What we also observe - and this to an ever greater degree - is the spread of contractual forms of cooperation between enterprises of different nations. By contractual forms we mean relationships going beyond a spot contract of exchange. The behavior patterns of both contractors are directly influenced by this form of international interdependence, which implies a certain time span of the relationship, a certain risk-sharing in the joint exploitation of common resources, as well as a qualitative change in the contents of the transaction.

2.4 The Entrepreneurial View: New Forms of Internationalization

As postulated at the outset of this chapter, the three perspectives are not mutually exclusive. Whereas the trade and FDI views are more or less complementary, the NFI perspective is an attempt at synthesis. Conceptually, synthesis can be achieved by integrating the logical foundations of the first two views. Trade is focused on the nation state, FDI on the multinational centralized organization. Trade transactions operate through open markets but cross national borders. FDI-related transactions are governed by the hierarchical relations within a central ownership and management structure. While FDI-transactions cross national borders, they remain within the "sovereignty" of the enterprise. It follows naturally to view these two cases as polar opposites, leaving a lot of room in between for the establishment of a variety of relationships between independent firms and/or foreign subsidiaries of MNEs located in different nations. The common denominator of all these relationships is their contractual nature (instead of exchange at arm's length) on the one hand and property-related central control on the other. New Forms of Internationalization are, of course, not really "new" as such. What is new, however, is:

- the fact that these forms are rapidly spreading and partly replacing classical trade and FDI
- the conceptual notion that trade and FDI are special (extreme) cases in a framework of contractual interdependence among enterprises.

We prefer the general term "New Forms of Internationalization" to either "New Forms of Investment" or "New Forms of Cooperation" because both the latter have a normative ring to them, implying some kind of improvement over traditional sales and investment relationships. The term New Forms of Internationalization (NFI) refers in a neutral and general way to the different forms of international transactions. It is, however, certainly true that at the aggregate level these (not really new) NFI boil down to the same thing. Goods, services, capital, returns on investment, etc. flow from one country to another and shape the structure of the balance of payments and the economy as a whole.

But the theoretical interpretation is radically different. The question of international competitiveness in a NFI-framework is basically one of competitive advantages of companies i.e., of organizations internalizing exclusive skills and exploiting them globally by very different strategic routes. Since this concept will be fully developed in Part III, the following characterization of the NFI-view must suffice at this stage:

- The international actors can be either the classical transactors of the trade view or the MNE of the FDI perspective. To the extent that they deal with each other according to the assumptions of either view, these perspectives remain perfectly adequate models.

- The transactions in an NFI-context are executed according to contractual arrangements leading to a mutual influencing of the behavior of all partners involved. This may entail, for instance, rearranging risk-sharing in R&D or production oriented joint ventures, tying management responsibilities to capital goods, or engageing in bilateral barter or buy-back agreements in order to finance exports.
- This not only increases the potential number of international transactors - opening up internationalization strategies by non-export means for SMEs - but also the potential range of what is "tradable". Since the NFI perspective includes control by property (FDI) or pure exchange (export sales), it is a much richer concept for analyzing international transactions. At the same time, it definitively shifts the focus from nations or giant MNEs to enterpreneurial internationalization strategies in general. The role of the nation state is therefore not necessarily diminished but conceptually changed: The nation is no longer primarily a geographical category containing given resources and "interfering" more or less with the rules of international exchange, but rather a creator of more or less favorable parameters ("Rahmenbedingungen)" for the creation of firm-specific competitive advantages and permitting their world-wide exploitation in appropriate forms.
- Commodities, finance, and technology transfer become fully interdependent. They can be initiated by a multitude of actors and in a practically unlimited variety of combinations and forms for all types and sizes of enterprises. NFI is nothing less than the second or most important dimension of innovation, the first being the accumulation of technological skills or know-how.
- International interdependence is thus a process fed by changes in the social and political environment and by the creative response of firms. But which changes in the technical, political, social, and cultural environment lead to which forms of internationalization? Which types of firms in which countries employ which NFI? In our view this is the relevant question. It replaces RICARDO's question: Why does Portugal export wine to England and England cloth to Portugal? At the same time this question replaces the traditional question of the (production) theory of the firm: How much of which commodities should be produced?
  "The crucial decision for a firm is often not what type of final product or service to produce, but what particular functions in a certain production and distribution system should be performed in one specific country, rather than another, and also what the firm should produce itself and what it should buy from other firms" (LINDBECK, 1981:393). This is all very well said, but LINDBECK does not go far enough when he speaks of international location of firm functions and of "buy-or-make" alternatives. What is missing here is the organizational and contractual dimension: the question of how (in what form) functions can be shared with other partners and of how inputs can be acquired from and outputs transferred to contractors of all kinds (transferred - not just bought and sold).

2.5 Opportunities for New Forms of Internationalization in the Future

Despite increasing conflicts, growing politicization, and rising levels of government intervention, the internationalization of entrepreneurial activities is not decreasing. On the contrary, internationalization is becoming more accentuated, albeit in a variety of forms. Just as increasing trade restrictions led to the expansion of international production in the 1970s, so too will increased government intervention, export requirements, and regulations regarding local production usher in a new phase of internationalization. We can expect the multinationals to become involved in more diverse and rewarding forms of transnational cooperation. Moreover, the increasing pressure to internationalize will also spread to small and medium-sized companies.

The traditional real theory of international economics has concerned itself primarily with two forms of international operations: trade in goods via open markets and direct investments by multinationals. Both forms clearly dominated the development of the period of growth experienced by the world economy between 1950 and 1973. The changes outlined above have, however, considerably restricted the amount of leeway enjoyed by both big multinationals and small and medium-sized nationally operating companies which rely heavily on export specialization. Given the demand by the developing countries for a new world economic order and the growing trend to enforce (neo-mercantilist) special interests in the industrialized countries, the free play of market forces in the areas of trade, direct investment, monetary agreements, and financial matters has been definitely restricted and replaced by administrative regulations. There are parallels between the restrictions imposed on free international trade and those on free international direct investment: bilateralism, direct barter agreements, re-export regulations, and local production requirements are making what is already a tough life even harder for both the pure exporters and the traditional multinationals.

The precarious balance of payments and debt situation of many countries is increasing the incentive to pass on the heightened financial risks wherever possible to a local partner, the host country, or an international financial organization. In addition, many multinationals have taken advantage of the fact that their local partners have the necessary knowledge and connections to allow them to penetrate more effectively protected domestic markets. Last but not least, the higher political risks (criticism of low wages and inadequate social benefits, responsibility in the event of lock-outs and relocations) and/or the general reproach of exploitation can, in certain cases, be fobbed off on local firms or governments. A comparative analysis of exports and direct investments reveals that they are both extreme cases of a wide spectrum of forms of international operations. Between the two lies a broad gamut of internationalization options which may be termed "New Forms of Internationalization" or just "New Forms".

Whilst export transactions at arm's length can be carried out with a relatively low risk factor, foreign direct investments involve a long-term, sometimes even permanent, commitment of the parent company to assume all risks. Seen in this light, international transactions within the framework of "New Forms of Internationalization" may be placed somewhere between the two extremes. This becomes even clearer if we also consider the aspect of controlling the product and process know-how, which is particularly important for maintaining firm-specific competitiveness. The direct investor does not abandon his/her control of knowledge either in regard to the product or in regard to the production technique. The exporter, on the other hand, loses all control over the destiny of his/her products. "New Forms of Internationalization", however, allow many combinations of risk sharing, transfer of know-how, and profit-sharing among and between the various partners.

Chapter 3
Global Forces Behind New Forms of Internationalization

The transition process within the world economy has been dubbed a phase of "international economic disorder" (HELLEINER, 1980) or a "non-system" (WILLIAMSON, 1985). This phase, following the break-down of the Bretton Woods exchange-rate system on the one hand and the weakening of the GATT-related free trade arrangement on the other, is leading to a new kind of world order. This new order, of course, resembles neither the phantom of the propagandists of a "New Economic Order" nor the ideals of free world markets for goods, services, capital, and resources of all kinds. Since both camps - "the new economic order propagandists" as well as the "free trade champions" - carry a heavy ideological cargo, some systematic clarification is badly needed. This is quite clearly recognized in the case of the first group, but quite often covered up behind the tenets of scientific objectivity in the case of the latter. At the government level there is a wide cleavage between the rhethoric and the deeds, but this is even more true of private entrepreneurs, many of whom are protectionist - if not in their minds then at least in their hearts. Specifically, some representatives of multinational corporations have shown strong resentment against "New Forms of Internationalization", arguing that NFI are Trojan horses destined to serve socialist-inspired changes in the world economic order: away from a free and open market and towards bilateral bureaucratic arrangements. Do these entrepreneurs not see what is so evident and so aptly phrased by CAVES (1982:36) that "forces restricting trade encourage foreign investment"? In a world of purely free trade, there would simply be no need and no room for multinational corporations. Their very existence is the consequence of market imperfections (mostly government restrictions on trade) and strategic potential (mostly monopolistic advantages). CAVES' verdict can be equally applied to the new forms. Forces restricting trade and foreign investment encourage NFI. NFI are the symptoms of these new forces, not exogenously imposed modes of international operations. Inasmuch as these forces are - from the point of view of the firm - detrimental to their interests, it is quite understandable that the managers affected resent these developments. But such a point of view does not suffice to reshape company strategy or to redirect economic policy.

Therefore, it is necessary at this point to look briefly at the forces which restrict trade and FDI. "Modes of international industrial cooperation are changing under pressure from host countries to achieve greater political and economic control over their development, and from multinational firms to achieve a return on their investment in creating, developing and transferring knowledge." (BUCKLEY, 1983a:216). The actual new economic world order is not yet clearly shaped by such forces, but it is evolving in this direction. For the purposes of this book, we restrict ourselves[1] to identifying those forces which at the global level favor the transition of interdependencies from classical trade and/or FDI to NFI. In our view, the following trends are symptomatic of these forces:

- The displacement of global growth dynamics from the Atlantic to the Pacific region.
- The technical revolution in communication, transportation, production, and the resulting increase in the speed of technology diffusion.
- A speed-up of structural adjustment processes with adverse affects on the traditional industrial countries (aging economies).
- The continuing financial imbalances between debtor and creditor countries.

3.1 The Displacement of Global Industrial Dynamics

After World War II the world economic order was centered on the superpower of the USA and the Western capitalist societies. Politically and technologically, this focus on one center has since given way to a polycentric constellation. The dissolution of a clear-cut North-South dichotomy was made possible first by export-oriented industrialization in the Latin American and Asian NICs, secondly by the rapid rise of Japan to a world economic power and thirdly by the trend away from economic dynamism to welfare state conservatism in the industrial nations of Western Europe, and, to a lesser extent, North America. As a result, the uncompromising logic of the world market led to the displacement of the dynamic center of world economic development from the Northwest toward the East and the South - toward Japan and the NICs. These industrial, export-oriented countries have based their success on selling the products of their plentiful, low-wage labour forces, on increasing the qualification level of their work force, and on carrying out an open, expansive policy of economic growth.

Together, these measures have resulted in a newly-won comparative advantage for a broad spectrum of industrial activities. Until recently, redeployment had only hit the old shoe-making, textile, and watch-making regions of Switzerland. Today, however, one can also witness the decline of the West's comparative advantage in the automobile and electrical industries. In a sense there is little difference between the redeployment of the production of automobile components and sophisticated machine tools today and the redeployment of the textile and shoe industries a decade ago. At the beginning of the 1960s, there were no NICs. The export value of industrial goods coming from the Third World's industrial leader in 1960 - India - has been surpassed by the new leader of 1980 - South Korea - by a factor of 20. Hong Kong, Singapore, Taiwan, and Brazil have also overtaken India. In 1960, as well as in 1980, more than 80% of the total export of industrial goods from the developing countries came from only 12 countries, but by 1980 the total export volume from these top 12 was 25 times greater than in 1960.

Despite this phenomenal growth in exports, the developing countries as a whole account for only one-tenth of the world's industrial exports. But the dynamic lies in

---

1 See BORNER/WEHRLE (1984a), HESSE et al. (1985), BHAGWATI (1981)

the rates of growth. Worries about structural adjustment in the aging economies have arisen primarily in branches and regions where comparative advantage has been shifted to the NICs. For Switzerland, the fact that the developing countries exported only 1% of the world's total exports of electrical products in 1963 as opposed to 12% today is unsettling. The basis of the industrial success of the NICs and the developing countries no longer lies in the production of textiles, shoes garments, and other 'typical' developing country goods, but rather in the production of televisions, telephones, radar, household appliances, optical equipment, watches, automobiles, etc. The old industrialized countries must finally accept the fact that the high level of competitiveness of Japanese industry is no longer due to a cheap imitation of the West's technological innovations. Rather, industrial research and clever exploitation of the world market has allowed Japan and even some NICs to rise to the top.

3.2 Revolution in Information, Communication, Transportation, and Production Technologies and their Rapid International Diffusion

Technological change as the well-spring of industrial and entrepreneurial innovation is a very difficult and controversial subject. Historical analysis of technical change, theoretical modeling, and everyday experience only illuminate the complexity of causes and effects in the innovation process.[2] Technological forecasting is an even more risky and tricky business. Nevertheless, the following positions seem to be well confirmed by theory and empirical evidence:

- Technological (or scientific) inventions are a necessary but not sufficient condition for industrial innovations. They open up new production and marketing potential but do not guarantee new feasible products and processes in private industry
- The driving force of industrial innovation is dynamic competition among profit-seeking enterprises. The economic relevance of technological/scientific inventions hinges on their profitable employment by industrial enterprises. In order to be profitable, know-how must somehow be protected from imitation - be it by 'internalization' and/or contractual arrangements.[3]
- It is not clear how we can measure the speed and direction of overall technological change. In view of the internationalization of entrepreneurial operations, however, we can quite safely assume that the speed of diffusion of industrial knowhow has - both geographically and/or with respect to transfer modes - definitely increased and will continue to do so. This point is briefly elaborated below.[4]

The nature and speed of the diffusion process depends first on the political power structure, second on the nature of technological changes and, third, on the strategic orientation of firms engaged in global competition. As the debate concerning technology transfer reveals, non-Western countries (LDCs, NICs, and COMECON countries) are increasing their efforts to widen and deepen the inflow of technology into their industries. They do so either by tying the import of capital

[2] See AYRES (1984) and ABERNATHY et al. (1983)
[3] See Part III, Chapters 7-10
[4] See also AYRES (1984: 83 ff.)

goods to other elements of know-how (i.e., management contracts, services, etc.) or by unbundling the FDI of MNEs. Although the purely ideological or rhetorical demands for free transfer of technology are nonsense, the increasingly rapid diffusion of know-how – as a consequence of 'forced unbundling of FDI' and/or of combining imports of goods or capital with know-how components – is a reality.

In this respect, the regulatory efforts of technology importers (restrictions on "classical" imports and on "classical FDI") are complementary and reinforce each other. While we may not advocate these restrictions, we have to recognize their existence as well as their growing effectiveness. The effectiveness does not depend mainly on legal or bureaucratic measures as such. Rather it depends on improved pre-conditions for the absorbtion of modern Western technologies into other cultural or developmental settings. The critical factors, in our opinion, are the general "modernization" of human consciousness, of social institutions, and of material infrastructure on the one hand and the existence of an entrepreneurial class on the other. Again the latter is not primarily culturally or historically determined but depends to a great extent on the existence of a market-oriented domestic and foreign policy, at least in the case of LDCs and NICs.

Furthermore, the nature of technological breakthroughs has facilitated the global spread of innovations. Of critical importance are the fantastic advances in the fields of information, communication, and transportation. These have not only enhanced the central management capacity of world-wide operating MNEs, they have also led to the contractual route of transferring and sharing know-how between partners in very different corners of the world. The mobility of human capital has grown enormously, thus making complex relationships over great distances possible. Specialists can be dispatched to the point of difficulty within a few hours and at a reasonable cost. These forces of technological globalization are strengthened by global media and global marketing which shape the tastes and preferences of the peoples of the world in more uniform ways. This process is highly visible in the case of consumer goods but equally relevant for production processes. The marriage between the product/technology cycle theory and location theory, as developed by VERNON (1966), has ended, therefore, in divorce. It is not only in the stages of maturity or even obsolescence that Western corporations transfer so-called naked technologies (i.e. turnkey plants, licenses, etc.). Even early phases are quite compatible with technology outflow, be it through multinational optimization of sourcing or through new forms of international cooperation. Faced with high production costs and high risks of losing control over know-how – via imitation, parallel development, or pressures from more potent competitors – more and more firms in the advanced countries are trying to exploit their know-how in multiple and innovative ways, rather than incorporating it in exportable (hardware) products.

3.3 A Speed-Up of Structural Adjustment Processes with Adverse Effects on the Traditional Industrial Countries

The aging economies of the highly developed countries are experiencing – under the conditions described above – difficult tests of their ability to compete and their ability to maintain their welfare states. The cautious, status-quo-conserving ('Besitzstanddenken'), no-risk mentality of the majority and the new alternative values of a growing minority have weakened traditional commitments to world market-oriented structural change. In the meantime, the technological monopoly of the North has been weakened as industrial know-how has spread to all corners of the world. Since 1950, the number of independent countries has tripled. From an economic point of view the old picture of a rich North and a poor South has given way to a polycentric constellation which includes the OPEC oil cartel and the industrial export offensive of the NICs.

The social and political reactions in the North to this global competition have been ambivalent and even contradictory. On the one hand, there have been attempts to check foreign competition, thereby supporting inefficiency in some industries. On the other hand, attempts have been made to maintain full employment and the real wage level by reducing the profitability, mobility, and flexibility of individual firms. Politicians attempt to gain time by dividing up the non-existent dividends of future growth. Trying to maintain the present, we are sacrificing the future. When all social relationships have been thoroughly commercialized and when the democratic decision-making processes have been reduced to a pure form of interest group egotism, then the national political arena will disintegrate into a distributional battlefield - with "public welfare" ending up the main victim. A mentality of conservatism and conservation is spreading thoughout the North, but especially through Europe. Crises of democracy and a general decline in the level of economic performance are socio-political symptoms of crippled a capitalist economic dynamics in the Western industrial countries. Traditional technological and growth-oriented approaches to the future find themselves on a course of collision with changing social and cultural values and needs - people-oriented and environment-oriented values.

The classical strategies of hardware exports and direct investment are being increasingly confronted by strong nationalistic measures to protect, control, and structure economic activities. The phase of intra-industrial interpenetration (1950-1970) produced relatively weak pressures for structural adjustment. Specialization and product innovation were the major strategies of export-oriented Swiss firms. Such strategies enabled innovative processes and growth of production to take place without much redeployment and without the displacement of entire branches or product groups. Except for large-scale immigration of foreign labour, foreign trade and structural change took place 'without tears'. The political demands for locally-owned production units (the Lima Declaration of 1975), the growing attractiveness of industrial locations in the Southeast Asian and Latin American NICs, as well as the need to test promising marketing possibilities, have all combined to bring forth a true internationalization of production. The forms taken by such internationalized activities range from licensing to 100% controlled direct investments. The internationalization of companies is gradually replacing market-oriented foreign trade. Goods and services are exchanged internationally among the units of one firm. Strategic bundling of resources in non-market packaging leads to an 'invisible' international transfer of resources. Structural adjustment and the innovation process take place primarily inside the firm. Competitiveness has come to be based on 'private' absolute advantages internal to the firm. National resources and traditional indicators of competitiveness at the level of the branch or product group have been rendered virtually useless by this change in the form of economic competition, at least in the realm of knowledge and/or capital intensive manufacturing activities.

Even a highly developed country like Switzerland cannot just rely on the profitable sale of know-how from its patented reservoir of technological and human potential. The firm-specific internalization of knowledge goes well beyond anything that can be patented. Know-how which can be internalized and then internationalized includes the following: organizational capabilities, marketing experience, creativity, team-work, flexibility. World-wide sale of integrated packages of know-how services must take advantage of all forms of trade, investment, and cooperation. Just as the export boom was the key to financial success in the postwar period, today it is important to weave one's firms successfully into the diverse forms and types of international activities at all levels of company functions. Both classical export activity and direct investment have lost out to pressures for protection and local production. At the same time, the chances for exports from the traditional industrialized countries are disappearing rapidly, as the credit available to developing countries is cut and as these countries try to meet debt payments by increasing their own exports and by limiting their imports. The complexity of the world-wide economic structures and relationships will certainly continue to increase.

3.4 The World Debt Problem and New Forms of Internationalization

Just as in the case of the other main driving forces, the world debt problem cannot be fully analyzed here.[5] Again, we shall try to pick up only those threads which lead directly to NFI. As in the case of the world trading system, we are rather agnostic about a simple, clear-cut, and market-oriented system of global financing. In many respects, the debt issue is even more political than trade and technology problems. First of all, the question of national solvency (or insolvency for that matter) really boils down to the question: How far can living standards be depressed in order to pay off debts? "The real issue is whether their political systems and citizens can and should be made to stand the strain." (DORNBUSCH/FISCHER 1984: 1). Secondly, the discussions about long-term solutions in the framework of new and stable financial arrangements cannot be separated from trade conflicts. And it is obvious that depressed demand and severely restricted imports in the large debtor countries wipe out exports and threaten employment in the Western industrialized countries. Likewise, the increased efforts of debtor nations to promote exports in order to realize balance-of-payments-surpluses - the only way to pay off debt without outright swap of assets - meets political resistance against imports in those same nations which are blaming the debtor countries for their lavish policies.

This basic conflict has been well expressed by Lord LEVER:[6] "(Purely commercial lending) is defective in that it requires premature attempts at balance of payments surplus by the debtor countries not compatible with our political interests or

[5] The reader is refered to the vast literature on the subject. A prime choice includes CLINE (1984), DORNBUSCH/FISCHER (1984), KINDLEBERGER (1981), SACHS (1982).

[6] LEVER (1984), cited by DORNBUSCH/FISCHER (1984: 1).

theirs. Recent net transfers of resources from the debtors have been bought at the cost of economic slack and grave risk to political stability. They are too small to restore confidence but large enough to do serious damage to the debtors' economies and societies: they are neither desirable nor sustainable."

It is no wonder that practically all experts - economists and politicians alike - place their hopes in global export growth and liberalization of trade. But as we have argued consistently in this book, "there is no reason to believe that a much more liberal world trading system is around the corner. Nor is it reasonable to overlook the fact that DCs (= Developing Countries, authors' note) will be competing with each other in all markets." (DORNBUSCH/FISCHER 1984:51). The vast majority of observers is also skeptical about increasing the financial flows into debtor countries (especially NICs and LDCs) by more bank lending, by tapping the international bond market, or by transferring large sums of purely financial aid. From the traditional economic perspective, this leaves only FDI as a potent source of external capital inflow. And there are certainly signs that FDI is becoming more attractive and welcome in LDCs and other debtor nations. However, the high risks associated with the shaky political and economic status of debt-ridden host countries and the pressure applied to produce for export (re-exports) cannot be overlooked by the MNEs. Thus there will most likely be no grand design to solve the world debt crisis, i.e. the global financing problems. Neither large-scale debt-relief, the swap of real assets against IOUs, nor a one-shot increase in international liquidity represents an acceptable and sustainable solution. If we want to overcome the present path of "muddling through", we basically need more cooperation, more consistency in national economic policies, and also new ways of combining financing with other international transactions.

Discussing the pre-conditions and terms of better cooperation, SIMONSEN puts his finger on the sore spot: "Under what conditions (would) rational policy-makers in debtor nations ... prefer cooperation to retaliation? While precise rupture points are difficult to locate, a general principle remains valid: a growing economy with expanding exports hardly would seek confrontation with its creditors. In the same line, solvency at the expense of prolonged recession may be politically unsustainable."[7] But the critical assumptions of more rapid growth (with less inflation) and reduced trade restrictions are based more on hope than on probability. Their correctness would depend, first, on a different monetary-fiscal policy mix, especially in the USA, and second, on a turnaround of political attitudes in the "aging economies".

CLINE (1985) estimates the elasticity of LDC export growth in relation to real GDP-growth in the OECD countries to be about 3%. This places a high level of responsibility and a heavy burden on the shoulders of the industrialized countries and their economic policies. At this point, the connections between the debt issue and NFI should be clear.

NFI allow a bundling of one or more transactions - finance, technology, intermediate products, finished-goods components - which could not (or might not) be transferred individually under the given conditions. One of the worst aspects of the

---

[7] SIMONSEN (1984) cited by DORNBUSCH/FISCHER (1984:61)

debt crisis is the high concentration among debtors and creditors: the first being nation-states, the latter large, international banks.

NFI-strategies aimed at cooperation between debtor-nation firms and creditor-nation firms would most certainly be an improvement over pure commercial lending to governments by banks. We see the following potential advantages:

- The "lumpiness" of the credits can be decreased if exporters, suppliers, consultants, and their respective house banks take part in the financing.
- Countries with a high level of debt and therefore very bad "country ratings" may still have promising firms with potentially rewarding investment projects. These projects, however, can only be realized by some NFI arrangement.
- In most cases NFI establish a long-term relationship between the cooperating firms. Technology and marketing know-how transfers are usually more frequent than in the case of exports or FDI. The export position of the host country is thus strengthened.

NFI may even contribute to the erosion of protectionism by undermining the cheapest but most effective argument used by lobbies against structural adjustment necessitated by foreign competition. In the case of Switzerland, it is quite evident that the dichotomy between "we Swiss" and "them foreigners" cannot be maintained. International production by our MNEs on the one hand and the degree of internationalization within contractual frameworks of Swiss NFI on the other are too visible and too economically significant to be hidden behind nationalistic rhetoric.

Chapter 4

The Structural Adjustment Problems of the National Economy: Views on the "Competitiveness Debate" of Swiss Executives

Before probing more deeply and more systematically into theoretical and empirical analysis, we close this introductory part with some views on the structural adjustment problems faced by Swiss industry. The views presented here were expressed by top managers from industry, banking, trading and consulting.[1]

The main purpose of these interviews, each of 1-3 hours duration, was to get a first-hand, authentic impression of the perspectives of managers in charge of industrial development. We did not primarily expect hard facts and concrete results - but visions of problems, their potential solutions, as well as insights into the ways of thinking among those responsible for strategic decisions at the top level.[2] The topic of these 20 sessions was centered around the adjustment problems of Swiss industry, especially in regard to the new challenges to competitiveness which are "threatening" our enterprises from without and within.[3] The need for our industries to adjust to the new phase of international competition was not disputed by any of our discussion partners. This is not surprising when we take into account that none of

[1] These interviews based on a loose discussion guide were carried out by Prof. C. Pümpin (HSG) and Prof. S. Borner (Basle). The interview partners of Prof. Pümpin were:
P. Borgeaud, Präsident der Konzernleitung, Gebrüder Sulzer AG, Winterthur
Dr. D. Bührle, Präsident des Verwaltungsrates, Oerlikon Bührle Holding AG, Zürich
W. Frehner, Generaldirektor, SBV, Basel
F. Gerber, Präsident des Verwaltungsrates, F. Hoffmann-La Roche & Co. AG, Basel
Dr. H. Götz, Delegierter des Verwaltungsrates, Georg Fischer AG, Schaffhausen
Dr. P. Gross, Generaldirektor, SBG, Zürich
Prof. Dr. h. c. M. Hilti, Präsident des Verwaltungsrates, Hilti AG, Schaan
P. Hummel, Vorsitzender der Konzernleitung, BBC AG Brown, Boveri & Cie, Baden
R. A. Jeker, Präsident der Generaldirektion, SKA, Zürich
H. Maucher, Delegierter des Verwaltungsrates, Nestle AG, Vevey
Dr. P. Spälti, Delegierter des Verwaltungsrates, Winterthur
Schweizerische Versicherungsgesellschaft, Winterthur
D. Syz, Präsident der Konzernleitung, Landis & Gyr AG, Zug
The interview partners of Prof. Borner were:
Nicholas Hayek, Hayek Engineering AG, Zürich
Dr. H. U. Baumberger, Unternehmensberatung, Herisau
Benoît Ludwig, McKinsey, Zürich
Bruno Simma, ICME Unternehmensberatung, Zürich
Dr. Luk E. Keller, Unternehmensberatung, Zürich
Claus Nüscheler, Konzernleitung Siber Hegner, Zürich
Dr. Zumstein, Generaldirektor, UTC, Basel
Dr. U. Sigg, Konzernleitung Schindler Holding AG, Ebikon

[2] The main results of these sessions have been published separately by C. Pümpin (1985).

[3] This is a rather free re-interpretation with respect to the issues raised in this report, especially the nature and importance of internationalization from the perspective of individual firms.

the managers interviewed was rooted in the purely cartellized and protected sectors of our economy. Just as in the semi-popular and also professional literature, the causes for losses in competitiveness were discussed in a diverse and ad hoc fashion. This was even more true in the case of the managers' discussions of proposed remedies. On the following points a certain level of consensus seems to have been reached:

- Many traditional needs are satiated, with the corresponding markets displaying a tendency to shrink rather than to grow. This forces enterprises to adjust their scale of operation (redimensioning) in a situation of depressed returns.
- Protectionism in all shapes and sizes is mentioned again and again as a source of first-rate troubles. As long as unemployment and/or indebtedness remain high in so many key countries, there is little hope for a turn-around in trade policies towards free exchange and open markets.
- The third problem area mentioned by practically all those interviewed is technological changes which require new industrial and entrepreneurial structures.

What shall we make of this? We share the conventional economic wisdom that "satiation" is a poor diagnosis of current structural problems. This is obvious in view of "global needs" and the fact that most people do not opt for less work with less pay, which would be the logical solution to over-abundance of industrially produced and market-distributed goods. If we interpret the first point as a lack of effective demand, then we run into the rival hypotheses of cyclical slump versus structural weakness within certain industries in specific countries. "Protectionism" and "technological change" are both catchwords for extremely complex processes, which are certainly not exogeneous in any meaningful way. Protectionism is mainly the outcome of the political struggles in an adjustment crisis and thereby indirectly an outcome of the entrepreneurial dynamic itself. Technological change originates directly in entrepreneurial strategies of growth through innovation and therefore it is even less defensible to view technological change as a purely exogenous change in the environment.

Contrary to what might have been expected some years ago, no one explicitly or implicitly favored a purely macroeconomic approach for diagnosing structural weaknesses. In other words, the cyclical components of weak demand, over-capacity, and all the market consequences thereof were taken into account, but not considered to be decisive.[4] In the same way, the conservative supply-side view characteristic of macroeconomics was not supported, at least not in any dogmatic, simplistic version. In a certain sense, taxes are always too high for business, regulations are always too extensive, and government expenditure too lavish. Lower taxes, lower government expenditure, fewer regulations, and more incentives are always welcome to business and managers. But in the Swiss case, few if any managers felt strongly that a radical approach à la REAGAN would really solve the basic problems.[5]

[4] This picture may be influenced by the fact that our interviews took place in 1985 when the dollar was at its maximum "overvaluation". Thereby, Swiss industry was blessed with a macroeconomic edge in international competitiveness.

[5] We suspect the same is true for US business, where businessmen fear the consequences of the high REAGAN deficits. The hard-core supply-siders are mainly ideologically-oriented academics or politicians.

While focussing more narrowly and deeply on the causes as perceived by individual enterprises, three categories of explanations for loss of competitiveness dominated. In order of importance, they are:

- "Social sclerosis" as a very general tendency of "aging" organizations: Organizations and organized groups seem to become progressively more bureaucratic, more rigid, while the individuals shaping them seem to become more and more defensive and protective.
- Bad management in various forms: Whereas US analysts deplore the degeneration of the overall top-manager to a financial monger of investment portfolios,[6] the Swiss version of bad management focusses mainly on the success of yesteryears as the main cause of present and future difficulties. Success came easily under the favorable growth climate of the 1960s and early 1970s. Management attributed this lucky draw to its own geniality. Unbroken growth performances nurtured ideas of infallibility. The lack of outside pressure to change led to an entrepreneurial culture which is not geared to change. This cultural climate attracts and promotes managers who lack long-term vision, who lack the ability to design basic strategic innovations, and who lack the capacity to motivate teams to engineer and carry out the necessary changes.
- Technological development: Here the basic hypothesis is that there has been a slow-down in R&D, especially in basic research and scientific education. Many managers said that the falling-behind of the Swiss is basically explained by the catching-up of others (the Japanese, the NICs) on the one hand, and by the more radical drives for basic scientific innovations in the US on the other hand. This is viewed as a common European predicament and not a typically Swiss aspect of the problem.

The most valuable information was distilled from discussions of proposed remedies. The general outlook of our 20 managers can be captured in the following matrix:

Necessity of changing corporate strategies and cultures	Sources of Structural Difficulties: Firm level	Sources of Structural Difficulties: Outside Environment
High	(Type A)	
Low		(Type B)

Fig. 4-1. Strategies to Raise Competitive Advantage

6 See especially AYRES (1984)

Type B is clearly the minority in our sample. These managers tend to favor a combination of improving the external conditions of firm operations (such as influencing the exchange rate, lowering taxes and social security contributions, promoting free trade, or, on the contrary, cartellization) and of making relatively defensive and passive adjustments within the firm (such as cost control, termination of non-profitable operations, adaptation to shrinking markets, etc.).

The more prevalent group (Type A) does not overlook the fundamental changes in the political and economic environment which entail new forms of competition and regulation. For them, these changes are either quite natural or not really reversible - at least in the short run and from the perspective of the individual firm. In order to increase flexibility, international composition, and selection and development of a management which considers change to be the "normal state" and innovation to be the "normal response", these business leaders advocate a basic reorientation of entrepreneurial culture and company strategies. We will return (cf. PÜMPIN 1985) to these issues in the final part of this study.

In contrast to technological and political bureaucrats, (successful) business leaders seem to support the hypothesis put forward earlier by BORNER: that innovation is a process which starts in a particular climate and which requires specific organizational structures; the result is the development of new skills (technical innovations in the narrow sense).[7] This hypothetical chain of causation is presented schematically in the following matrix:

The decisiveness of the cultural dimension of competitive advantage was clearly emphasized both by those who felt they had established an innovative culture and those who criticized the stubbornness with which mainstream Swiss management clings to the principles and strategies of yesteryears. The issue of the relationship between technological and organizational aspects of innovation, especially in view of international operations, remains a subject of debate. Our contention, supported especially by outsiders (consultants, traders), is that many Swiss firms are either "under-internationalized" or not optimally utilizing the entire range of forms of internationalization which are available.

This strong emphasis on the organizational dimension of entrepreneurial behavior will be explained in more detail in subsequent chapters. Nevertheless, its position in the very center of the matrix implies the following crucial considerations:

- There is a two-way linkage between the technological and cultural dimensions of firm-specific competitive advantages. Cultures, philosophies, visions, etc. are easy to design and proclaim, but they are only relevant if they are embedded in an appropriate organizational framework. In the same way, R&D expenditures are easy to make, but they become economically successful only when guided and absorbed by an appropriate organizational framework.
- The same is true for strategic elements. Purely technologically or culturally oriented strategic efforts get stuck either in fancy hardware and/or paper-software if they are not backed up by a powerful organization which is able to put into effect what is strategically envisaged.
- The central organizational cell "scope" (cf. Figure 4-2) is clearly less "flashy" than the more "heroic" ones in which the business giants of "technological" or

[7] See BORNER (1984b), BORNER/SIMMA (1984), BORNER/WEHRLE (1984b)

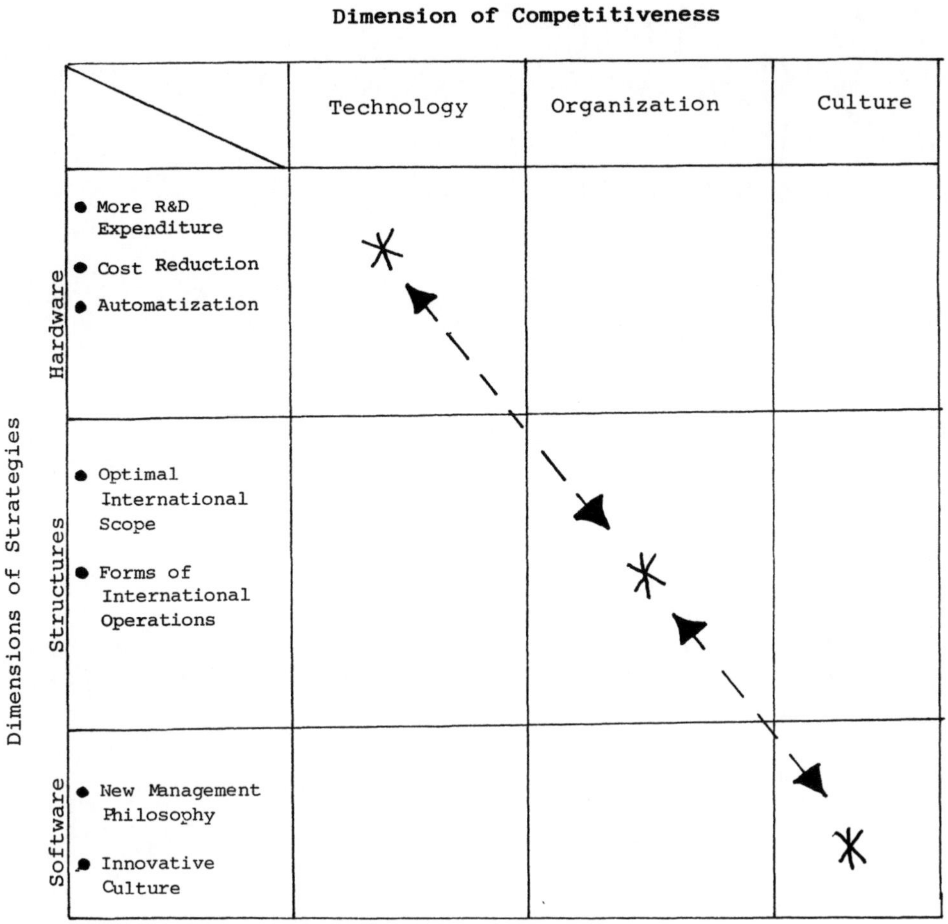

Fig. 4-2. Firm-Specific Competitive Advantage

"cultural revolutions" like to place themselves. This lack of attractiveness is, in our view, more than compensated for by the high degree of "doableness" - in German, "Machbarkeit".

Whereas geniuses and giants only appear at random (with a high probability of failure in their own fields), "organizational scope" - the bundling of skills in the realm of know-how with forms in the realm of operations - is a clearly manageable task. In fact, this is the central managerial function.

Part II

A Taxonomy of New Forms of International Investment and Export Financing

Chapter 5

New Forms of International Investment

Our conceptual framework for research on New Forms of Internationalization (NFI) rests on a basic distinction between two fundamentally different forms. On the one hand we investigated New Forms of International Investment (NFII) and on the other hand New Forms of Export Financing (NFEF). Both are aimed at reducing the transaction costs of internationalized entrepreneurial activities, that is, at reducing the transaction costs of the two classic forms of internationalization: exports and direct foreign investment (DFI). In fact, exports and DFI can be conceptualized as polar opposites on a continuous spectrum of forms of internationalization which in some way or the other are a combination of these two "pure" forms. More specifically, all New Forms of Internationalization are designed to serve the following purposes:

- internationalizing profitability of the core skills of a particular entrepreneurial unit or firm
- internationalizing various business activities and services
- internationalizing marketing strategies
- overcoming protectionist regulations and other barriers to trade.

Depending on the nature of the strategy chosen and followed, we can designate forms of internationalization either primarily as export financing strategies or primarily as international investment strategies (cf. Table 5-1). In some cases the nature of the combination of the two makes the situation difficult to characterize as NFII or NFEF. In this chapter we shall discuss specific New Forms of International Investment; Chapter 6 is devoted to New Forms of Export Financing.

Table 5-1. Taxonomy of New Forms of Internationalization

New Forms of International Investment (NFII)	New Forms of Export Financing (NFEF)
1. Licensing	1. Barter
2. Sub-Contracting	2. Long-Term Commercial Framework Agreements
3. Consulting	3. Counterdelivery
4. Contractual Cooperation	4. Offset
5. Joint Ventures	5. Junktim
6. Group Investment	6. Turnkey
	7. Buy-Back

5.1 Licensing

Licensing permits a plant or a firm to carry out an "activity" - the rights to which are in fact owned by another firm. In the case of industrial licensing this means that a firm can purchase the right to use know-how and/or trademarks developed and owned by a firm which holds a de facto or de jure monopoly over both. Licensing contracts concern the use of immaterial goods. In Western Europe licensing contracts per se are not subject to specific legal regulations. The two partners are free to formulate the contract as they wish, providing they do not break anti-cartel laws and/or laws against illegal competition. "The licensing contracts can thus contain elements of a purchasing contract and a rent contract" (WIDMER 1980:25), thereby containing elements of "leasing" (HUG 1983:3). The essence of the license is the right to use an object - the object is not bought or sold. The licensor waives his monopoly rights in return for payment of a fee.

Objects of licenses are patents, know-how without formal protection, industrial and ornamental designs, trademarks, and copyrights. These objects can be licensed singly or in combination. According to a study of 3,500 licensing agreements registered with the European Commission (POLEY 1978:88), only about one-third (35%) are "pure" licenses, i.e. having one object only (27% are patent licenses, 5% know-how, and 4% trademarks). Thus, 64% are "mixed" licenses: know-how and trademarks 35%; patents, trademarks, and know-how 15%; patents and know-how 12%; patents and trademarks 2%. Know-how was involved in 97% of the agreements, rights to use trademarks in 56% of the contracts, and patents in 45% of the cases.

There are two basic motives which lead to licensing agreements among entrepreneurs: the opening-up of new markets and/or the further penetration of old markets on the one hand and the establishment of market security on the other. Market expansion is an offensive strategy, market security a defensive strategy. Less important motives include monetary receipts from the sale of know-how itself - e.g. in the case of research spin-offs. Licenses also serve as mechanisms for transferring profits from branch plants to headquarters of MNCs.

5.2 Sub-Contracting

A number of concepts are often used as synonyms despite the fact that they are not really identical: contract-finishing, redeployment on a contractual basis, sub-contracting, contract manufacturing, off-shore assembly, etc. For our purposes these concepts may be used as synonyms if they conform to the following definition based on UNIDO (1975): Sub-contracting agreements take place between independent enterprises; the contract is always based on specifications defined by the contractor. This definition also covers regular custom-made procurement. Even though in this sense sub-contracting is an externalization of productive activities, we add the following four restrictions:

- The contract deals with the "processing or finishing of parts provided by, and returned to, the primary company" (UNIDO 1975:23) and/or the contractee "carries out certain operations or manufacture(s) parts and components according to the specifications and under the technical responsibility of the main contracting

firm" (UNIDO 1975:45). The latter two conditions can be met both individually and jointly.
- The marketing of the end product is done by the contractor.
- The contractor and the contractee are located in different countries.
- Sub-contracting activities are limited to the industrial production of commodities. (Thus we do not include production contracts for retail chains).

The literature dealing with sub-contracting focusses mostly on North-South sub-contracting, with the contractor in the industrial North and the contractee in a Third World country. Yet the concept does not exclude North-North or South-North sub-contracting. Using the UNIDO typology (UNIDO 1975:23/24) we distinguish among the following:
- Cost-motivated sub-contracting: The contractor is able to realize cost advantages.
- Specialized sub-contracting: The contractor utilizes the specialized know-how and infrastructure of the contractee.
- Surplus sub-contracting: The contractor cannot or will not expand his facilities.
- Peak demand sub-contracting: The contractor needs reprieve from short-term increases in demand.
- Marginal-sub-contracting: Insignificant or one-time orders are contracted out to other firms.

Sub-contracting is possible only when the production process can be decomposed into a succession of intermediate goods - and when the value/weight ratio of the intermediate goods in question is relatively high: "International sub-contracting is usually easier in electronics than for electrical goods, and easier for electrical goods than for most mechanical engineering" (SHARPSTON 1975:111).

5.3 Consulting

Consulting can consist of pure technical advice or it can apply to all types of organizational, marketing, and financial questions. During the course of our research we did not investigate the following types of consulting: the sale of consulting services by specialized consulting firms, consulting as a strategy for firm diversification, and consulting as a customer service. Rather, our investigation was aimed at consulting activities with a long-term investment character. In such cases the consultant offers his or her capabilities - know-how and know-why - to a particular company. The company in turn becomes somewhat dependent on the consultant. Usually, however, the remuneration is partially based on long-term success. Thus the dependency relationship does not remain one-sided.

We are talking about "permanent consulting". The consultant works closely with the customer and gives him instructions. SCHAUB (1979:53) describes such consulting work as follows: "First goal-oriented creative work is done. Prior to this, sometimes large amounts of information have to be gathered, information which then serves as an input for the "headwork" that has to be done. Depending on the specific task, this thinking is oriented to purely technical, purely business, or a combination of entrepreneurial problems. Finally, the results are embodied in the form of reports, tables, diagrams, sketches, and plans to be utilized by those whose job it is to transform the ideas into action."

Both management consulting and technical consulting can take one of a variety of forms: from the one-time job to sporadic consulting to continuous or permanent consulting. Management consulting can lead to a high level of participation and even to the installation of the consultant on the company's board of directors. It should be obvious that such consultancy relationships cannot be classified as "sales operations". At the same time such consulting agreements are not direct investments in the traditional sense either. Rather, they are forms of foreign operation which bind specific resources and have an investment character.

5.4 Contractual Cooperation

Contractual cooperation is the most heterogeneous form of internationalization. Under full contractual freedom two legally - and from the point of view of capital - independent firms join together to carry out particular activities. Leaving out cartel agreements, we concentrated on activities resulting from two types of motivations: first, pre-competitive cooperation and complementary oriented cooperation. Pre-competitive cooperation refers to the situation in which two firms supplying the same market cooperate in certain research and development activities. This may be accompanied by cooperation in purchasing, warehousing, and after sales service. From a macroeconomic point of view pre-competitive cooperation strikes a delicate balance between the promotion of technological and developmental cooperation and the prevention of a reduction in the level of competition. Secondly, firms in the same industry can assist each other by bringing together complementary structures in all types of entrepreneurial functions - research and development, purchasing, warehousing, production, marketing, sales, services, administration - thereby achieving higher levels of cost effectiveness, market presence, and innovative performance. Complementary cooperation can occur between firms possessing either the same or substantially different levels of know-how. In the latter case the object is to aid the weaker partner in expanding production facilities and marketing capacity under the condition of abundant sources of labor, raw materials, or energy (cf. SCHMOLL/GOLDBERGER 1983: 12-24).

Here again the literature concentrates on cooperation between firms in the Western industrialized countries on the one hand and firms in developing countries, the NICs, or in the Eastern European countries on the other. We note, however, that a more intensive use of existing know-how - especially among OECD or, more specifically, Western European firms - could result from more frequent contractual cooperation. Despite the great variety such contracts can take, certain features are common to all (cf. SCHMOLL/GOLDBERGER 1983: 21-24):

- the intention of two or more firms to undertake one or more tasks together
- the basically unlimited time horizon for the cooperative task
- mutual obligation to provide complementary goods and services - rather than to purchase from each other against payment
- the maintenance of the partners' legal and financial independence.

5.5 Joint Ventures

The claim that "a joint venture is any contract you have to live with", given the restriction that "there is an ongoing service responsibility or relationship" (TRUMPY 1984a:2) may seem useful to a practitioner. For our purposes such a definition is too general. A joint venture[1] is "a separately incorporated enterprise in which investors from two or more countries commit capital assets, share some degree of management responsibility at some level and participate jointly in the full risks of the enterprise." (ROBINSON 1980:65). The partners do not necessarily need to bring financial capital into the venture. Technical and business know-how - e.g. by way of licenses - can form a sufficient basis for participation. The activity and operation of the venture can be grounded in a complex contract between the two main participants on the one hand and with other local firms on the other. A robust legal framework between trustworthy partners can circumvent the necessity of a high level of capitalization.

Leaving aside one time projects - "ad hoc" joint ventures - we must still distinguish among the various economic functions of long-term joint ventures: the politically tricky ventures between two firms who supply the same markets and joint ventures designed to integrate and coordinate firms with complementary positions within a specialized division of labor. As in the case of other NFII we do not consider cartel arrangements as joint ventures. Rather, we investigated joint ventures designed to coordinate productive resources - from supplying raw materials and intermediate products (cf. HAUSER 1981:180) to research and development, the launching of new marketing strategies, and the elimination of overlapping productive capacity.

5.6 Group Investment

Various firms from one or more countries enter a joint venture in order to guarantee or achieve cooperation on a third market. The team can be project oriented or have a permanent status. Group investments as NFII refer only to investment oriented, long-term ventures. For example, production joint ventures without local participation, marketing joint ventures, or various types of turnkey operations. However, group investments can also be operated as NFEF: arm's-length transactions which have an extended time horizon but which lack typical investment traits.

[1] Cf. TRUMPY 1984a, HAUSER 1981, ROBINSON 1980, WALMSLEY 1982

Chapter 6

New Forms of Export Financing

6.1 Barter

Barter is certainly the oldest form of international economic exchange. The following definitions of barter serve to situate barter as one form of minimizing the higher transaction costs of bilateral exchange in comparison with monetized exchange. (For the legal aspects cf. FONTAINE 1982 and JACKSON 1969.)

- "Barter is the direct exchange of goods between an East European and a Western partner. There are two important differences between barter and all other forms of countertrade: no money changes hands and no third party is involved." (Business International 1984a: VI-3).
- Barter is the "échange direct et simultané de marchandise de valeur équivalente qui ne donne lieu à aucun réglement financier ou transfert de fonds et fait l'objet d'un contract unique." (ACECO 1983: 27).
- "Barter is the exchange of goods or services between two parties without resort to money-swapping." (R. WEIGAND 1980: 34).
- "'Classical' barter denotes a once-only transaction which is bound by a single contract that specifies the goods to be exchanged to an equivalent value. Of all forms of countertrade it is the closest to the traditional pure barter, except that today money is normally used." (G. BANKS 1983: 160).

Despite the fact that the four authors agree that barter in its bilateral form consists of one single contract, the definitions differ in their answers to the following questions:

- What is the nature of the values exchanged - commodities or services?
- Can the responsibilities agreed to in a barter contract be passed on to a third party?
- Does barter just consist of the exchange of goods and services or can finances be involved as well?

In the following paragraphs various forms of barter will be described, starting with the simplest form, the bilateral exchange of goods.

6.1.1 Classical or "Pure" Barter

"The most radical form of bilateralism is the bilateral exchange of real goods." (PÜTZ 1959: 270). This form of bilateralism means that the domestic exporter does not receive money as compensation - he receives commodities in exchange for his product. With the exchange of goods for goods all the advantages of a monetarized economy are eliminated. Despite the relationship between the terms of trade and the ratio of the domestic price level, a price is not attached to the goods exchanged. Since barter agreements - as opposed to export operations - have a longer binding period (OECD 1981:18) - up to three years - new types of risk are added to the classical export risks (cf. VERNON 1983). The major risks include:

- that the real exchange rate - relative prices - will change to the disadvantage of domestic exporters
- that the quality of the compensatory goods will be lower than promised and that the commodities received in exchange prove to be difficult to market. (The marketing risk can be high even in cases where high quality goods are delivered on time and "at the right price". Since the commodity received in exchange is seldom an input in the production process for the domestic exporter, the exporter must market his partner's goods.)
- that political events will prevent or delay the delivery of the compensatory goods (political risk).

6.1.2 Barter with Contractual Participation of a Third Party

The inclusion of a third party requires the insertion of a transfer or third party clause in the agreement. "This transfer clause is essential to Western suppliers who will not themselves settle the countertrade commitment. Even if the Western exporter originally intends to use the East-European goods in-house or for resale through his own trading division, inclusion of the transfer clause is cheap insurance against eventualities." (BUSINESS INTERNATIONAL 1984b: VI-22). The transfer clause says for example: "The western company commits itself to buy or to have bought through a third party goods from . . .". (ACECO 1983). For the foreign importer such a contract is as if it were pure barter. The domestic exporter, however, is paid directly for his commodities.

6.1.3 Parallel Barter

Parallel barter "is a form of compensation dealing (which) is characterized by the fact that in contrast to classical barter, each delivery is paid for in cash" (SCHUSTER 1980:62).

6.1.4 Triangular Barter

Triangular barter is a form of pure barter, parallel barter, or barter with participation of the banking system. It differs from the forms described above in that the foreign importer delivers to a firm in a third country.

6.2 Long-term Commercial Framework Agreements

A large company or trading firm contracts with an export trading firm of a foreign country to handle the exports of an entire industrial sector. Such an agreement, sealed with a letter of intent, is made when, for example, the Western exporter is practically a monopoly supplier of products which have a high priority in the import planning of an Eastern European country. Besides the countertrade component, many elements of subcontracting are included in such a framework agreement. The difference lies "... in the full size of the contract ..., the involvement of government organizations in East European countries as intermediaries for the firm, the lack of flexibility in the program decided upon which must fit in with the East European country's economic planning, and the secondary role played by financial settlements in equalising such transactions." (OECD, 1981:22). The multifunctionality of a framework agreement allows not only flexibility in supply, it also permits long-term cooperation - where technology transfer is not necessary - in the area of production. Used in combination with Junktim, framework agreements permit the booking of imports as a form of prefinancing for one's own exports.

6.3 Counterdelivery

Counterdelivery is in principle similar to parallel barter. In contrast to parallel barter, however, three separate contracts are necessary:
- the contract of sale of exports from A to B,
- the contract of sale of exports from B to A,
- a head of agreement, which maintains that the first two contracts were signed within the framework of a bilateral agreement. Often a product list - with a list of possible compensation commodities - is included so that the exporter can reduce the risk of receiving poor quality goods or goods which are difficult to market. In the head of agreement, the possibility of transferring the compensatory responsibilities to a third party can be agreed upon.

Why is counterdelivery the most common form of countertrade transactions? (cf. GMÜR 1980, and BUSINESS INTERNATIONAL 1984c). The separation of the agreement into separate contracts brings significant advantages.
- The export contract between A and B can be insured, either privately or through government programs, against various risks of doing business abroad.
- The export and refinancing instruments of the banking system can be used.
- Compensation can be transferred to third parties, thus allowing the terms of the basic export contract to remain secret.
- The existence of three separate contracts means that the Western exporter "gets full payment for his deliveries at once or under credit arrangements, while his own purchases in Eastern Europe have to be paid for only when suitable products have been found and a contract signed" (BUSINESS INTERNATIONAL 1976: VI-4). "Separating the contracts protects the original seller because payment for his goods cannot legally be withheld if problems arise in the execution of the second contract." (WELT 1984:16)

The mere existence of separate contracts results in a re-distribution of risk to the advantage of the exporter.

6.4 Offset

With the responsibility of finding buyers for the products of one's trade partner, the exporter takes on the allocation functions of a trading company. This form of trade is called off-set. Offset is often confused with counterdelivery (cf. BELTRAMO 1985). The differences between offset and counterdelivery are:

- The partners in offset are a government (the buyer) and a large multinational firm or the government operated weapons industry in the exporting country.
- The exporter does not function as the purchaser of commodities in return. Rather, he lets the importer use his marketing know-how and his world-wide trade and information network.
- For the most part offset is limited to the defense industry. The monetary value of such offset deals runs into the billions (BUSINESS RESEARCH INTERNATIONAL, 1984).
- The buyer's country government, as purchaser, profits from the offset mechanism only indirectly - increased tax income, employment effects, balance of payments - through the offset induced increase in demand for other products.
- Offset is not a vehicle for selling otherwise non-marketable goods. Rather, it is an instrument to open up markets for competitive products or to overcome neo-protectionist trade barriers.
- Offset, as a memorandum of understanding, allows counterdeliveries to operate as if they were classical exports.

6.5 Junktim

Junktim is the mirror image of counterdelivery. It is defined as follows: "Achats, sous-traitance ou services dont la réalisation precède celle d'exportation prévisionelles pour lesquelles une contrepartie est envisagée." (ACECO 1983: 33). A firm uses Junktim as an instrument within a long-term internationalization strategy. The following variations can serve to balance accounts:

- One considers debts as pre-financing with the possibility "that all the Western firm's purchases (...) can qualify for a credit to be offset against subsequent deliveries." (OECD, 1981: 20). In this way one avoids the risks stemming from future countertrade demand and supply.
- Further, one can book the debts as imports - with the compensatory obligations of other exporters. This leads to the use of International Trade Certificates - marketable securities which guarantee the holder export rights.
- Another possibility is the pre-financing of New Forms of Internationalization with the objective of redistributing the risk.
- Foreign demand can be met through payments.

Through booking imports with the value of one's own exports, Junktim redeploys export risks to the advantage of the exporters. In combination with buy-back, Junktim enables the reduction of the credit and/or in-house financing necessary to span the period between the moment of production and that of marketing the buyback commodities. The risk of marketing the counter-goods is transferred to the contract partner. Exports of huge construction projects can be pre-financed through countertrade. The basic problem with this financing mechanism (cf. ENGELHARDT/SCHUSTER, 1980) is the high search and marketing costs associated with selling the compensatory goods.

6.6 Turnkey

"Under a turnkey contract, the contractor is responsible for setting up a complete production unit - factory, energy plant, etc. - or infrastructure project." (OMAN 1984:15). There are three basic forms of turnkey:

- Clé-en-main: the project must be technically ready for operation.
- Product-in-hand: the obligation is fulfilled as soon as the plant is functioning with local personnel and the output has reached, qualitatively and quantitatively, the agreed upon level of performance.
- Marché-en-main: the exporting firm takes on the responsibility of evaluation and realization of the marketing mix. Thus, besides output objectives certain sales objectives must be met, a situation which in fact makes the exporter responsible for success.[1]

6.7 Buy-Back

Buy-back is defined as a "form of countertrade (which) involves the sale of machinery, equipment, production know-how and/or licensing of patents or trademarks, and in return receiving the output of production as payment." (ALTMANN/CLEMENT 1979:50). This definition makes clear that buy-back and turnkey can be combined effectively. Such a package of technology transfer, export, and financial mechanisms covers the whole spectrum of internationalization strategies: from redeployment - as a substitute for direct investment - to the guarantee of raw material supply, from the sale of a packet of core skills to the overcoming of tariff barriers. (Depending on the nature of the buy-back goods, one can characterize buy-back deals by the type of counter commodities.) Particularities of this type of financial internationalization are the long-term contractual obligation - up to 15 years (cf. BANKS 1983) - and the participation of the exporters in the risk of success. In this way buy-back is very different from forms of commercial compensation (cf. MCVEY

[1] In most cases, turnkey is accompanied by either Junktim and/or buy-back to reduce the exporter's credit risks (cf. OMAN 1984:63): "What evidence we have suggest (... that) in the manufacturing sector per se loans to finance turnkey plants more often than not consist primarily of suppliers' credits from the supplying firms' home countries." And: OMAN (1984:103): "As long as the investment project can be financed with local savings and depends largely on host-country demand, there is no inherent problem. But what happens when financing depends on major borrowing from international capital markets, or when long-run viability of the project depends on the project's export competitiveness? (...) One result could be a long-run disequilibrium in global supply and demand. This undoubtedly explains and may well be exacerbated by the increasing interest (...) approaching the new forms of investment in these industries as sales operations - via turnkey and management contracts - rather than as investment operations." The Swiss case studies (cf. Chapter 12.2) confirm OMAN's interpretation, so that turnkey is considered as a form of countertrade.

1980, 1985). "The most basic problem is that so much finance carries a fixed repayment schedule, that is, one that does not vary according to the borrower's capacity for pay (...). For projects, loans are needed with some of the conditions normally associated with equity, that is, debt service that varies with the surplus or profits of the projects" (HARVEY 1981:2). In contrast to stock-holding, buy-back allows the "sale" of management and technical know-how without the necessity of owning part of the project. In addition, debt service is connected with success.

Part III

Economic Theory and New Forms of Internationalization: Toward the Synthesis of a General Model

Chapter 7

Introduction: Synopsis of Theoretical Development with Regard to Trade, Foreign Direct Investment (FDI), and New Forms of Internationalization (NFI)

Vis-à-vis the problems raised in Part I and the great variety of international business operations described in Part II, the state of the art in economic theory is highly underdeveloped and therefore unsatisfactory. The main reason for this is the nature of the research strategies which currently dominate mainstream economics. These strategies deviate from a useful approach to theory building in the following ways:

- by trying to transform political economy into an axiomatically based hard science
- by setting standards of rigour and relevance which are based on the sophistication of the statistical methods applied and the robustness of the results obtained
- by squeezing history as well as the study of institutions out of the research agendas.[1]

In international economics, this yawning gap between ever-increasing interdependencies in the real world and the ever-narrower focus on special aspects which characterizes most scientific output is especially visible - and at the same time destructive. This is not the place to review these issues. We have done so elsewhere (BORNER 1983, 1984a, 1984b).

The survey of the literature reveals interesting insights. By shedding the illusion that there is one and only one theoretical structure for all times and all places we were able to identify useful contributions. In a very eclectic manner, we tried to pick up those pieces which fit into the perspective presented in Part I, Chapter 2 and which also fit together as a patchwork of facts and sensible ideas concerning NFI. Our patchwork-synthesis of microeconomic theory of the internationalization of business operations is presented in the following synopsis. The framework presented in Table 7-1 will serve as basis for organizing and presenting our approach.

Our critical review of the orthodox positions, including their extensions, is not reiterated here. We also take for granted that the reader is familiar with what we have coined paradigmatic breakthroughs: First, the industrial organization or "control" explanation of FDI by HYMER (1976), second, the COASEian theory of the firm and the market which is based on the transaction cost approach to both of these modes of coordinating economic activities (COASE 1937), and, third, the transaction cost relationship to the terms of trade (MEADE 1955). Unfortunately, HYMER did not really incorporate the COASEian view of the firm into his framework. He definitively exposed the inappropriateness of theories of international trade and finance for MNEs and their FDI. Moreover, HYMER succeeded convincingly in explaining FDI

[1] See, for example, SOLOW (1985) or STRANGE (1985)

Table 7-1. Microeconomic Theory of the Internationalization of Business Operations

<table>
<tr><th>Theories / Development Phases</th><th colspan="2">International Trade</th><th colspan="2">International Capital Movements FDI</th><th colspan="2">The Firm</th></tr>
<tr><td>Traditional Orthodoxy</td><td colspan="2">International market exchange based on (national) comparative advantages</td><td colspan="2">International flows of capital based on arbitrage of different rates of return</td><td colspan="2">Atomistic firm acting under perfect competitive conditions</td></tr>
<tr><td>Conservative Extensions</td><td colspan="2">Refinements in types and nature of comparative advantages (neo-factor, neo-technology)</td><td colspan="2">Asset pricing approach to international capital markets and global portfolio adjustments</td><td colspan="2">Imperfect competition barriers to entry/exit special assets and monopoly</td></tr>
<tr><td>Breakthrough of New Paradigms</td><td colspan="2">MEADE (1955)
Political economy of protectionism and neo-protectionism</td><td colspan="2">HYMER (1960)
Industrial organization approach to FDI/market power explanation of MNE</td><td colspan="2">COASE (1937)
Transaction cost approach to the firm (internalization) and the market (externalization)</td></tr>
<tr><td>Building Blocks for NFI-Perspective</td><td>Transaction-cost approach to exchange: barter, counter-trade and other bilateral contracts
(1)</td><td colspan="2">Structural market failure approach to MNE based on market power advantages
(2)</td><td colspan="2">Efficiency approach to internalization based on transactional advantages
(3)</td><td>Strategy approach to business planning and organization based on firm-specific competitive advantage
(4)</td></tr>
<tr><td>New Synthesis: Transaction Cost and Contract Approach</td><td colspan="6">Eclectic Theory of International Business Operations:
General approach to trade, FDI and NFI based on firm-specific ownership, competitive advantages of firms, a transaction cost approach to exchange and control and a dynamic competitive environment</td></tr>
</table>

as a means for controlling and exploiting monopolistic, firm-specific competitive advantages. By neglecting the transaction cost dimension of internalization, he one-sidedly promoted the further development of the building blocks (2) and (4). The former interprets internalized control of monopolistic advantage as a structural market failure: The firm wields market power and suppresses alternative market transactions. In line with traditional welfare judgments of monopoly, the MNEs and their FDI are therefore inefficient and thus undesirable. Building block (2), the route mainly taken by HYMER himself, led therefore to the so-called inhospitality tradition of MNEs.[2]

[2] TEECE (1985:235) expresses this as follows: "What is needed, and what is not supplied by HYMER, was an assessment of the comparative welfare properties of multinational firms and the market alternatives. HYMER's comparison of the MNE with the frictionless market fiction was inapposite and fueled host country antagonism towards the MNE."

This was challenged by authors like WILLIAMSON (1975), RUGMAN (1981), TEECE (1981, 1982, 1983), and CASSON (1983), who stressed the efficiency aspects to internalization which could result from market failure and lead to (efficient) vertical integration with plants in different locations. But there might also be transaction advantages in horizontal international integration. This is the case where a firm owns some kind of special asset or bundle of special skills which warrant international exploitation but which cannot be transferred through markets, because markets for these kinds of transactions do not exist (and presumably cannot be expected to develop). Again, the welfare consequences differ from the purely monopolistic interpretation since these internalized transactions, not being able to take place on markets, have no market-equivalents. Building block (3) is therefore a much needed counter-balance for (2). Contrary to RUGMAN's claim, these elements are not sufficient for a general theory (cf. RUGMAN 1981). The main deficiency is the short-circuiting of firmspecific competitive advantages with FDI, the only channel for the transfer outside or beside narrowly defined markets. There are clearly other organizational modes for exploiting transaction advantages internationally. The dichotomy between market and non-market modes of organizing international transactions is inappropriate. Exports and FDI are just the extremes of a broad spectrum of possible transaction modes. In other words, building blocks (2) and (3) allow the establishment of a partial eclectic theory of FDI. But a theory of internationalization of firm activities as such is still missing. This partial integration has been masterly achieved by DUNNING (1981). DUNNING summarizes his interpretation as follows:

> "Today it is widely recognized that theory of FDI (i. e. international production) is primarily about the transfer of non-financial and ownership specific intangible assets by the MNE, which needs to appropriate and control the rate of use in its internalized advantage(s), ..."
> (DUNNING/RUGMAN 1985: 228).

Building block (1) can be added relatively easily to the synthesis of (2) and (3). The basic ideas are very similar to those leading to the efficiency approach toward MNEs and their FDI. Once we acknowledge market imperfections and/or transaction costs of using the market - here for multilateral exchanges of goods and payments - we realize that barter, or more generally countertrade, is not a priori inefficient and detrimental to the functioning of the international economy. This is really symmetrical to the interpretation in building block (3). Additional welfare complications arise, however, from the fact that many if not most transaction costs in markets for goods and services are barriers to trade set up by national governments: to protect local industries, to restrict competition, or simply to link market with non-market allocation systems. Nevertheless, the simultaneous application of the transaction approach to FDI by MNEs and countertrade by national firms opens up new alleys of insight. While in the former case, FDI is seen to supersede non-existing markets, in the latter case existing markets are replaced by contracts, thus implying some form of "cooperation" and/or mutual influence on the behavior of the contractors. Even assuming that we all agree that free trade would be the optimal solution (which is not the case) (see BORNER 1985), we must still analyze what a (former) exporter will decide when faced with increasing transaction costs in the international goods and/or financial markets. What can he do? In fact, he can do quite a lot. He can give up the market in question altogether. He can go the route of the MNE and substitute his exports by FDI and therefore establish foreign production. Or he can explore the middle ground of contractual arrangements: from New Forms of Financing Export (NFEF) to New Forms of International Investment (NFII). From the viewpoint of the firm, this is no different than the situation pictured in building block (3).

This leads us finally to building block (4): the theory of business strategy. By this we refer to the work of specialists in business administration such as TEECE, CAVES, and especially PORTER, who – unlike most popular strategy sellers – are firmly and safely rooted in the industrial organization tradition and who are therefore perfectly familiar with modern developments in the theory of industrial structure and competition.[3] TEECE (1985:237) points out the critical links between the FDI and the business strategy literature:

> "Clearly, transaction-cost economics must be married to organizational decision theory if the dynamics of channel selection (for transfers S. B.) are to be better understood ... Progress in this area is unlikely to be rapid until our understanding of the internal resource allocation and governance processes within firms begins to match our understanding of how these processes work in markets."

PORTER (1980, 1985) has done pioneering work in this direction. Whereas most of the strategy literature is just simply unscientific and therefore prone to never-ending cycles of fads and fashions,[4] PORTER integrates the notion of scope as developed by BAUMOL into the strategy discussion.[5] Thus he assigns the competitive advantage to the firm, i. e. its primary and support activities. Furthermore, he extends the scope aspect far beyond the traditional (COASEian buy-or-make) perspective by including the degree of integration, the geographical location, and coordinated competition in related industries. Most interesting for our synthesis is his emphasis on "coalitions":

> "A firm can pursue the benefits of a broader scope internally, or enter into coalitions with independent firms to achieve some or all of the same benefits ... Coalitions are long-term agreements among firms that go beyond normal market transactions but fall short of outright mergers." (PORTER 1985:57)

What PORTER calls "coalitions" are, in our view, better understood as "contractual agreements." Their purpose is "broadening scope without broadening the firm." (PORTER 1985:57).

At this point in our analysis we are in a position to link up the elements of our integrative perspective in order to create a theoretical synthesis. Thereby we can put our taxonomy of NFI into theoretical perspective and render it empirically operational. The theoretical synthesis is anchored in the transaction aspect of internationalization: modes of organizing the transfer of goods, capital, and technology by enterprises planning and acting in a framework of dynamic (innovative) competition and national regulation.

---

[3] See CAVES (1982) and WILLIAMSON (1975)

[4] This is, in our opinion, also true for PETERS/WATERMAN (1981) who wrote a stimulating story of successful companies but who fail any tests of systematic analysis beyond the "post hoc ergo propter hoc" type.

[5] Cf. BAUMOL/PANZAR/WILLIG (1982). See also BORNER (1983, 1984b)

Chapter 8

The Transaction Cost Approach to New Forms of International Investment (NFII)

8.1 Introduction

"It can be assumed that the distinguishing mark of the firm is the supersession of the price mechanism." (COASE 1937:389). This is a very pragmatic position and does not mean that the existence of firms is a response to market failures. Rather "the main reason why it is profitable to establish a firm would seem to be that there is a cost of using the price mechanism." (COASE 1937:389). In other words, the utilization of the market simply has its own costs. ALIBER (1983:248) argues that COASE has identified the motive for a firm's growth: "Firms expand and grow because the costs of avoiding the use of the market are less than the costs of using the market."

The orthodox theories of internalization - with their two-pronged modification of neo-classical theory - were an attempt at an internal critique. That is, these theories tried to improve neo-classical theory without abandoning its basic principles. First, a perfect market is no longer seen as the norm. Market imperfections are seen as exogenous hindrances which in turn raise costs for buyers and sellers. The second point of the critique has to do with the existence of multis, a phenomenon which cannot be explained by neo-classical trade theory. "If the world were characterized by a model of free trade, there would be no need and no room for the MNE. The modern theory of FDI suggests that the MNE develops in response to imperfections in the goods or factor markets." (RUGMAN 1980:366-367). Multis are thus perceived as a second best solution. Moreover, their profitability depends on how successfully they replace the first best solution. Competitiveness and profitability of the MNE depend on its ability to increase the efficiency of world-wide resource allocation (cf. CASSON 1979:45). An important way of doing this is to overcome the problem of very expensive or non-existent external markets by internalizing transactions. Analogous to the HECKSCHER-OHLIN model, where national comparative advantages lead to international trade, firm-specific advantages lead to the MNE. The importance of internal markets lies primarily with intermediate rather than finished products. Intermediate products can be divided into the tangible (hardware, semi-finished products, resources) and the intangible (software and know-how information). The higher the information content of the intermediate products and the higher the danger of information diffusion, the more important the control of the transaction. Software and know-how are thus particularly delicate products for selling on the market.

In the area of information, transaction costs are also especially high. Economists speak of buyer uncertainty. This implies that the purchaser is not really in a position to judge the value of the commodity he or she is purchasing. If the supplier can maintain his/her property rights mainly through secrecy, then the potential buyer of the information must either trust the supplier or the supplier must offer a type of insurance or guarantee. Again, transaction costs rise. As a matter of fact, transaction costs are generally so high that there are practically no markets for technology and information as such.[1]

In sum, we can conclude that each hindrance in the functioning of the market mechanism leads to an increase in transaction costs: the higher the transaction costs, the greater the incentive to internalize. The creator of the information integrates "forward" that is, products which contain the information are manufactured (and marketed). This explains the existence of multis. The high level of R&D, which is especially characteristic of industrial multis, is nothing more than the logical conclusion of an internalization policy. "Ultimately, the MNE is always a creature of internalization." (RUGMAN 1980:374).

From this perspective, licensing and contractual arrangements are the opposite of internalization. They are not internalization strategies - they are market solutions and are used and preferred in situations where the risk of diffusion of the entrepreneurial advantage is small. "To a large extent licensing occurs when the requirements for internalization are weakest. Once we have a theory of the MNE we also have a theory of licensing; that which need not be internalized can be licensed (or exported, if the conditions for free trade were to hold)." (RUGMAN 1982:14-15).

Given that the main characteristics of the multis are their internalization of advantages and their head start in know-how, a MNE is by definition a monopolist. "Thus, contractual arrangements are fraught with danger for the MNE." (RUGMAN 1982:15).

8.2 NFII in the Categories of Internalization Theory

Nonetheless, this chapter deals with the theoretical explanation of New Forms of International Investment (NFII). The usual explanation is a negative one. Licensing and contractual agreements take place when there is no necessity to internalize. While we accept this explanation as our working hypothesis, we shall try to build up a more differentiated set of arguments. At the same time, we must not idealize transfer efficiency vis-à-vis other forms. This would mean subjecting ourselves to the same rigidities as the HECKSCHER-OHLIN trade theorists. The higher the pedestal, the harder the fall.

Neo-classical transaction theory begins from the assumption that firms and markets are alternative coordination mechanisms for production. While markets are characterized by specific and short term contracts (the futures markets being an exception), firms are characterized by hierarchical structures, long-term organization, and less specific relationships. In principle, the firm has no temporal limits to its operation. A firm allocates resources according to the decisions of management. Transactions are numerous and cannot be forseen or specified. Market transactions on the other hand are typically short term and specific. The firm is thus a system-specific response to the uncertainty of the real world. Where the conditions for mar-

[1] Cf. HYMER 1960/76, BUCKLEY/CASSON 1976, MAGEE 1977, RUGMAN 1982, KINDLEBERGER 1984.

ket transactions no longer exist, transactions are internalized, that is, removed from the market. Internalization can occur through forward or backward integration into the respective functions. In order to categorize NFII we must create an imaginary spectrum – with the market and the firm at either end. The non-equity NFII could be located closer to the market end of this spectrum.

Concretely, we shall discuss licensing, sub-contracting, business and management consulting, technical assistance, and contractual cooperation. The highly idealized short-term nature of market transactions does not characterize any of these forms. Nonetheless – and in contrast to internal functions – there are temporal limits to such agreements. This temporal aspect marks a clear but not an important difference between an internalization strategy and NFII. Numerous firms have a shorter life-span than many contracts. Nonetheless, the longer the time period of the contract – the higher the transaction costs. "The two behavioral assumptions on which transaction-cost analysis relies – and without which the study of economic organization is pointless – are bounded rationality and opportunism." This means that the economic actors are "less competent in calculation and less trustworthy and reliable in action" (WILLIAMSON 1981:1545), than the homo oeconomicus. "If the contract is spot and effected cash on delivery then the only risk arises from deliberate misrepresentation of product quality, and this can usually be dealt with by testing on the spot a sample of the product." (CASSON 1979:49).

Thus long-term contracts imply higher costs. "Pure long-term contracts are costly or impossible to write, a reflection of bounded rationality and assymmetric information." (POLLAK 1985:583). Where rationality is limited and opportunism cannot be ruled out, categories of the unexpected must be defined. In other words, all eventualities must be made explicit. "The cost of closing loopholes will depend on the number of contingencies and this in turn will reflect the complexity of the product and the variety of its uses. Transactions involving sophisticated products may prove very costly to organise in external markets." (CASSON 1979:49). TEECE points out (1977) that firms which transfer technology must, in fact, be able to formalize the object of transfer. The more idiosyncratic and individually bound the object of transfer, the more difficult it is to reach a formalized description – the result: rising costs. Yet, at the same time protective control is easier and hence policing costs lower.

The corollary is that the objects of NFII are typically older, more simple types of technology and information. These objects of transfer are divisible and can be formalized. The temporal length of the negotiations and the contract itself, as well as the scope of transfer and thus costs, can be clearly limited. Sub-contracting is good example. It is specific, has a temporal limit, and all eventualities can be dealt with contractually. In the case of licensing, however, there are problems with property rights and there may be problems of buyer uncertainty. If property rights can only be ensured through secrecy, then the transaction costs will be high. Control problems are also greater than in the case of sub-contracting.

Technical consulting as a transfer of know-how is similar to licensing in that buyer uncertainty is relatively high. Moreover, once the advice is given it becomes, by its very nature, the property of the buyer. Contracts are specific in that at least the maximum scope of the work can be determined. From the supplier's side, however, a proper market transaction actually exists. On the other hand, the buyer is at the outset not always in a position to evaluate what he is purchasing. The necessarily small number of interactions carry a real danger of buyer dissatisfaction. Contracts tend to lack details and usually deal with process technology or back-up information. The same problems characterize management consulting agreements.

The most heterogeneous type of foreign engagement is contractual cooperation. Such an arrangement fulfills all the demands of a market transaction. In particular, the boundary line between utilization of the market and internalization are clear. Diffuse and uncontrolled cooperation is not likely. Rather, contractual cooperation tends to occur horizontally between units exercizing the same entrepreneurial functions. Vertical cooperation on a contract basis is not realistic.

8.3 Critical Review of Orthodox Internalization Theory

Within the theories of internalization and transaction costs there is little room for investigating the depth and intensity of NFII. Implicitly, internalization theory postulates that firms do not turn to NFII unless they are forced to. In an historical sense this is true. But such an assumption is not sufficient for understanding the nature of firm behavior in detail or for explaining offensive strategies of foreign involvement. In order to do this the strategic element of firm behavior must be included in the analysis.

The theory of firm-specific advantage rests on a differentiation of the level of technological expertise (i.e. superior vs. inferior know-how). Thus internalization theory concentrates almost solely on the forward link: from research and development to production. This explains the large number of studies on research intensive multis. Two problems, however, were left by the wayside: MNEs which are not research intensive and New Forms of International Investment. Consequently, the internationalization problems of SMEs were also left off the research agenda. The lack of consideration of smaller firms is due to the fact that international actors have had a choice between internalization and the market sale of firm-specific advantages. The choice made was determined by the respective transaction costs. The ability to make this choice implies strong product or process based monopoly characteristics and a rather solid capital base. To rise above this rather one-sided perspective, one must go beyond a simple comparison between transaction costs and costs of internalization. One must look at the respective discounted profitability of the various possibilities at hand. In this way, one can include smaller firms - not just multis - in the analysis.

Dunning (1982b) distinguishes ownership advantages from internalization advantages, thus allowing us to gain a more differentiated idea of firm behavior. "In the language of the eclectic theory of international production

- ownership advantages stem from the ability of a firm to gain an economic rent by the creation or acquisition of assets, goods or services, which, because of barriers to entry, other firms cannot create, or acquire on such favourable terms; and
- internalization advantages stem from the benefits of a hierarchical organisation to exploit these advantages relative to the market or contractual route" (Dunning 1982b:4).

This definition touches upon one of the weakest points of the orthodox internalization theory. It is unable to grasp fully the essence of the multi. On the one hand, the MNE is seen as a parallel market; an internal price mechanism compensates for major trade obstacles or even non-existent markets. On the other hand, MNEs have a strict, hierarchical form. KAY argues, however, that multis do not face a simple choice between internal and external markets. "The creation of internal markets requires decentralised decision-making and a considerable degree of decomposability of units. On the other hand centralised hierarchical decision may be appropriate in the case of highly synergistic systems in which separability of units is difficult or impossible to achieve." (KAY 1983:306). There are fine shades of difference which form a gradual bridge between the conglomerate multi and the integrated system. But economists have a natural desire to emphasize internal markets and prices: "An economist without a price is a sorry sight, like a doctor without a stethoscope." (KAY 1983:306).

ROBINSON (1981) takes the final and essential step. He defines the difference between the international and the multinational firm. The goal of the international firm is to develop and implement the best strategies of entering and performing profitably in individual markets, whether through exports, subsidiaries, joint ventures, contract manufacturing, or other NFII. In this way the firm seeks to maximize profits: "No one in the firm is being rewarded nor has the technical competence to set up or sustain a globally integrated production system requiring a much higher level of central control." (ROBINSON 1981:20). "The objective - and reward system - of a true multinational . . . induces its decision-makers to exploit the advantage of its internal market via either regionally or globally integrated, production-marketing systems." (ROBINSON 1981:20). Through this characterization ROBINSON indicates the dual character of the MNE. He believes that the enormous amount of capital locked into these integrated systems immobilizes these organizations, that is, they are at a disadvantage in relation to parallel markets and international firms with less FDI.

8.4 Attempts to Integrate NFII into a Theoretical Framework

In building up a theory of New Forms of International Investment we must not look upon these forms simply as market solutions. It is true that NFII may come into being through the market and that non-equity forms can also be dealt with via the market mechanism. But even non-equity NFII can and usually do serve as an incentive for establishing deeper ties between business partners. All NFII go beyond a pure trade or simple exchange relationship. "Licensing involves continuing expense on the part of the licensor to ensure successful transfer (of technology) and 'police' his rights. Several studies . . . have emphasized the continuing transfer of skilled personnel in cementing the know-how. In other words, licensing is a relationship rather than an act. Interaction between recipient and seller is both essential to successful transfer and a continuing element of cost." (BUCKLEY 1983a:211-212). With each NFII there is a certain level of participation in another enterprise. The depth of this participation cannot be measured exactly. Rather, one must visualize the level or intensity of participation on a scale which ranges from very little to 100% ownership.

Our case studies show that the depth of cooperation and the level of participation is a function of the level of trust between or among the parties involved. BRADA (1981:217) speaks of degrees of intimacy between two partners, which in turn determine the position of the operation between the two extremes: the market solution and FDI.

At this point we must deal with the question of control. Licensing, as an alternative to FDI, offers a rather low level of control. The issue is primarily directive control. In a study on the hotel industry (DUNNING/MCQUEEN 1982), NFII other than licensing were investigated for the first time. Despite the fact that these two authors overlook the influence of combinations of NFII on control potential, they correctly and clearly show that NFII can bring to bear firm-specific advantages just as effectively as full ownership. "Received theory tends to assume that the extent of internalization (which is provided by the degree to which the transferor of resources continues to exercise control over the use of these and complementary resources owned by the transferee) and ownership stake are closely correlated with each other ... Little attention has been given in the literature to alternatives to equity investment as a means of retaining control over the use of an intangible asset." (DUNNING/ MCQUEEN 1982:95). From a legal perspective de jure control is really a function of the percentage of equity participation. But DUNNING and MCQUEEN (1982:96/97) found "that some MNE involvement ... through the non-equity route has the characteristics usually associated with direct investment in the sense of providing de facto control. To determine whether and how such internalization is de facto practiced, one therefore needs to look at the control procedures of equity-based control and the terms of contract of contract-based control." In other words, they suggest that our scale of participation should be a two dimensional matrix of international production, the two axes being "degree of control" and "percentage of capital ownership." Each cell on the grid then represents a specific combination of the two elements.

Our statement that firms of all sizes can become international becomes clearer and DUNNING's eclectic theory proves itself superior to internalization theory. The distinction between internalization advantages and firm-specific advantages proves more fruitful than the determinism of "monopoly through ownership". The step from internalization as a principle to internalization as a theory seems of little use. The framework is basically symmetric and allows for both internalization and externalization, at least implicitly (KAY 1983:306–309).

Depending on the situation, the task of gathering information is more or less costly. The demand for information arises "when a good or service is transferred across a technologically separable interface." This transfer, according to WILLIAMSON (1981:1544), constitutes the transaction, whereby information costs are a part of transaction costs. "Like other business decisions, decisions about foreign operations are based on opinions, and opinions are to a large extent based on the existing stock of relevant knowledge." (CARLSON 1975:10). Transactions across international boundaries are apt to raise the level of uncertainty or in other words such transactions raise the level of necessary information. The need for information and the level of transaction costs increase as cultural distance grows (CARLSON 1975:13; cf. ROBINSON 1981:19). All other things being equal, an accumulation of foreign operations in culturally similar areas is the result. Foreign operations in areas with a high cultural distance remain a domain of the multis. "It also explains in part why decisionmakers are reluctant to invest in fixed assets in a given foreign market until they are personally familiar with that market". (ROBINSON 1981:19). International operations are built up step by step. The necessary know-how for the next step is gained through learning by doing. The path from entry into a foreign market through occasional sales to the establishment of a marketing subsidiary and then the start of local production is a long one, a path which demands much experience but a path on which NFII can be regularly used.

The particularities of a product group can make it necessary to overcome "cultural distance" (cf. KINDLEBERGER 1984). If the firm is a small one, then - in order to pay the higher transaction costs - costs of other entrepreneurial functions must be reduced. The internalization-externalization question cannot be avoided. Small firms are pressured from two sides. They can be so specialized that they must operate internationally. But their capital base and/or their management base is usually too limited to allow them to open subsidiaries in all important markets, which sharpens the problems of protective and directive control. Here our case studies have shown the importance of a particular ability typical of the capitalist entrepreneur - the ability to work with the likes of himself or herself, i. e. the ability to work with other capitalist firms on a basis of mutual trust. While such arrangements are not limited a priori to small firms, they seem more likely to arise when two owner-operators are working together. The factor "human trust" is important because it is a way of establishing "quasi-subsidiaries". The personal relationships and responsibilities can aid in both directive and protective control. At any rate, mutual trust is a good substitute for a massiv array of contracts between two private bureaucracies (cf. MACAULAY 1963). In our case studies personal contacts served as a bridge, even - or especially - in situations where cultural distance was great.

CASSON was one of the first economists to work on a theory of confidence (CASSON 1982b:40–41). He started by analyzing multis which offered no differentiated products. This meant studying firms which could not draw on ownership-specific advantages of the technological type. MNEs in the hotel branch, food multis, and banana multis are good examples. CASSON localized their monopolistic advantages in the integration of "market making" and production - that is, not in the integration of R&D and production. The purpose of this integration is to raise product quality and to guarantee quality control. Buyer uncertainty is decreased: buyers can "afford" to have confidence in the firm. This in turn reduces transaction costs. "Buyer uncertainty is overcome most efficiently by giving the buyer confidence in the seller's competence and integrity. The buyer's knowledge of the seller's personal characteristics acts as a surrogate for knowledge of product quality. Typically this confidence is built up by the successful repetition of trades." (CASSON 1982b: 41). In the case of know-how this mechanism, according to CASSON, does not work. In contrast to yogurt and hotel services, know-how transfer is associated with few transactions but a high volume of exchange. "This makes it extremely difficult for confidence to be built up and hence for buyer uncertainty to be overcome." Here, CASSON's excellent theoretical analysis is clearly confirmed in reality. For small firms in particular immediate ad hoc transfer of technology is a very rare occurrence. Even larger firms shy away from such transactions. The successful repetition of contact, say, in hardware trade or even in non-exchange interactions, is also a means of establishing trust prior to a possible know-how transfer.

Highly diffusable technologies are not appropriate for transfer, except through wholly owned subsidiaries. Such is the case for both very abstract know-how and for highly formalized know-how. Conversely, protective control of idiosyncratic technologies is easier to maintain; but the technology is more difficult to transfer! This accounts for the modest significance of pure market forms of licensing. Either the control possibilities are too limited or transfer problems arise. Pure licensing is only used in highly segregated markets which are characterized by oligopolistic competition in established technologies. This is also the case for spin-offs, organizationally foreign technology, and cross-licensing. (Cross-licensing is primarily an intraindustry phenomenon having to do with related technologies.) Only under the pre-condition of tighter cooperation are large volumes of NFII transactions possible. By definition, the closeness of the relationship is dependent on the number of transactions. NFII are only of interest as long as the marginal transaction costs are lower than the costs of internalization (assuming, of course, that the firm has the financial capacity to internalize). This tautology can only be disturbed by the introduction of the factor "confidence".

In the context of inter-system cooperation between West and East, BRADA concludes that the transfer of process technology will be the object of cooperation (BRADA 1981 and 1977; cf. COUGHLIN 1983). BRADA hypothesizes a relationship between the type of technology and the type of management structure. Firms primarily dealing in product innovations are most likely to be centralized and vertically integrated. Firms characterized by process innovations are more decentralized and horizontally integrated. The reason for this lies in the pressure to internalize product innovations and to take advantage of the uniqueness of the product. BRADA argues that the costs of product development cannot be assigned to one specific product. Moreover, uncertainty about the market life of a product is a further obstacle to transfer of product technology. Process developments on the other hand are part of product costs and can be calculated. (BRADA defines process technology as containing know-how in both production and marketing.) This means that process technologies are more mobile between firms than product technologies. The cooperative utilization of process technology between two firms can, however, lead to product innovation. According to BRADA, the pharmaceutical industry is characterized by integrated, centralized firms which compete in the realm of product innovation. In contrast, agricultural machinery is produced by decentralized firms competing in the area of process innovation.

In the case of the Western industrial countries, other factors - oligopolistic competition in particular - can influence the use of NFII. Market relationships can force even product innovators to use NFII. The pharmaceutical industry is a good example. Because they lack ownership capital, small firms must also begin to use NFII when they do not want to slow down a growth impulse. New Forms of International Investment permit international activity without complete internalization and at the same time without restricting international activities purely to sales operations.

Chapter 9

The Transaction Cost Approach to New Forms of Export Financing (NFEF)

9.1 Introduction

In this chapter it is our aim to show that New Forms of Export Financing (NFEF) are not merely an inefficient inversion of the long-term historical trend away from barter and toward a monetarized economy. Rather, it is our task to show that NFEF can be explained rationally by the transaction cost structure of the international market economy. Analogous to the theory of MNE, most economists interpret the existance of NFEF as the result of so-called structural market imperfections, such as protectionist measures. Though it is impossible to draw a sharp line between structural market imperfections and efficient barter arrangements, it is essential to recognize that - unless we ignore all transaction costs - NFEF are not a priori a second best solution. In the context of the international market economy contractual arrangements - NFEF - must be seen as one element of a coordinated and rational entrepreneurial strategy to maintain and increase competitiveness.

In traditional foreign trade theories NFEF have not been understood as multifunctional internationalization instruments. Monetary theories of foreign trade concentrate primarily on the problems of explaining price structures, income structures, and foreign exchange rates as they figure in trade relations among nations. Such theories thereby ignore the more basic issue: what motivates monetarized trade? In contrast, our point of departure is to examine the reasons for the continued co-existence of both a monetarized and a natural exchange system within the global economy. What are the concrete determinents of an exchange system? What transaction risks and transaction costs are associated respectively with the various exchange systems? What motives lead an entrepreneur rationally to favor a barter arrangement over a monetarized market transaction?

9.2 Transaction Costs and Risks as Determinants of Exchange Systems: the Niehans Model

In a completely monetarized world economy, where all non-monetary systems of exchange are assumed to lead to greater costs for the trade partners, it is not clear a priori why trade partners would choose not to employ the traditional two step monetarized exchange procedure. Nonetheless, in today's world of international trade such transactions are losing ground. By using one step barter, credit granting exporters attempt to transfer or insure against the Delcrede risk, as well as the risks of inflation, foreign exchange, and political change. The NIEHANS model is an attempt to assess the advantages and disadvantages of both monetarized exchange and barter in terms of the nature of the goods exchanged. A two-level national economy forms the basis of the model: the first level is that of brutto transactions, the second, netto market transactions. The interdependencies between the partners in a trade relationship can be dealt with via various systems of exchange. Barter or direct exchange of goods demands the double coincidence of mutual wants. For monetarized exchange only a single coincidence is necessary. The two step process of monetarized exchange allows the functions of exchange and possession to be carried out with the same medium. NIEHANS develops a general theory of trade in which barter and monetarized exchange appear as the two poles of an entire spectrum of possibilities.

At the first level, net sales of all economic units are determined in an auction of the general equilibrium type. At the second level, the simple world of bartering commodities is left behind to permit examination of the various simultaneously existing systems of exchange. At this level brutto transactions are examined: who exchanges what with whom? Here exchange appears as a resource-consuming activity and the societal choice between monetary and non-monetary exchange systems appears clearly as a question of the optimal utilization of resources (NIEHANS 1980: 122). All commodities which are to be resold function as potential means of exchange. Thus in the two level model two types of commodities exist: goods which are sold on the market and goods which, in addition to possessing use value, are employed as means of exchange.

Two price systems also co-exist. The commodity prices at the first level result from the activity of commodity sales. At the second level, shadow (efficiency) prices exist for commodities which function as means of exchange. Since each bilateral exchange transaction demands a quid pro quo, "a given WALRASian system of exchange flows, together with a complementary monetary or non-monetary exchange system, depends only on the transaction costs structure." (NIEHANS 1980: 122). Consequently, if the transaction costs for a particular commodity drop, the probability of its being used as a means of exchange rises. Trading partners who, due to institutional factors, have a scale of transaction costs lower than that of other economic actors are able to make transactions more cheaply than their competitors. In turn, this comparative advantage is used to constitute a trade center. The trade center then appears as "a substitute for a means of exchange." (NIEHANS 1980: 128). Depending on the structure of transaction costs, it is possible for a number of different exchange systems to co-exist within the same national economy. The explanation is simply the rational attempt by individual economic units and/or actors to minimize transaction costs.

In an integrated national economy the two level nature of the exchange system represented in the model disappears. All economic actors are participants on the market and solve their optimization problems in a decentralized manner. For n commodities there are (n(n-1))/2 markets for barter and (n-2) monetarized markets. The fundamental question is which of the (n(n-1))/2 markets are actually utilized? The answer is consistent with what one might expect intuitively. Depending on the transactions cost structure, "all markets could be active or all markets – with the exception of one – may remain unused." (NIEHANS 1980: 134). The concrete pattern of the transaction costs structure determines which exchange system is used. Even in the model of an integrated economy, multiple, parallel exchange systems co-exist as an expression or result of the optimization processes of individual economic units.[1]

9.3 Tariffs, Subsidies, and Deficient Market Transparency as the Determinants of Countertrade

After having established that the price structure of transaction costs determines the nature of the system of exchange, we shall delve in more detail into two other aspects of this question. On the one hand, we want to examine the effects of countertrade on the terms of trade - under the assumption that the transactions could be realized via monetarized exchange (cf. section 9.3.1). On the other hand, we want to examine the problem of market transparency and show how variations in the means of exchange lead to alternative conditions of market equilibrium (cf. section 9.3.2). The surprising result of this model is that under certain sets of circumstances countertrade permits a greater volume of exchange than a fully monetarized system of exchange.

9.3.1 Countertrade in Situations of Bilateral Monopoly

In principle, international commodity flows can be influenced quantitatively and qualitatively (structure and direction) through import, export, production, or consumption tariffs, subsidies, and/or purely quantitative restrictions.
The utilization of these instruments produces a different equilibrium than would be the case under the conditions of a free market. The following peculiarities hold:

- Tariffs and export subsidies lead directly to increased revenue for the state. In the case of quotas, government income only arises from import licenses. Import restrictions which are designed to protect domestic production do so at the cost of higher prices on domestic consumer markets.
- By definition, quotas limit the volume of transactions on a particular market. Tariffs and subsidies, however, do not eliminate the interaction of supply and demand unless a prohibitive tariff is set consciously.

Quotas cannot be sabotaged via countertrade; smuggling is the only viable alternative. But through bilateral dumping and price discrimination it is possible to overvalue goods sold on other markets, thereby compensating for exports to restricted

[1] "It is obvious that there is always a price structure for transaction costs which is high enough to make it advantageous not to use a particular means of exchange. The result is the substitution of direct exchange for indirect exchange. If this procedure is repeated over and over again, eventually the point is reached where only direct trade, i.e. barter, continues to exist. It is generally accepted that such a situation results in an increase in economic costs for society as a whole. This, however, is not true in general, since, given the incorporation of particular technologies in certain groups of transaction cost structures, barter can, in fact, be the most efficient exchange system." (NIEHANS 1980:35).

markets. Only when markets can be differentiated and when arbitrage is impossible can such a strategy be effective. Under these circumstances countertrade is a perfect substitute for protective tariffs or export subsidies. MEADE (1955) analyzed countertrade in terms of such politically determined trade barriers and demonstrated that barter naturally and regularly replaces monetarized exchange if and when one of the trading partners can thereby improve his or her terms of trade. The model developed by MEADE is a "numerical and geometrical representation of some barter deals". It examines barter within the framework of two state-owned trading companies, that is, under conditions of bilateral monopoly. This simplified assumption is not only analytically useful, but, in light of our case studies, it is a realistic assumption. The countertrade options of a buyer who faces several potential suppliers are such that the buyer is in a position to negotiate a favorable contract.

The model examines countertrade on two levels: through the direct comparison of barter with monetarized sales and through the elimination of all potential contracts which do not meet the criteria of PARETO optimality. In the following paragraphs we present a short summary of the MEADE model.

- "In (a) so-called bilateral monopoly the State import monopoly in A and the State export monopoly in B must come to agreement upon some barter deal between (x_B) (which B is exporting) and the dollars (x_A) with which A is paying and which represent purchasing power over the general output of A-products." (MEADE 1955:178).
- The trading company B purchases x_B on the free domestic market for price p_B. The accounting price of the barter deal which results out of the terms of trade (as a consequence of export subsidies, for example) does not need to be the same as p_B.
- A sells the received goods x_B in his or her respective domestic market at price p_A. The price p_A must not be identical to the accounting price p^* of the barter deal (the price may be altered through import tariffs, for example.)

"It is clear (...) that all the barter deals (...) are advantageous to both A and B. (...) If we assume that any bargain which will be struck by the two State-trading monopolies will be one which does not permit both of them to become better off simultaneously by striking another bargain, we are confined to the barter deals." (MEADE 1955:585).

To determine the quantity of goods actually exchanged one must examine the price relationship p_A/p_B. A priori it is clear that in cases in which $p_A \neq p_B$ no transaction will take place. In the case of under-trading ($p_A > p_B$) an expansion of trade in the A market would mean a price drop for commodity x_B, while B would receive more units of x_A for each unit of x_B. The resulting increase in the volume of transactions produces an increase in welfare. The inverse is true for over-trading, where $p_A < p_B$.

Thus there are three relevant constellations of prices which must be examined:

$$p^* = p_A = p_B \quad (1)$$
$$p^* > p_A = p_B \quad (2)$$
$$p^* < p_A = p_B \quad (3)$$

According to the first variation, barter corresponds to an "optimum optimorum". Neither A or B gains from a bilateral arrangement. The terms of trade of a bilateral deal are the same as for exchange on the open market. There is no motivation for countertrade. In the second case, A utilizes import subsidies and/or B demands an export tax. The net result is a transfer of capital from A to B. In the third case, a market price which differs from p* for commodity x_B is retained through a tariff in A and/or an export subsidy in B. A net capital transfer from B to A is the result.

Since this model implies a zero-sum game, there must also be a motivation on the part of the trading partner who stands to gain less from barter. Possible motives include:

- possesion of buying power[2] on the part of one of the trading partners (over-capacity of the suppliers, buyer's monopoly, protectionism)
- price discrimination by suppliers (splitting demand between a market with regular monetary exchange and a market on which dumping can be camouflaged by countertrade, through cartel agreements, state regulated markets, etc.), and/or
- lack of market transparency.[3]

9.3.2 Countertrade as a Rational Strategy for Combatting a Lack of Market Transparency

Market transparency means that all actors who participate on a particular market possess the necessary and essential information for making their economic decisions. A lack of market transparency implies decision-making under conditions of uncertainty. Buyers cannot determine whether or not there is a suitable supplier; suppliers cannot estimate whether or not buyers will react appropriately to market signals. From a theoretical point of view the premises of OKUN (cf. section 9.3.2.1) and MURRELL (cf. section 9.3.2.2) will be used to analyze countertrade as a consequence of deficiencies in market transparency.

9.3.2.1 The Invisible Handshake: Okun's Theory of Implicit Contracts as Applied to Countertrade[4]

OKUN's macroeconomic analysis of implicit contract theory examines the market behavior of suppliers and buyers who find themselves forced to choose between short-term adaptation to changing market relations and the costs or advantages which might result from cooperative long-term continuity of contractual ties. OKUN's considerations are primarily directed at explaining why "restrictive macroeconomic policies have the seemingly paradoxical effect of reducing output and increasing unemployment while doing little to slow inflation". (OKUN 1981 : 7). Here,

---

[2] "Economic power is the ability to change objective economic parameters, to force business partners to make concessions, to subdue competition, to effectively utilize information, in moments in which other actors lack information, and to influence the economic framework established by governments - all in order to gain economic advantages without adding to the social product at the expense of other economic units." (ARNDT 1973 : 101).

[3] In MEADE's model market transparency is a premise. The consequences of a lack of market transparency will be discussed in the next section.

[4] Since in our research we were not concerned with countertrade as a once-in-a-lifetime purchase, we shall concentrate on OKUN's hypothesis. Cf. OKUN (1981 : 1-26 and 134-81) for a discussion of commodity markets.

however, we shall attempt to use OKUN's hypotheses concerning commodity markets in order to understand the phenomenon of countertrade.

In contrast to the neo-classical analysis of auctions markets, OKUN assumes that "in fact, most products are sold with price tags set by the seller and through a process of shopping by the buyer." (OKUN 1981:138). When evaluating the offers of various suppliers, the buyer calculates his search costs - opportunity costs - as part of his purchasing costs. If we assume that the buyer has a good idea of supplier prices but does not know where the cheapest supplier is located, the supplier - even in the case of homogeneous goods - holds a monopolistic position which allows the setting of prices. Moreover, the supplier has an edge on future sales: "If (the buyers) have a favorable assessment of the terms of their last supplier, and if they believe that the information obtained from the last purchase is still relevant they are likely to return to that supplier as customers. Presumably, the buyers made their last purchases with satisfaction about the price and other dimensions of the offer; unless they were subsequently disappointed, they can be expected to repeat the decision." (OKUN 1981:140). Commercial compensation and especially industrial compensation contain elements of implicit contract:

- Exporters who are looking for access to sales markets via countertrade or who enter into contractual agreements on existing export markets expect a deepening of business relations through the establishment of subjective demand preferences. Subjective preferences can also play an important role in periods when there is no countertrade activity. From this perspective countertrade is not simply a necessary evil. "To view countertrade as a necessary cost implies that there is only a single motivation for the Western partner, suggesting that in every contractual arrangement with the East, the Western partner is in a defensive position and must make concessions." (ALTMANN/CLEMENT 1979:164).
- Each tied transaction means the establishment of mutual dependence. In the case of commercial compensation, analogous to classical export, the exporter completely loses control of the product and process know-how embodied in the commodity (cf. BORNER/WEHRLE 1984a:183). Mutual dependence, however, arises out of the specific terms of risk sharing which is contained in the countertrade agreement. In the case of industrial compensation, the financing of the original capital goods technology transfer is guaranteed in the long run through the successful sale of the goods produced by the mutually established production unit. This means the exporter shares the risks. The interests of long-term continuity dominate short-term considerations. The exporter must take an active interest in the successful application of the goods and services exported.

This explains why countertrade arrangements almost never include highly innovative or high-tech products and processes. The application of standardized product and process technologies guarantees the level of quality in outputs which is necessary for refinancing. (In general, a high level of standardization goes hand in hand with an extensive division of labour. Thus, variations in the quality of labor result in variations in the quantity of output). Since standardized technologies are globally more or less homogeneous, there is a strong motivation on the part of buyers and sellers to engage in implicit contract agreements, such as countertrade.

9.3.2.2 Countertrade as a Reaction to a Lack of Market Signals on World Markets

MURRELL's hypothesis stems from market-signal theory[5] (MURRELL 1982; cf. AKERLOF 1970, NELSON 1974, SPENCE 1974). Due to the existence of information costs, market transparency appears as a factor-using activity. Informative (vs. motivating) market signals increase the market transparency on a given market, whereby supply is directed to points where demand is greatest. The volume of transactions on a given market appears as a function of the respective level of market transparency, that is, as a function of access to accurate market signals. For our analysis the market signal par excellence - the price of a commodity - is not of major concern. Our hypothesis is that a competitive supplier looks for buyers but that as a result of subjective preference, i.e. prejudices - "newcomer", "Eastern goods", etc., the buyer closes himself/herself off ex ante from particular suppliers. Accordingly, suppliers have to look for alternative market signals. The question is whether or not countertrade can serve as such a market signal.

MURRELL situates his model in intersystemic trade. "The average quality of items supplied will increase with price because sellers usually know quality. These assumptions will imply that less trade takes place when buyers do not know quality than when quality is easily ascertainable" (MURRELL 1982:590). When product quality is uncertain, the rational buyer usually underestimates the quality of the product in order to minimize risks. In the case of trade with the Eastern bloc countries, buyers often assume an imaginary country-of-origin standard. A priori the buyer assumes that the suppliers will offer goods of a particular - lower - standard. As a result, competitive suppliers from Eastern European countries must develop alternative market signals for the product quality of their products. It is MURRELL's hypothesis that buy-back can be interpreted as a quality signal. MURRELL's model is based on the following premises:

- Suppliers from centrally-planned economies search for ways and means of launching their products on world markets.
- Each buy-back agreement per se is a market signal for the quality standards of the buy-back commodities.[6]
- In cases where the terms of the contract have not been met, the capital goods exporter can demand financial retribution.
- The quality of buy-back goods is seen as a function of the transferred software - reliable access to spare parts, services, training, etc.
- The suppliers' brand names and trademarks can be used on the buy-back goods.

MURRELL's model takes bilateral East-West commodity trade as its starting point. In an "all or nothing" offer the choice is between 100% buy-back and "purchase of the unit". The exporter is the taker in the arrangement. From the point of view of the Eastern country partner, the object is to maximize output. MURRELL's model is summarized graphically in Figure 9.1.

The countertrade solution will only be chosen when the price elasticity of demand is small enough. If the price elasticity were too great, quantity x_3 would be

[5] "Market signals are activities or attributes of individuals or goods in a market which, by design or accident, alter the beliefs of, or convey information to, other individuals in the market." (SPENCE 1974:11)

[6] "By placing themselves in a position of mutual dependence, the two parties are signalling the reliability of their future conduct." (MURRELL 1982:593).

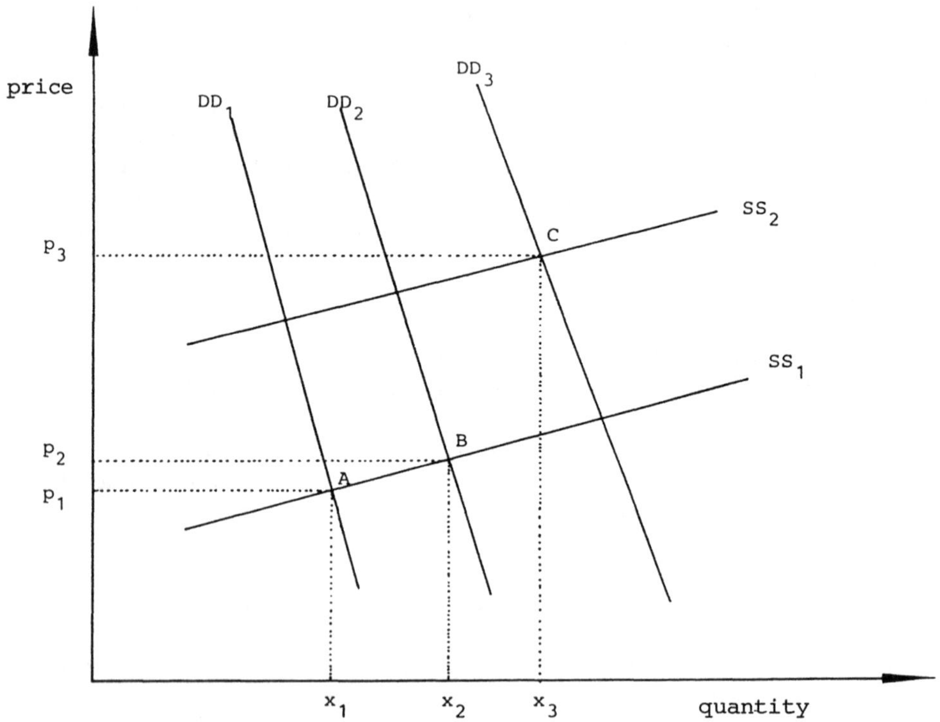

Fig. 9-1. Graphic Interpretation of the MURRELL Model.
The value q_1 is the product quality standard in the country of origin, which, due to the lack of alternative market signals, is assumed by the buyer. With an information cost K, however, the buyers are in a position to establish the real state of product quality q_2 ($q_1 < q_2$). (K is a linear function of the quantity demanded.) If buy-back is agreed upon, the supplier can signal the value q_2 through trademarks and the information costs disappear. DD_1 (p,q_1) corresponds to the demand for the buy-back commodity at the point of departure. $DD_2(p,q_2,K)$ is the level of demand under conditions of market transparency. Since information gathering is factor-using, the quantity demanded under buy-back ($DD_3(p,q_2)$) will rise, while product quality will become ubiquitous for the buyer. The two supply curves SS_1, SS_2 mirror the difference in cost to suppliers between imports (SS_1) and sale of the means of production (SS_2). Thus points A, B, and C, are the relevant points of equilibrium for a comparative-static analysis

smaller than x_2. Countertrade takes place only if the absence of market signals implies high information costs. Otherwise DD_2 and DD_3 lie so close to each other that x_3 would be smaller than x_2 and countertrade would be rejected. If, however, both of these conditions are fulfilled, rationally behaving economic actors will choose a form of industrial compensation independent of the institutionalized system of exchange.

Not only institutional parameters (intersystemic trade, protectionist measures, etc.) but also a lack of market transparency on free markets can lead logically to countertrade solutions. This is due to the implicit contract implied by countertrade and/or the effects of market signals. In addition, countertrade raises the export volume of both partners. In a countertrade arrangement - as opposed to export, risk sharing is tied to an implicit contract, thus favoring the application of standard technologies within an industrial compensation agreement. This allows the exporter to realize multiple profits on his core skills.

In comparison to exports, the higher equilibrium price of a countertrade transaction does not a priori imply inefficiency. Moreover, our analysis has shown that such an assumption is not accurate in the case of imperfect markets. Industrial compensation is a substitute for direct investment in imperfect markets. Industrial compensation is capital extensive and implies risk sharing with the local producer. At the same time the SME does not lose control over the product and process know-how which is transferred. Intra-firm trade is thereby replaced by buy-back arrangements.

Chapter 10

Competitive Advantage and Technological Change from the Strategic Perspective of the Firm

So far, we have analyzed fundamental changes in the nature of global economic, political, and technological forces which are leading to multidimensional interdependencies cum internationalization. We also looked closely at the theoretical interpretations of international business operations, ranging from classical exports to classical FDI and in-between including the whole spectrum of NFII and NFEF. At this point, we want to focus on the concepts developed to explain NFI from the strategic perspective of the firm. We see the firm as the main actor in the field of technological change on the one hand and of international business operations on the other. It is obvious that our synthesis of NFI theory has rather severe implications for the concept of "competitiveness" as well as for policies to foster competitiveness.

"Can America Compete?" is the title of a well-documented study by LAWRENCE (1984). Its orientation toward a traditional national (endowment) perspective is exposed by this title. Moreover, the title implies an orthodox research strategy based exclusively on export and import shares at the level of the industrial branch. If – as is the case in Switzerland – value-added in international production exceeds the total value of exports, traditional market-share analysis overlooks right from the start the largest part of international operations. Furthermore, it is well established that the growth of a highly industrialized nation is inextricably linked to the successful transfer of technology by all means and in all possible forms. "Nevertheless, economists have been remarkably slow in addressing themselves to the economics of international technology transfer." (TEECE 1977:242). The explanation for this misdirection of research efforts is easily discovered. Industrial branch data on trade, production, and consumption are readily available, whereas other forms of international operations and technology transfer are hard to grasp conceptually, let alone to measure empirically. "(S)hortcomings of the data have blocked the right kinds of research design." (CAVES 1985:45). In addition, we do not find industry-based studies of competitiveness[1] very informative. There are enormous differences among individual technologies and levels of entrepreneurial performance in any given industry. Moreover, modern enterprises are a priori multi-product firms generating and exploiting know-how. World trade for modern industry is based more on differences in technological, managerial, and marketing skills than on differences in factor endowments. "Indeed, the importance of technological or organizational factors (i.e. intangible assets) continues to increase." (KOJIMA/OZAWA 1984: 2). In a small and highly interdependent country like Switzerland, it should surprise

[1] See KNESCHAUREK/MEIER (1983), BORNER/WEHRLE (1984a), BORNER (1984b).

no one that the actual and potential internationalization of practically all entrepreneurial functions is a natural and logical response by firms faced with tougher competitors on the one hand and higher barriers to entry in markets on the other. A short summary of our previous analysis of competitiveness in global markets reveals the following major points as decisive for firm strategy:

- Except for dying and decaying old industries producing standardized products and/or operating with degenerated production technologies, competition is dynamic and innovative. Know-how, know-what, and know-why are the critical factors. It takes substantial resources to make a new process or product economically feasible, i. e. profitable.
- Technological and managerial know-how has very little to do with national endowments. It is neither "given" nor "immobile". On the contrary, it is not only generated by costly R&D and systematic learning; it is also deployed globally by those enterprises capable of appropriating and integrating the critical elements of know-how.
- Competitiveness is, therefore, no meaningful attribute of a nation state. Competitiveness is firm-specific. What really determines the winner of the innovation-imitation race is the absolute advantage of one firm over the other(s). In this respect, we do not only have to consider the costs and risks associated with the "production" of know-how (R&D), we must also consider those of "diffusion" to other domestic plants and firms in other nations. This has two very important implications:
- Competitive (absolute) advantage can only remain firmspecific as long it can be "protected" by the respective firm. In other words, know-how is primarily attributable to a formal organization (centralized hierarchy = internalization) or exclusively assigned via a contractual framework between cooperating individual business units. Know-how is not primarily owned by individuals, nor is it primarily embodied in technological hardware (be they processes or products). Know-how is a bundle of skills, developed, packaged, and deployed by a managerial system with a goal-oriented organization.
- The second implication is that the core skills of firms are necessarily different and differentiated from those of competitors or partners. Furthermore, competitive advantages are highly uncertain at the moment of decision. Competitive strategies are, therefore, heavily influenced by perceptions of and attitudes toward risks. The function of competition is mainly to select those organizations which are best adjusted to the environment of markets and regulations. "In market economies, decisions to export, sell industrial knowledge or set up production facilities abroad are made (...) by industrial firms in a non-identical manner, not by the central authority." (KOJIMA/OZAWA 1984:2).
- Innovation is the key to success, but innovation must be interpreted as any adjustment to new requirements in the relevant environment. Strategies of innovation have three distinct but at the same time closely inter-related dimensions:
  - the development of firm-specific skills
  - the organizational bundling of these skills into entrepreneurial scope through internalization/externalization
  - the global exploitation of skills and scope through all channels of technology transfer according to the costs associated with the various alternative modes of diffusion.

- The purpose of strategic management is to develop these three dimensions of competitiveness in a coordinated, consistent, and systematic way. Thus a competitive strategy must do the following:
  - "cultivate", develop, and appropriate a set of exclusive skills which gives the firm an absolute (monopolistic) competitive advantage (SKILLS),
  - bundle and protect these skills by internalizing the critical assets and relationships in a hierarchical organization and/or contractual network (scope). Control over these skills can be exercised in many different ways, such as property rights (e.g. patents), human capital (research teams), physical capital (process technology), organization (division of labor), and/or contractual cooperation (sharing assets, combining know-how components) (SCOPE),
  - exploit the skills and scope of the firms in local, regional, national, and/or global markets according to their specific characteristics (size, regulations, competitors, etc.) on the one hand and their transaction costs at the other (PROFILE OF INTERNATIONALIZATION).

Competitiveness is the result of such an entrepreneurial strategy. Accordingly, innovation cannot be understood in terms of skills or even technological skills only. On the contrary, organizational/contractual innovations designed to adjust the scope of the firm to its economic and political environment and innovations in the form of international operations are more important. Why is this? Purely technological skills (embodied in hardware or individuals) may quite often be a necessary condition for an entrepreneurial innovation, but they are rarely at the same time a sufficient one. Skills of this sort diffuse quite easily by imitation unless they can be protected by clearly specified legal rights (such as patents, trademarks, etc.). In all other cases, only the appropriate "scope" offers sufficient protection from diffusion of competitive advantage. And only adequate modes of transaction allow a multitude of technology transfers in bundled or unbundled form. Both scope of internalization and/or cooperation, as well as modes of transaction safety, place the skills as such in an "intangible asset" setting.

A blueprint can be copied, a specialist can be bid away, a capital good can be bought, a new product can be "reverse-engineered", while general scientific knowledge, a quasi-public good, is of no economic value to the firm. Moreover, the price of a well-defined good can be undercut by competitors. The true elements of firm-specific and protected competitive advantage lie in the organizational dimension of scope and the strategic exploitation of all forms of operations. This is especially true in the case of multi-purpose or multi-product firms whose skills are know-how based. Just as economies of scale decide the competitiveness of the one-product firm, so the economies of scope determine the competitive advantage of the multi-product enterprise. Scope defines the time and space dimension of "managerial control". Our theoretical approach to competitiveness demonstrates how "scope" can be altered - by "COASEian internalization" (supersession of market transactions by hierarchical organization), by coalitions (PORTER), or through contractual arrangements of various types (BUCKLEY 1983a). This world-view of competitive strategy makes life more difficult for strategic management - and also for those consultants who are busy selling the same prescriptions to everyone (market share, learning curve, portfolio analysis, etc.). At the same time, however, the range of innovative options open to firms of all sizes and industries seems greatly enlarged.

"The transactional model of the MNE ... implies that the firm is a contractual coalition of heterogeneous assets - long-term employees, physical capital, intangibles. Although transactional ownership links avert market failures in transactions in these intangible or heterogenous assets, the internal organization of the MNE itself incurs costs and 'organizational failures' ..." (CAVES 1985:91).

Together with many other studies, our own empirical investigations show that a minimum level of "scale" puts a lower limit on the size of FDI operations. For small and intermediate-sized firms, the contractual route for sharing intangible assets, and thus competitive advantages, in coalition or cooperation seems especially promising.

Part IV

Empirical Research on the Impact of New Forms of Internationalization on Swiss Industry

Chapter 11

Empirical Research Concept and Data Base of Our Swiss Study

11.1 Empirical Research Concept

The empirical part of our study follows an even more modest approach than that followed in the previous theoretical and conceptual chapters. In our modern age of statistical sophistication and ready-made data-bases, empirical research has become even more routine than theory building. The weakness of theory in the field of international entrepreneurial operations is not only a consequence of the high degree of complexity and the rigidity of dogmatic-axiomatic model structures. Probably the most important impass to research is the almost total lack of data, or simply, of information. Modern technologies of computation and "informatics" have taught us how to build, service, and use existing data. But they remain more or less mute when confronted with the task of generating information, especially of generating from scratch data on new phenomena.

The information required is not only evasive but politically sensitive. Even firms involved in NFI-operations are mostly unable to quantify the significance of these operations. In some instances, firms are quite unwilling to reveal the little they know themselves. Hence, the empirical material presented below is extremely crude, certainly incomplete and fragmentary, in short, very provisional and uneven. Nevertheless, our contacts proved that we were touching interesting aspects of present and future business trends.

Additionally, limitations of space made a concentration on the most important points necessary. More empirical material and more lengthy interpretations thereof can be found in the respective monographs by Bürgin (1986) and Hämisegger (1986).

What we present in the following chapters is an outgrowth of our research philosophy of explorative empiricism. Our work profited markedly from the work done at the OECD Development Center by the coordinator of parallel projects, Charles Oman, but we hope it goes further. Whenever the reader gets desperate, we kindly ask him or her to turn to page 1 and reread the motto ...

11.2 Data Base

The data used for our empirical study of New Forms of Internationalization among Swiss industrial firms was a new primary data base which we generated by the development, mailing, and evaluation of a written questionnaire. The questionnaires were filled out by company representatives in the spring of 1984. (Cf. the results in Chapters IV/13 and IV/14.) In addition, we carried out in-depth interviews of some of the responding firms during the months of October, November, and December 1984. (Cf. Chapter IV/12.) The questionnaire was divided into three sections: exports; new forms of internationalization, economic policy, risk management; and general data on the individual firm. The written survey consisted of 34 questions on 14 pages. The firms were encouraged to supplement their multiple-choice answers with additional comments.

For the following industrial branches the Swiss Federal Census Bureau provided us with the address of every third firm in its register of industrial plants with 10 or more employees:

- the textile industry (including the apparel and shoe industries)
- the chemical industry (including basic chemicals and pharmaceuticals)
- the machinery industry.

Altogether, 1524 questionnaires were sent out and 1456 reached their addressees. The German language questionnaire was mailed during the first week of April 1984 and the French language questionnaire in the second week of April. Both groups of firms were asked to return the questionnaires by the middle of May. The chemical, machinery, and engineering firms were sent a reminder in the second week of May. Due to technical problems, we were not able to send reminders to the French language addressees or to any of the textile firms. 281 questionnaires were returned and 272 were included in the evaluation process. Thus 18.7% of the firms which received questionnaires are represented in the analysis.

The method of selection was to take every third firm in an alphabetical list, thereby permitting us to assume that the sample is representative. The composition of the responses, however, cannot be considered representative. Some of the more serious biases are: relatively too many large firms and a significant underrepresentation of textile firms. From the point of view of branch structure, it was not our intention to strive for any representivity. Rather, we concentrated on the main Swiss exporting industries. Our sample consists of 44 textile firms, 44 chemical firms, 177 machinery firms, and 7 firms not assignable to any particular industry. Table 11-1 indicates the distribution of these 272 firms according to the category "size of firm".

Our sample includes 9.4% of the total number of Swiss industrial firms: 3.1% are textile and garment firms, 1.1% chemical firms, and 5.1% machinery firms.

All three branches included in our analysis can be considered typical export industries. Among the firms in the sample, 85% exported goods and/or services, while another 4% were planning to do so. All three of these branches were hit by the global recession of the 1970s. In addition, the textile industry was challenged from Third World competition and underwent a thorough restructuring in the last decade. While the machine industry had, in 1984, not yet regained its 1977 zenith of production, the chemical industry has been continuously growing in output since 1975.

The case studies concerning NFEF consist of firms which could be regarded as representative firms employing different forms of countertrade. The aims of the in-depths interviews include the following:

- reconstruction of history, character, and problems of an exemplary NFEF-operation

Table 11-1. The Sample According to Branch and Size of Firm in Comparison to the Statistical Population of the Swiss Firm Census

Number of Employees	Total	Textiles	Chemicals	Machinery
Base (100%)	272 100.0 (100.0)	44 16.2 (33.2)	44 16.2 (12.0)	177 65.1 (54.8)
10- 49	109 40.1 (65.9)	14 31.8 (67.2)	15 34.1 (63.6)	77 43.5 (65.6)
50-499	120 44.1 (31.6)	25 56.8 (32.3)	24 54.4 (33.4)	72 40.7 (30.7)
500-999	18 6.6 (1.4)	4 9.1 (0.3)	1 2.3 (1.2)	11 6.2 (2.1)
1000++	19 7.0 (1.2)	0 0.0 (0.2)	4 9.1 (1.8)	15 8.5 (1.6)
No Information	6 2.2	1 2.3	0 0.0	2 1.1

The corresponding figures of the Swiss Firm Census are in brackets. (Source: Schweizerisches Jahrbuch für Volkswirtschaft und Statistik 1984:172)

- "testing" of the hypotheses developed during the course of our theoretical work.

The case studies in the realm of NFII consisted of thirteen firms: one textile company (a converter), five chemical and pharmaceutical companies, four electronics manufacturers, and three firms from the machine industry. We examined these firms' utilization of various forms of foreign involvement. The aim was to verify and amend the theory presented in Chapter 8.

Finally, to build a bridge between our previous project "Global Structural Change and International Competition Among Industrial Firms: The Case of Switzerland" (cf. BORNER et al. 1985 and BORNER/WEHRLE 1984a) and the project described in this report we again surveyed the largest Swiss multinational corporations in the manufacturing sector. The purpose of this second survey was not a quantitative analysis but rather a qualitative evaluation of the importance of NFII to multinationals. Unfortunately, some of the companies refused to release any information on their NFII activities: some for reasons of confidentiality but some because of political fears.

Chapter 12

Case Study Results

12.1 Case Studies of New Forms of International Investment (NFII)

Our case studies were not designed to provide a representative profile of the internationalization process in Swiss industrial firms. Rather, we focussed on single forms of foreign operations carried out by individual firms and examined why these forms were strategically selected and how they were put into practice. The case study sample consists of 13 firms, representatives of which had already filled out our postal questionnaire: one from the textile branch, five from chemicals and pharmaceuticals, and seven from machinery and electrical goods, whereby four of the latter produce electronic or telecommunications equipment. There were 10 medium-size firms - with between 50 and 499 employees - and three large companies - with over 500 employees. One of the firms could be considered to be a small multinational. The export share of our case study sample differed from that of the written survey: for chemicals and machinery it was lower, while for the textile firm it was above average.

None of the medium-size firms have redeployed production on the basis of full ownership. For technical reasons one firm was compelled to carry out certain elements of its processing abroad. Its internationalization potential is thus nearly exhausted. Firms which absolutely require market proximity or firms which have a very high export share (over 90%) have sales operations abroad. The two largest firms prefer to keep tight control over foreign operations. While the one is trying to eliminate old non-equity forms, the other is being forced to increase local value-added. In a high-tech sector with a high percentage of purchases by government agencies, the firm can easily be put under pressure.

Our interviews show that foreign production with 100% ownership lies either beyond the capacity of SMEs or it stands as a direct trade-off to more participatory forms of operation. That is, small or medium-size firms can support either one branch plant or several New Forms of International Investment, but not both. Since there were no cases of cost motivated redeployment, market access the dominant reason for foreign engagement. Which basic form of foreign operation - 100% ownership or NFII - is preferable cannot, however, be determined theoretically. Quantitatively, the success of foreign engagement depends on the relationship between market potential and the means necessary for effective marketing. That is, market density and demand structures determine the optimal strategy. Qualitatively, elements such as knowledge of the market, relationships to local partners, capacity of local partners, and the goals of the individual enterprise determine the specific form selected.

In the analysis of NFII a distinction must be made between distribution oriented and production oriented forms. Engagements with purely marketing and sales motives raise no problems in respect to protective control. In cases where production activities are involved the firm must be assured of a sufficient level of protective control over its know-how.

Firms tend to invest their capital where their expertise makes it possible to enjoy a satisfactory rate of growth and a satisfactory rate of return. Contrary to common theory, firms do not invest wherever profit levels are highest (cf. CLIFTON 1977). At the same time the firm must consider which steps in the production process it must and can control directly, which steps should be the object of cooperation with other firms, and which steps could be given over to the market mechanism. The ever-changing boundary lines among these three alternatives produces the internalization/externalization profile of the individual firm (BURGENER 1983b:33).

In the following paragraphs we present and discuss the results of the case studies in terms of various analytical categories common in the literature on industrial development and change: branch, technology, ownership, export, and markets.

12.1.1 Utilization of New Forms of International Investment and the Branch of Industrial Activity

The textile firm in our case study sample is a converter and thus has virtually no process or product technology to internationalize. This firm's NFII are limited to design and marketing. Success on textile markets demands an intensive network of market contacts and extremely high levels of knowledge about the functioning of specialized markets. Thus, this firm is represented on all important markets by a subsidiary. Licensingout only comes into question where market density is low; hence no particularly important functions can be given over to NFII.

Because of their technological and know-how characteristics, certain machine and chemical firms seem particularly suited to cooperative forms of foreign engagement. So long as important areas of know-how - core skills - can be kept under control, process and product technology can be transferred. Certain segments of the chemical and pharmaceutical industries are specialized in internationalizing through licensing. Many pharmaceuticals - both prescription and over the counter drugs - stemming from small firms are produced locally and sold locally through licensing agreements. The same is true for small markets like Switzerland. This pattern can also be found among producers of household chemicals.

In contrast, there is resistance toward cooperative forms of internationalization in the electronics branch. Nonetheless, small firms are forced to employ some NFII if they hope to sell their products abroad. Frequently, a conflict arises between long-term NFII contracts and increased desire for direct control. In the electronics industry NFII are often limited to precompetitive cooperation and complementary cooperation in marketing and distribution, that is, in areas where problems with protective control cannot arise.

12.1.2 New Forms of International Investment and Technology

It is usually assumed that highly modern technologies are not objects of NFII because, according to the product/process cycle theory, such technology still contains the advantages of monopoly pricing. This, of course, remains true. Nonetheless, another factor cannot be overlooked: the danger of diffusion of such technologies. The more abstract and theoretical a technology is, the less it depends on experience and, thus, the less "idiosyncratic" it is. Less idiosyncratic technologies imply the danger of the firm's being deprived of its monopoly situation before the costs of research and development have been covered. Easy transmission of the technology means fewer chances for employing NFII. High tech as such does not preclude NFII, but neither are "lower" types of technology necessarily free from the danger of diffusion. Wherever there are low levels of resistance to transmission of knowledge, the danger of rapid diffusion exists. Yet, as the firms we interviewed confirmed, production experience in the machine industry offers more protection from lost monopoly gains than does such experience in pharmaceuticals, electronics, and telecommunications.

12.1.3 New Forms of International Investment and Management Structure

The composition of management is decisive. Is the firm directly managed by the entrepreneur, is it run by a hired manager, or is the management structure a mixture somewhere between the two? There is a positive correlation between direct management and interest in NFII - especially participatory forms such as joint ventures. Typically, it is the entrepreneur who personally initiates the joint ventures and, through relationships of mutual trust, who is able to bring such ventures to successful fruition. Such ventures are usually carried out between firms of more or less the same size; often a personal friendship exists between the two entrepreneurs. It is interesting to note that joint ventures and minority control are looked at skeptically by hired managers. They tend to favor 100% ownership and prefer fewer markets but more intensive marketing, that is, greater initial investment, but no need to share directive control - "sovereignty" (RICHARDSON 1972) - and profits.

12.1.4 New Forms of International Investment and Export Activity

The firm in our sample with the lowest level of exports still shows 80% of its sales abroad - namely through licensing. Consumer products are sold in dense markets, where advertizing and brand names play an important role. In most cases the foreign partners are responsible for production - using mature technologies, sourcing, and sales. In order to achieve a homogeneous product image the Swiss firm delivers packaging materials and takes care of advertizing. Licenses are awarded for production, distribution, and the use of brand names. It took Swiss firms some time to learn to take advantage of their control potential. It is generally true that NFII - including sub-contracting and joint ventures - are used to achieve higher levels of product distribution.

Participation in a foreign unit of production by way of NFII is usually undertaken by firms with an export share of around 30%. This is true for products for which the firm commands a large share in a stagnant domestic market or in cases where the Swiss market is too small or inappropriate. Usually, the products require a comparatively high level of market proximity. Such internationalization processes are not at all limited to mature technologies! The important point is, again, the relatively small export share. An internationalization strategy relying on NFII seems to be characterized in general (cf. Chapter 13 below and BERGER/UHLMANN 1983) by early entry into foreign markets without the firm's committing a large part of domestic capacity to export production.

12.1.5 Market Characteristics of Firms Utilizing New Forms of International Investment

Basically, our research showed that SMEs' competitive advantages - gained through vertical quality competition - can be realized on foreign markets. Marketing can be made easier via new forms of foreign engagement. Technically oriented firms - as Swiss industrial firms tend to be - concentrate their innovative potential in technological activities. Swiss firms are often reserved and even helpless when it comes to market-oriented innovations. Exceptions are to be found where the individual entrepreneur works actively toward a new future for the company and/or where there is an agile and flexible director of foreign operations. In such cases a more or less carefully structured strategy for internationalization can be expected. The more precise and conscious a firm is about its own advantages and core skills, the better it is able to control and utilize these advantages in foreign markets.

For the most part firms in our case study sample are striving to create and maintain company specific competitive advantages in oligopolistic markets. This is clearly a strategy for avoiding the pressures of price and process competition. When the price component in domestic markets gains in importance - due to the pressure of imports - firms are forced to utilize their competitive advantages abroad as well. New Forms of International Investment play an important role in this strategy. Moreover, saturation of domestic markets instigates firms not threatened by imports to become involved in foreign markets. One comes to the conclusion that Swiss industrialists show little inclination to be drawn into pure price and process competition.

12.2 Case Studies on New Forms of Export Financing (NFEF)

In this section we present three case studies, all selected from our sample of chemical and pharmaceutical companies. The cases were so chosen as to allow a comparison between the countertrade operations of SMEs and MNEs. Furthermore, we selected those firms which applied practically the whole spectrum of possible contracts.

12.2.1 The Chemical Industry

The firm which we investigated in detail is engaged in producing finished goods for the market. The firm has 450 employees. Between 1978 and 1984, its export share oscillated between 85% and 95%. Following a drop in sales in 1980, the firm has almost fully recovered. Since 1979, annual gross investment has averaged 8.7%. The most important export markets in order of importance are the Common Market, the USA, the COMECON countries, Brazil, Argentina, and developing countries in Africa. The firm has utilized countertrade measures world-wide on all of its export markets.

Outside the OECD the firm's products which are exported via countertrade face a quasi demand monopoly. On the supply side the situation is one of competitive oligopoly. In non-OECD countries any one of these oligopolistic suppliers is able to satisfy the entire national demand. Thus negotiations take place with a monopoly supplier facing a buyer's monopoly. The buyer negotiates contracts with each supplier but in the end only ratifies the one which is most advantageous. Given that most suppliers seem to be willing to offer export credits - in some cases with government assistance - our case study firm feels compelled to utilize countertrade in order to maintain competitiveness. From the point of view of this Swiss firm such agreements primarily serve to support and expand its marketing mix or to take advantage internationally of the firm's core skills through buy-back. Countertrade is not necessarily used to internationalize sales operations. Multilateral countertrade agreements are often made in collaboration with a multinational firm which has a specialized countertrade division producing complementary goods for the same market. Cooperation with a specialized trading firm is another frequently used alternative.

In Figure 12-1 we have sketched the major steps which must be taken, as well as the relationships among the partners, in a classical monetarized three-way barter deal.

The value of Swiss exports - commodity flow (1) - was compensated for by foreign importers in the following way:

- through the use of a bilateral payment agreement between countries A and B - (2) and (3)
- through sales of counter goods via a trading company - (4) and (5)
- through direct payment - (6).

The splitting of the payments - (3), (5), and (6) - permitted the refinancing costs to be minimized.

In another case (November 1984) the exports of the firm and those of the cooperating Swiss MNE were split into 12 parts, which were to be delivered to a developing country over a period of 24 months. The total value of the deal was 28.25 million Swiss francs. The deliveries on both sides were based on parallel barter and financed through Swiss exporters who advanced payment. The credit risk was divided between the two firms according to their respective portions of goods delivered. The compensatory commodities - raw materials - were channelled into the free market by the countertrade department of the MNE. At least two additional parts of this parallel barter served to finance exports of other Swiss consumer and investment goods. The exporters of these goods, though not participants in the large

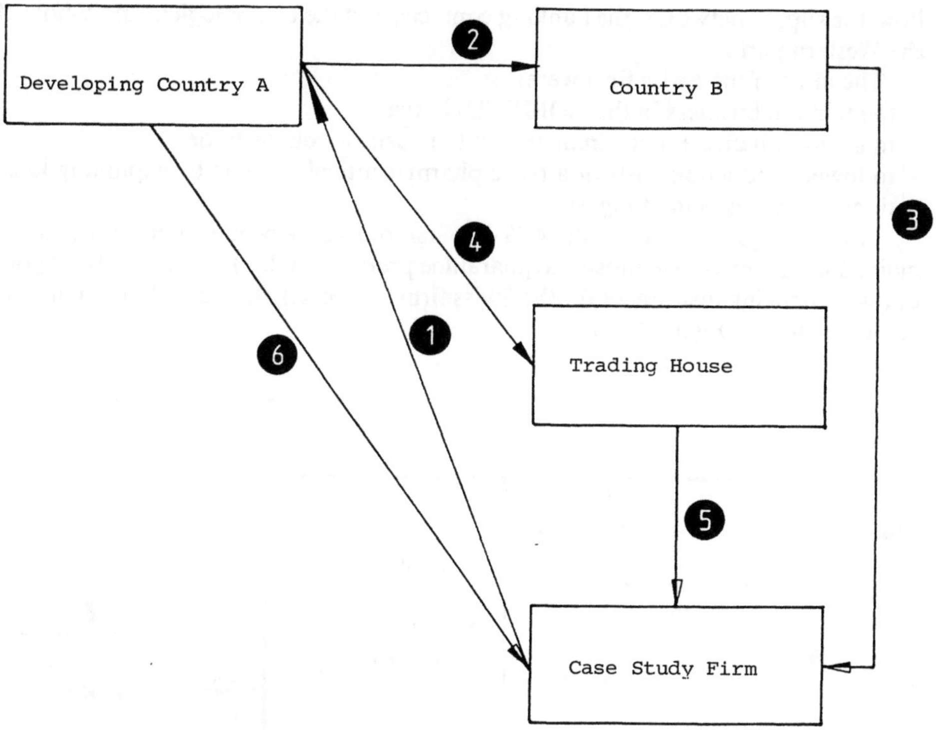

Fig. 12-1. Classical Monetarized Trilateral Barter

countertrade deal, were thus enabled to sell on markets which would otherwise have remained closed to them (the Delcredere risk having been too high).

12.2.2 The Pharmaceutical Industry

The firm we examined here is a subsidiary of a large multinational Swiss chemical company. Export destinations – in order of importance – are: OECD countries, COMECON countries, Brazil, Argentina, Peru, Syria, Jordan, Indonesia, Japan, the Philippines, some African countries, and Australia. Western Europe and the COMECON countries account for 85% of export sales, Latin America for 8%, and Asia 6%. The gross investment rate has been about 5% since 1977. When compared to the average for all firms in our sample, the firm's sales record is above average.

The starting point for this firm's involvement with a COMECON country was the revision of a law on "economic association with foreign participation" in Hungary. This revision allows for joint ventures with foreign companies, whereby the foreign firm was permitted only up to 49% ownership. Profit transfers and free market prices were guaranteed by contract. The aim of the Hungarian partner was to increase the use of modern technologies, as well as of new organizational and managerial know-how. In addition, the firm wanted to step up its marketing efforts abroad. All in all, the Hungarians wanted to take advantage of the marketing know-how, the supply networks, the banking contacts, and the technological know-how of the Western partner.

The aims of the Swiss firm were:

- to maintain business in the COMECON area
- to institutionalize export financing on the basis of countertrade
- to lower production costs of a basic pharmaceutical product by exploiting locational advantages in Hungary.

Through a joint venture with 49% ownership, a turnkey agreement (produit-en-main, that is, know-how transfer to guarantee product quality), and a buy-back policy (as a financing instrument for the Swiss firm's exports), the aims of both partners could be met (cf. Figure 12-2).

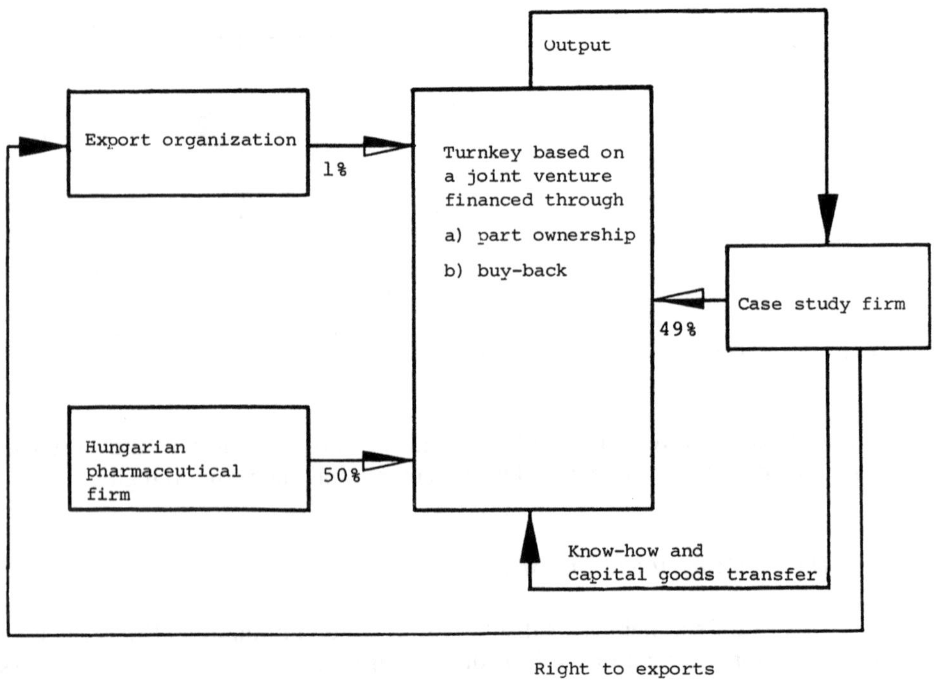

Fig. 12-2. Diagram of a Buy-Back Agreement on the Basis of Joint Venture and Turnkey

12.2.3 The Chemical and Pharmaceutical Industries: the Case of a Multinational Firm

In the following description the term "trading house function" refers to the intertemporal allocation of compensatory commodities, that is, the use of existing markets or the creation of new markets for the sale of traded goods. In the organizational structure of a multinational firm, this trading house function can be internalized or externalized. The following options are listed in order of decreasing degrees of externalization:

- purchase of the services of a trading house on the open market
- establishment or purchase of a trading house as a subsidiary
- minority ownership in a trading house established by firms in a particular branch of industry to coordinate compensation business
- establishment of a countertrade department within the firm to control the organizational and business aspects of trade agreements and the quality of compensatory goods which must then be sold through a trading house
- in-house countertrading division which cover the trading house functions for the firm.

Confronted with a growing volume of countertrade, the MNE we examined established a countertrade department in 1984. This countertrade department was conceived as a cost center. With the exception of personnel, all costs associated with any concrete trade agreement are charged to the respective product division. Since countertrade is used as a multi-functional, and thus offensive marketing instrument, a profit center approach would have - via the transfer of trading house functions to a third party - meant the diffusion of competitive advantages.

The company in question is the most important Swiss exporter. By 1984, more than 10% of this company's exports from Switzerland implied some form of countertrade. As is the case within the branch in general, a significant expansion of North-South countertrade is taking place. Despite the undermining of cartel agreements and dumping in the branch as a whole, the firm was able to realize short-term price reductions as a result of the sale of compensatory goods. In some cases the compensatory goods had an unexpected competitive advantage and were successful in a particular market niche.

In the analysis of countertrade, the global situation is quite different for the chemical industry than for the machinery industry. For the chemical industry the volume of countertrade agreements has risen not because of the protection of industrial imports, but rather because of the protectionist policy against agricultural imports. This agricultural protectionism hits the Third World and has been accompanied by a worsening of developing countries' terms of trade. The result is a lack of foreign exchange. Consequently, there has been an increased tendency for the developing countries to turn to countertrade agreements. Since most European and American firms are willing to enter into countertrade agreements, Swiss firms - if they are to maintain their competitiveness - must also participate. As mentioned above, each supplier can cover the entire demand of a developing country. Thus the developing country can choose among the firms offering bilateral agreements.

Chapter 13

Results of the Survey on New Forms of International Investment (NFII)

13.1 An Overview of International Activities

Of the 272 firms which returned the questionnaire, 230 firms - 85% of the respondents - reported export activity. An additional 4% were planning to export in the near future. 94% of the exporting firms made sales in Western Europe and/or North America, 37% in the developing countries, 15% in the NICs and Japan, and 14% in Eastern European countries. The unweighted average of exports as a percentage of total turnover (1983) was 56%. A fourth of the firms which returned the questionnaire showed an average export level of under 20% and another fourth of over 80%. 29% of the small firms, 48% of the middle-sized firms, and 63% of the large firms exported over 60% of sales. The intensity of export activity clearly increases with the size of the firm. Table 13-1 compares the export activity of firms in our sample and the export activity of Swiss industrial firms as a whole.

Despite the fact that the figures are not wholly comparable (the average for our sample is unweighted, GDP and turnover are not parallel concepts) the difference in the figures for the chemical industry are too significant to be ignored. The smaller firms which dominate our sample are obviously domestically oriented. The role of the large Basle-based companies in determining national averages hides the reality of the branch as a whole. To a far lesser degree this applies to the machine industry as well. In the case of the textile industry the figures are practically identical.

BERGER and UHLMANN (1983:24) identify the following types of direct investment:

- acquisition by equity purchase
  - up to 50%
  - over 50%

Table 13-1. A Comparison of Export Shares in Percent of Production According to Industrial Branch, 1983

	Textiles and Apparel (TEX)	Chemicals (CHE)	Machinery (MACH)
Unweighted Average for the Sample	59*	47	55
For Swiss Industry	62	80	62

Note: The export quota in our sample is a percentage of turnover. The export quota for Swiss industry as a whole is a percentage of GDP for the respective industry.
* = 1982

- establishment or expansion of firms or branch plants
  - single-handedly
  - jointly with other companies

Even though this categorization of direct investment allows a more differentiated analysis, our approach was somewhat different. We asked firms to distinguish between minority, majority, and 100%-ownership on the one hand and joint ventures on the other. (The latter will be treated below.) The responses clearly indicated that companies preferred 100% ownership. Of the 39% of our respondents who had capital invested abroad, 39% had minority ownership, 27% majority ownership, and 71% had activities with 100% ownership. For the individual branches these figures were: textiles 46-9-64; chemicals 40-26-65; machinery 30-28-76. As for geographical distribution, the OECD countries dominate. Between 85% and 90% of majority (including 100%) ownership activities are located within OECD countries. However, only two thirds of the minority holdings are located in OECD countries (cf. Table 13-2).

We surmise that the rather high number of firms with minority holdings in developing countries is due to the ever growing legislative restrictions for foreign dominated companies. These restrictions are easiest to enforce in the field of capital participation. Whether or not entrepreneurial control of "core skills" is really hampered by such legislation is another question. But our interviews lead us to conclude that only when forced by government restrictions do Swiss firms forego investment with 100% ownership.

Of the 272 respondents to our survey, 129 firms, 47% of the respondents, reported New Forms of International Investment (NFII). 63 firms (23%) had experience with New Forms of Export Financing (NFEF). 18% (48 firms) indicated experience with both forms, 20% (54 firms) experience with international investment alone, and 5% (14 firms) experience with export financing alone. This means a total of 143 firms or 53% had some kind of involvement with New Forms of Internationalization (NFI). If we include firms which in the past have had such involvement but which have no such engagement at present, then the figure is 60% or 163 firms with experience in NFI.

Of the 129 firms with experience in NFII we distinguish between "inward" and "outward" forms of activity. In the case of an inward form - sometimes referred to as a passive form - the firm is on the receiving end of an arrangement - i.e. licensing-in. With an outward form - sometimes called an active form - the firm is "selling" or "giving" i.e. licensing-out. We choose to use the terms inward and outward rather than passive and active because both forms are in fact elements of

Table 13-2. Geographical Distribution of Equity Participation in Percent of Occurrences in Each Category

	Industrial Countries	NICs + Japan	Developing Countries	Total
Ownership				
Minority (up to 50%)	66	13	21	100
Majority (51-99%)	88	8	4	100
100%	90	6	4	100

Table 13-3. Outward and Inward Forms of International Investment Among Firms in the Sample

Outward or inward	47%, absolute 129
Outward	38%, absolute 102
Inward	32%, absolute 86
Inward and outward	23%, absolute 62

an active strategy of technology management. Table 13-3 shows a breakdown of our sample firms according to the inward or outward nature of their foreign involvement.

All in all our survey results indicate a relatively high frequency of NFII among Swiss firms.

13.2 New Forms of International Investment and Traditional Categories of Industrial Analysis

In this section we investigate New Forms of International Investment in terms of more standard categories for analyzing the foreign oriented operations of Swiss firms. Thus, we examine the relationship of NFII to exports, FDI, size of firms, industrial branch of activity, technology, and host-countries.

13.2.1 New Forms of International Investment and Exports

In our questionnaire we asked for information on exports for the years 1970, 1975, 1979, 1980, 1981, 1982, and 1983. It is clear that the number of responses for the later years was higher. Nonetheless, the results are consistent. The average export share for these seven years oscillates between 52% and 58%. Firms without any NFI (i.e. New Forms of Internationalization comprising both NFII and NFEF) show export shares of between 31% and 36%. The average for firms with NFII (but without NFEF) fluctuates between 47% and 65%. Lastly, companies employing NFEF instead of NFII have a very high quota – between 69% and 74%. The seven-year average, as well as the correlation with FDI, is presented in Table 13-4.

Table 13-4. Forms of Internationalization and Export Shares

Basic Forms of Internationalization Applied by Firms	Export Shares Seven Year Average in Percent
no NFII, no FDI	31
no NFII, FDI	67
NFII, no FDI	58
NFII, FDI	64
NFII, no NFEF	50
no NFII, NFEF	72

Firms engaged in NFII are evidently located somewhere in the middle range, which – taken together with the knowledge gained through our case studies – leads us to the conclusion that firms 'select' between three basic strategies: (1) a supplementary export strategy, (2) an all-out export strategy, and (3) an internationalization strategy.

The first approach is characterized by a basically domestic orientation. Exporting has a buffer function; the export department is somewhat understaffed; export shares in total turnover may be erratic. Strategy number (2) is employed by firms for which the domestic market is far too small and for which foreign production is not a viable alternative. In this context countertrade solutions (NFEF) are often unavoidable. Finally, the third strategy comprises both FDI and NFII. Strategies (2) and (3) must be clearly distinguished since some FDIs have sales functions only and should therefore be classified as belonging to export strategies.

An internationalization strategy in the context of Swiss enterprises aims primarily at gaining market access via the establishment of local production (cf. BORNER/WEHRLE 1984b and HUNZIKER 1983). Either NFII or FDI may be used; if both forms are applied, they corelate with an export share in the middle range, for NFII alone the figure may even be lower. Interestingly, our results are in harmony with a similar study carried out by the Ifo-Institute for the Federal Republic of Germany. "It is evident that in the course of export growth companies supplement their exports or maintain some degree of export stability by employing various forms of foreign engagement. However, the most intense engagement in foreign countries is shown by firms with an export quota of between 31% and 50%." (BERGER/UHLMANN 1983:33; author's translation). Taking into account the generally lower average export quota of German firms (cf. Table 13-5) we would stretch this range to

Table 13-5. Comparison of Export Shares of the IAER/SNF Study for Switzerland and the Ifo-Institute Study for the Federal Republic of Germany, 1982

Firms in percent 'Switzerland'	Export shares up to					
	20%	40%	60%	80%	more than 80%	Total
• With international investment	17	17	13	16	37	100
• Without international investment	34	15	9	18	24	100
'Federal Republic of Germany'	20%	30%	50%	75%	more than 75%	Total
• With international investment	33	22	28	23	5	100
• Without international investment	76	11	9	3	1	100

Note: The export percentages shown are not the same: 20%, 40%, 60%, and 80% in the case of Switzerland, 20%, 30%, 50%, and 75% for the FRG.

60%. Considering the small size of the Swiss market, strategies (2) and (3) may both be indispensable for small firms on their way to becoming larger enterprises.

Table 13-5 compares the NFII and export behavior of German and Swiss firms. We must, however, pay attention to the following: The Ifo-study was based on a much larger sample and also included additional industries.[1] Moreover, our sample is slightly biased toward larger firms. Nonetheless, the data substantiate the hypothesis that Swiss firms have a higher level of 'internationality'. Only 21% of the German firms reported current or planned application of what we call NFII. Among the Swiss firms, 38% currently employed NFII and another 9% planned to engage in such activity in the future, thus totalling 47%.

Against the backdrop of the macroeconomic export quotas for Switzerland and the FRG, these data become more meaningful. Where hardware exports are concerned, these quotas are roughly alike. Hence, we are led to assume that the international relations of German industry are heavily concentrated among large firms, whereas Swiss companies are forced to go international at a much earlier stage of development or smaller scale of operation.

13.2.2 New Forms of International Investment and Foreign Direct Investment

According to Table 13-6, the relative frequencies of NFII and FDI are practically the same.

That small firms show less financial and personal freedom in undertaking foreign activities - especially in the form of direct investment - seems logical. Nonetheless, as BURGENER (1983b) showed, and as our survey confirmed, there is a great deal of variation in the success with which small firms penetrate into other cultural zones - like Japan and Brazil - and a great variety in the form such engagements take.

For very small firms NFII seem to be preferred as a route to internationalization. In general, medium-sized firms as well as the textile and apparel industries seem to prefer FDI. Of all the firms reporting equity participation (FDI) abroad,

Table 13-6. Internationalization by Direct Investment and New Forms of International Investment: A Comparison According to Industrial Branch and Size of Firm, 1983 (in Percent of All Firms)

	Industrial Branch			Size of Firm (number of employees)				Total
	TEX	CHE	MACH	10-49	50-499	500-999	1000+	
• Foreign Direct Investment	25	46	40	11	48	78	100	39
• New Forms of International Investment	18	43	39	21	37	72	100	38

[1] These are the metal and wood industries.

Table 13-7. Relationship between New Forms of International Investment and Foreign Direct Investment (Figures in Percent)

		Ownership		
		Minority	Majority	100%
Firms with Equity Participation Abroad	NFII yes	45	30	70
	NFII no	25	11	70

only one-fifth do not employ NFII. Since the subsidiary or branch plant must be licensed to use technology, designs, moulds, dies, etc., licensing as one type of NFII must come into use.[2] The corollary is that about one-fifth of FDI occurrences are exclusively designed for international marketing purposes. We think that this is particularly true for medium-sized enterprises.

The Swiss textile firms possess hardly any production facilities abroad; their FDI activities are in the field of marketing and distribution. In other branches and for both small and large firms NFII and FDI seem to go hand in hand.

The relationship between FDI and NFII - cf. Table 13-7 - shows that majority ownership is less common than minority or 100% ownership. Reasons for this finding may include the following: Majority participation is simply unusual for the foreign partner of local enterprise. Where the laws allow, 100%-ownership is sought. In regard to the question of control, the difference between majority and minority holdings is minimal.

The preference for 100% ownership is obvious. Hunziker (1983:155) confirms this result and remarks that Swiss industry, by clinging to complete ownership, reduces its own elbow-room. We are led to infer that FDI in the form of 100%-ownership is also preferred to NFII. But Table 13-8 reveals that FDI as such may well be more frequently utilized than NFII. Yet per se NFII is more widespread than any one of the three forms of FDI.

13.2.3 New Forms of International Investment and the Size of the Firm

Table 13-8 confirms a somewhat banal truth: In general, the 'internationality' of firms is a function of firm size. This is true for exporting, FDI, and of course NFII. Our sample consists of 229 smaller firms (109 firms with 10-49 employees and 120 firms with 50-499 employees) and 37 larger firms (18 firms with 500-999 employees and 19 firms with over 1000 employees). 29% of the smaller and 86% of the larger firms employ NFII. The overall average is 38%.

For the smallest firms equity participation is of marginal importance, but more than one-fifth of these firms are engaged in NFII. In general, NFII are employed more frequently than 100% ownership. But it would be myopic to conclude that NFII are more significant than subsidiaries in terms of value added or turnover.

---

[2] There are exceptions, cf. Hämisegger 1986.

Table 13-8. Internationalization by Size of Firm (in Percent of All Firms)

Number of Employees	NFII	Equity Participation			Exporting	Export Share (Ø for 1982 in %)
		Minority	Majority	100%		
10– 49	21	6	3	3	74	43
50–499	37	14	12	35	90	57
500–999	72	33	28	56	100	57
1000+	100	53	26	100	100	68
10–499	29	10	7	20	83	
500+	86	43	27	78	100	

Firstly, NFII are used as instruments of participation in foreign units of production. The output imputable to NFII is nearly impossible to measure. Secondly, and not infrequently, the utilization of NFII (NFEF even more so) is frowned upon and the 'noble' forms of internationalization, i. e. exporting and 100%-FDI, are clearly preferred. Thirdly, the generation of jobs, output, value added, etc. by the subsidiaries of large Swiss multinational corporations is voluminous and rather easily measurable. For smaller firms (10–499 employees), however, NFII are no less important than FDI in shaping international involvement.

13.2.4 New Forms of International Investment and Industrial Branch

Coarse-grained statistical evidence cannot do justice to the peculiarities of the Swiss "textile system". Almost completely decentralized (cf. SCHAFFNER 1982 and BURGENER 1983b) into small and medium-sized firms, the majority of companies is not in touch with the final consumer. Therefore, foreign sales are primarily executed by specialized trading companies and converters. (The standard deviation of the export quotas is correspondingly high.) This structure, in conjunction with the fact that the textile industry is now[3] heavily concentrated on taking advantage of Switzerland's location-specific factors, influences NFII behavior. The industry as a whole is highly capital-intensive and oriented toward maintaining flexibility and producing very specialized, high-quality products. The industry makes use of low interest rates on the one hand and an excellent infrastructure and a well-trained, well-adapted labor force on the other. Production outside Switzerland is rare and limited to apparel and shoe manufacturers. As a consequence, we cannot expect a high level of NFII. FDI is limited to marketing and distribution as well as to some service-like manufacturing activities, e. g. sewing of garments for interior decorating purposes.

The chemical industry, which includes the pharmaceutical industry, shows a high level of international commitment, both in the realm of FDI and NFII. Although the industry-wide export quota is rather low, our case studies suggest the ex-

[3] "Now" means after the substantial down-sizing of this industry in the aftermath of the revolution of the Swiss franc and the international structural change of the 1970s.

Table 13-9. Internationalization According to Industrial Branch (in Percent of All Firms)

Branch	NFII	Equity Participation			Exporting	Export Share (Ø for 1982 in %)
		Minority	Majority	100%		
Textiles	18	11	2	16	73	59
Chemicals	43	18	11	30	89	44
Machinery	39	15	11	30	84	55

istence of extensive international cooperation, particularly in pharmaceuticals. Despite the fact that product and process technologies in the pharmaceutical branch are easily diffused, a tight patent-protection policy within a number of Western countries allows extra-firm realization of firm-specific advantages (cf. Chapter 8 above and HÄMISEGGER 1985). Outside these countries NFII operations are more delicate. Here FDI or "no-shows" are prevalent. Cooperation occurs mainly as a means for overcoming smallness, be it the small size of the firm, of the product, or of country markets. In the chemical industry NFII mainly cover process know-how. The 'intimacy' of cooperation is a function of the degree of experience-intensity of the technology transferred and of the potential of the local market. Markets characterized by intense competition - e.g. household chemicals, cosmetics, and OTC-drugs - are conducive to the use of NFII. In such cases NFII extends to the products themselves. As our case studies suggest, a number of manufacturers producing such products rely on NFII and show few hardware-oriented exports.

In the case of the machinery industry, the adjective "new" in "New Forms" is most misleading. New Forms have a long history, particularly in the national, but also in the international context. According to an industry representative (cf. also SULZER 1984), NFII have been practiced "ever since". Sub-contracting appears to have a long tradition as a trade cycle buffer. The other New Forms have had a significant impact on internationalization behavior because processes are highly divisible. Compare the batch and bulk production in the chemical industry. Owing to the idiosyncratic nature of many NEWTONian technologies, control is ensured without recourse to patenting. In electronics and telecommunications resistance to NFI is high because of the abstract and scientific character of the technology. But local production is bound to increase vis-à-vis world trade in markets where suppliers are abundant or too abundant and where technology has passed its innovate stage and is dispersing rapidly. Where high-tech is involved, countries go out of their way to acquire and master know-how. All these factors contribute to a high level of NFII in the entire machinery industry.

At this point we must note one important limitation of our primary data base. Each type of foreign engagement per firm per region could only be counted once. That is if one Form of International Investment was employed 10 times by the same firm in the same region, it was only counted once. Thus our data must be interpreted as "trends", not as actual frequencies. Our case studies revealed that the actual frequencies per firm per region are often greater than one, so that our figures are underestimates rather than overestimates.

13.2.5 *New Forms of International Investment and Host Countries*

If we examine the geographical distribution of foreign engagement more carefully, we see clearly that the industrialized or OECD countries are the primary host countries for New Forms of International Investment carried out by Swiss firms. This is hardly surprising. If the great majority of our exports go to European countries (cf. HÄMISEGGER 1985) and if that is where by far the most FDI-workplaces are situated (cf. BORNER/WEHRLE 1984a), one has to expect a large percentage of NFII to be hosted in Western Europe.

More interesting, however, are the deviations. While in most categories 90% or more of the firms have NFII in industrial countries, this is not true for the small enterprises and the textile firms. The larger the firm, the more evenly distributed are its NFII in the world's regions. This is an obvious result of the financial and managerial limitations of smaller companies. They have to select carefully where they commit their resources, while large enterprises can afford to be represented in more regions. Owing to the higher transaction costs, small firms are less inclined to get involved in culturally distant countries (cf. CARLSON 1975 and ROBINSON 1981). Where the textile industry is concerned, only a few (!) apparel and shoe manufacturers have production sites in developing countries. COMECON-countries are of little importance for this branch.

For the chemical branch the Eastern bloc plays a much greater role as a host region than the developing countries. We assume this is due to the technical competence of some of these countries as well as to the existence of the necessary infrastructure, particularly in heavier chemicals. Additionally, demand in these countries is similar to that in the West.

Other data computed from our questionnaire (which, however, do not lend themselves to tabulation - occurrences per positive interview), imply that it is the more experienced internationalists who dare to undertake NFII in developing countries. On the other hand, single occurrences predominate in Eastern countries (cf. also Table 13-11).

Table 13-10. Geographical Distribution of New Forms of International Investment According to Industrial Branch and Size of Firm (in Percent; Base = Firms Currently Engaged in NFII)

	Current Engagements (in %)						
	TEX (100%)	CHE (100%)	MACH (100%)	10–40 (100%)	50–499 (100%)	500–999 (100%)	1000+ (100%)
• Industrial countries	75	95	90	83	89	92	89
• NICs + Japan	50	47	48	39	39	54	72
• Developing countries	38	21	29	13	27	38	50
• Eastern European countries	25	42	26	22	36	8	39

Note: Multiple entries possible: figures do not add up to 100%.

Table 13-11. Geographical Distribution of New Forms of International Investment According to Branch and Size of Firm

	Average			Textiles			Chemicals			Machinery			Small Firms			Middle-Sized Firms			Large Middle-Sized Firms			Large Firms		
	1	2	3	1	2	3	1	2	3	1	2	3	1	2	3	1	2	3	1	2	3	1	2	3
IC	35	60	65	67	67	33	17	67	83	39	60	61	47	79	53	28	59	72	58	67	42	19	38	81
NI	55	72	45	25	25	75	67	67	33	67	88	33	89	100	11	65	82	35	57	86	43	38	54	62
DC	53	70	47	33	33	67	50	75	50	55	70	45	33	33	67	58	83	42	60	80	40	44	56	56
CC	76	86	24	100	-	-	88	100	12	67	78	33	80	80	20	75	88	25	100	-	-	71	86	29

1 = Percentage of firms with one occurrence in a region; *2* = Percentage of firms with one or two occurrences in a region; *3* = Percentage of firms with two or more occurrences in a region.
IC = Industrial Countries; *NI* = Newly Industrializing Countries plus Japan; *DC* = Developing Countries; *CC* = COMECON Countries

Interestingly, the NICs and Japan are important recipients of NFII from Swiss firms. Large firms especially place a heavy emphasis on this region. Table 13-11 presents the percentage of occurrences of NFII per world region. This table hints at the rather intense involvement of a small number of textile companies in the NICs and DCs and the more shallow character of NFII in the COMECON countries. The involvement of the smaller companies in the NICs and Japan is a more superficial involvement, whereas NFII realtions to LDCs are more complex. The large middle-sized firms exhibit a shallow pattern of NFII behavior in all regions. Except in the case of the Eastern European countries, the large enterprises show widespread use of NFII.

13.2.6 New Forms of International Investment and the Level of Technology

In the course of our theoretical discussion we hypothesized that there is a simple and straightforward relationship between NFII and the technological level that would rule out the use of NFII in the case of high-tech. This hypothesis was not tested via our questionnaire, but by our in-depth case-studies, of which we could carry out only a few. More research is certainly necessary (see Chapter 12). Nonetheless, we did try to assess the technological level of the responding firms. The statistical evaluation was, however, inconclusive. A further question was an attempt to estimate the firms' perception of technological change. Despite the limited reliability of these results, the statistical evaluation turns out to be quite useful. Table 13-12 gives information about the relationship between the speed of technological devel-

Table 13-12. Firms' Perception of Their Technological Environment*

	Average	Median
Textiles	53	58
Chemicals	63	66
Machinery	63	66
20- 49 employees	59	63
50-499 employees	60	57
500-999 employees	64	65
1000+ employees	75	79
Technically		
- passive	48	50
- progressive	65	72
Without direct investment	59	58
With direct investment	65	69
Without inward forms	59	63
With inward forms	65	65
Without outward forms	57	57
With outward forms	66	72

* Firms were asked to situate their judgement of the situation on a scale 0-100, with 0 indicating "no progress at all" and 100 indicating "very rapid and dynamic change".

opment and the employment of New Forms of International Investment as judged by the firms themselves. The textile industry is perceived by its member firms to be faced with an average rate of technological change, while the chemical and machinery industries are confronted by a more rapid pace of technological change. Firms with fewer than 1000 employees perceive themselves to be faced with a slower pace of change than the large firms.

Comparing the entrepreneurial perception of technological change with a firm's tendency toward outward or inward forms of foreign engagement, one discovers some interesting results. The firms with direct investments, NFII, and inward forms of engagement have a different perception of technological change than the rest of the firms in the sample: They observe a faster pace of technological change. Our explanation for this situation is the following:

- Firms employing NFII are more market-oriented.
- Proximity to the market - in the sense of supply and demand - enables firms to make a more realistic estimate of exogenous factors.
- In order to keep up with the pace of know-how development without sacrificing market proximity, firms are forced to cooperate internationally and to participate more intensively in foreign markets.

In other words, the closer the alliance achieved through NFII between Swiss industrial firms and foreign countries, the smaller the danger of operating with technological blinders seems to be.

13.3 The Various New Forms of International Investment in our Sample

Clearly, the most common NFII is licensing. Of all firms with experience in NFII, 57% - or 21% of all respondents - had experience in licensing-out. 47% (17% of responding firms) had contractual arrangements with foreign firms, 35% (13% of the respondents) had technical consulting services abroad, 31% (12% of respondents) sub-contracting. 24% have turnkey operations, 17% business consulting, and 9% joint ventures. All in all the "looser forms" of cooperation are used more frequently (cf. BERGER/UHLMANN, 1983). If we compare the significance of all NFII - eliminating exports - then direct investment with 100% ownership was the most common form (74 firms). 58 firms licensed out; 47 firms used contractual cooperation. Technical consulting with 42 firms and minority ownership with 41 firms were simularly popular. Sub-contracting was used by 38 firms, majority ownership by 28 firms, and turnkey by only 24.

"The basic statement about size-specific differences in respect to foreign engagement is that firms with 10 to 499 employees are less active than companies with 500 or more employees." (BERGER/UHLMANN 1983:52; authors' translation). We want to test to what extent the various forms follow this pattern. Using an indicator developed by BERGER/UHLMANN (1983:54), we compared the number of occurrences of one form (of the NFII) in two size-categories: "more than 500 employees" and "less than 500 employees".

This figure was then corrected by the cell count in each size-category:

$$\frac{A_l/k}{A_s/i}$$

"A_l" is the frequency of a particular NFII among large firms, "A_s" the same for small firms. "k" is the number of large firms in the sample, "i" the number of small firms. In our study "i" equals 67 (in the case of FDI: 70) and "k" equals 31 (in the case of FDI: 37). Thus, the higher the indicator, the more active the larger firms are. If the indicator has a value of less than one, this means that small firms are more active than large firms cf. (Table 13/13).

As expected, the majority of squares in the matrix is dominated by larger firms. This is particularly true for licensing and management consulting and, in terms of regions, the NICs and the developing countries. All forms of direct investment are a domain of the larger units. These findings of course are not surprising. The control and policing mechanisms in licensing-operations are resource-intensive. In the case of management consulting, management capacity is the crucial limitation of the smaller firm. This explains why technical consulting is also dominated by the larger companies. The know-how of smaller enterprises often rests in one or a few persons. As such, it cannot be codified and hence is not transmittable.

More surprising and interesting, however, is the relative lead of the smaller firms in sub-contracting and contractual cooperation and in activities in the Eastern block countries. It is typically the "looser", more informal NFII through which these firms - via personal contacts - establish an advantage. Although joint ventures are well suited to this size category, this form is met with suspicion, even when such an operation is successful. Since dealing with culturally more distant regions causes higher transaction costs, larger firms will be more numerous. In this respect

Table 13-13. Indicator of the Relationship between Size of Firm and New Forms of International Investment

	Industrial Countries	NICs + Japan	Developing Countries	Eastern European Countries	Future Plans
• Licensing	1.6	3.2	3.8	2.6	1.1
• Sub-Contracting	0.9	1.3	(0.7)	(0.4)	0.9
• Management Consulting	2.4	-	-	-	(0.4)
• Technical Consulting	1.1	1.9	2.16	(0.03)	0.7
• Joint Ventures	1.7	-	-	-	1.2
• Contractual Cooperation	0.9	3.6	1.8	(0.9)	1.6

Direct investment:
- Minority Ownership: 1.5
- Majority Ownership: 1.3
- 100% Ownership 1.4

Legend: ( ) = small cell count; - = cell count equals zero
Note: The indicator was computed from the number of occurrences of a certain NFII employed by larger firms divided by the number of occurences of the same NFII employed by smaller firms: the higher the value above unity, the greater the lag of small firms.
Source: Framework taken from BERGER/UHLMANN 1983:55

Table 13-14. New Forms of International Investment: Number of Occurrences of All Forms in Industrial Countries

	Total	1	2 or More
• All Firms	88		
• Licensing	49		
	100	22%	78%
• Sub-Contracting	32		
	100	16%	84%
• Management	16		
Consulting	100	(6)%	94%
• Technical	35		
Consulting	100	8%	92%
• Joint Ventures	9		
	100	0%	100%
• Contractual	43		
Cooperation	100	23%	77%

the Eastern bloc countries are culturally less distant and offer more opportunities for highly flexible small firms.

The response to our question about future plans suggests increasing activities of SMEs in NFII.

Tables 13-14 through 13-16 show the intensity of NF-interaction per region on the one hand and the function of the single forms in internationalization strategies

Table 13-15. New Forms of International Investment: Number of Occurrences of All Forms in the NICs and Japan

	Total	1	2 or More
• All Firms	46		
• Licensing	26		
	100	54%	46%
• Sub-Contracting	8		
	100	38%	62%
• Management	6		
Consulting	100	0%	100%
• Technical	15		
Consulting	100	20%	80%
• Joint Ventures	13		
	100	0%	100%
• Contractual	13		
Cooperation	100	46%	54%

Table 13-16. New Forms of International Investment: Number of Occurrences of All Forms in Developing Countries and in Eastern Bloc Countries

	Total	1	2 or More
• Developing Countries:			
• All Firms	30		
• Licensing	13		
	100	38%	62%
• Sub-Contracting	4	1	
	100	25%	75%
• Management	6		
Consulting	100	0%	100%
• Technical	12		
Consulting	100	25%	75%
• Joint Ventures	4		
	100	0%	100%
• Contractual	11		
Cooperation	100	36%	64%
• Eastern Bloc			
Countries:	29		
• All Firms			
• Licensing	11		
	100	64%	36%
• Sub-Contracting	7		
	100	57%	43%
• Management	1		
Consulting	100	0%	100%
• Technical	9		
Consulting	100	33%	67%
• Joint Ventures	2		
	100	50%	50%
• Contractual	7		
Cooperation	100	71%	29%

on the other. The tables condense the number of occurrences per region and form into "one occurrence" and "two or more occurrences". If one occurrence is indicated, then this form only is applied in the respective region.

Licensing and contractual cooperation tend to be the first NFII chosen by firms, especially for geographically distant operations. For all regions and for all types of firms these two forms are the most frequent. Where higher frequencies occur, technical consulting is significant. Sub-contracting shows a middle frequency, whereas management-consulting and joint ventures are reserved for the well-versed internationalists, though they generally hold a marginal position.

13.4 The Role of New Forms of International Investment in the Future

In the final section we requested firms to estimate the significance of New Forms of International Investment in the future. The results are presented in Table 13-17. The figures reveal that firms with experience in NFII forsee a greater role for NFII than firms with no experience. The exception is large firms. Large firms - with or without experience - anticipate an increasing role for NFII. The respondents from the chemical industry perceive a relatively lesser role for NFII than representatives from the textile and the machinery industries.

Table 13-17. Firms' Perception of the Future Role of New Forms of International Investment (in Percent)

Significance of NFII	Total	Textiles	Chemicals	Machinery	A	B	C	D
a) *All Firms*								
Insignificant	8	16	14	4	7	8	22	0
Diminishing	0	0	0	0	0	0	0	0
No change	10	2	25	9	13	9	6	11
Increasing	55	55	41	61	48	58	56	79
Heavily increasing	5	2	9	5	2	8	11	5
No opinion	22	25	11	22	30	18	6	5
b) *Firms with Experience in NFII*								
Insignificant	5	13	11	3	9	5	8	0
Diminishing	0	0	0	0	0	0	0	0
No change	10	0	26	7	4	14	8	11
Increasing	66	88	42	73	61	64	62	78
Heavily increasing	11	0	16	10	4	16	15	6
No opinion	8	0	5	9	22	2	8	6

Legend: A: Firms with 10- 49 employees;
B: Firms with 50-499 employees;
C: Firms with 500-999 employees;
D: Firms with 1000 and more employees

Chapter 14

Results of the Survey on New Forms of Export Financing (NFEF)

In this chapter we present, analoguously to the preceding chapter on NFII, the empirical findings on countertrade as derived from the answers to our written questionnaire. The data is presented in both graphic and tabular form.

14.1 Forms of Countertrade: their Frequency

Table 14-1 shows the frequency with which the 56 Swiss firms engaged in countertrade (i.e. about 25% of the exporting firms in our study) employed the various types of countertrade.

It is evident that pure barter is not a frequently used form of countertrade. Given the high level of risks involved, this result is not suprising (cf. Chapter 6). 26% of the respondents checked compensation. The high level of standardization of contracts which exists today, the collective experience of individual firms in East-West trade, and the opportunities for sharing risks account for the attractiveness of commercial compensation. Counterdelivery - 17% of the responses - has the advantage of including the legal separation of the two halves of the contract, but the disadvantage of a medium-term obligation for fulfilling the terms of the contract. The difficulty of finding markets for goods received, as well as the general reluctance of Swiss firms to carry out an active countertrade strategy, explains the fact that from over 100 respondents junktim was not mentioned even once.

Commercial compensation (i.e. barter, counterdelivery, junktim, multilateral countertrade) was indicated by 63% and industrial compensation by 37% of the respondents. This means that in a little more than one-third of the cases, an exchange

Table 14-1. New Forms of Export Financing: Frequency of Application

Type of Countertrade	Number of Occurrences in Percent (Base 100% = 119 Responses)
Classical Barter	3.4%
Barter with Third Parties/Parallel Barter	26%
Counter-Delivery	16.8%
Junktim	0%
Long-Term Commercial Framework Agreements	5%
Buy-Back	3.4%
Turnkey	28.6%
Multilateral Countertrade	16.8%

of commodities which was tied to know-how transfer (industrial compensation) took place. Firms engaging in industrial compensation saw themselves at a statistically significant rate as technologically more sophisticated than the average sample firm. The desire and the ability for employing organizational and technological innovation in order to maintain international competitiveness are highly correlated.

14.2 Forms of Countertrade: their Geographical Distribution

For Swiss entrepreneurs countertrade has become a global phenomenon. As shown in Table 14-2, about one-half of the respondents did business in the Eastern European countries. The developing countries and the NICs (cf. BLUM 1983), together with Japan, accounted for another third. The OECD countries (North-North countertrade) accounted for only 20% of the responses. Belgium, Denmark, France, Norway, Portugal, Australia, Canada, China, New Zealand, and last but not least the Latin American NICs and Indonesia are central to the growing countertrade activities. In the case of the developing countries,[1] it is above all the nations in the Near-East and the Middle-East (Iran, Irak) and in Africa which have countertrade relations with Swiss industrial enterprises.

Table 14-2. Frequency of New Forms of Countertrade According to Regions of the World

	Number of Occurrences in Percent (Base 100% = 119 Responses)
OECD without Japan	20.2%
NICs including Japan	11%
Developing Countries	20.2%
COMECON	48.6%

Fig. 14-1 shows the geographical distribution of countertrade from the perspective of the branch of industry to which the firms belong. Of the 119 responses, 81% stemmed from the machinery industry, 13% from the chemical industry, and 6% from the textile branch. While the machinery industry is engaged globally, the activities of the chemical industry show a concentration in the developing countries and in Eastern Europe. The textile firms were strongly concentrated in the Third World.

14.3 Regional Distribution of Various Forms of Countertrade

Our theoretical analysis of countertrade (see Chapter 9) implies that the geographical pattern of commercial and industrial compensation is dependent on the economic system on the one hand and on the state of development on the other.

[1] Basic aspects of North-South countertrade are described in SCHWENK 1985, JONES 1984, OUTTERS 1979, BUSINESS INTERNATIONAL 1983. For the East-West countertrade cf. for example, ECONOMIC COMMISSION FOR EUROPE 1979, 1981, 1983 and DIZARD 1983, KAIKATI 1976, 1981, FISCHER/HARTE 1985 discuss countertrade as a global phenomenon.

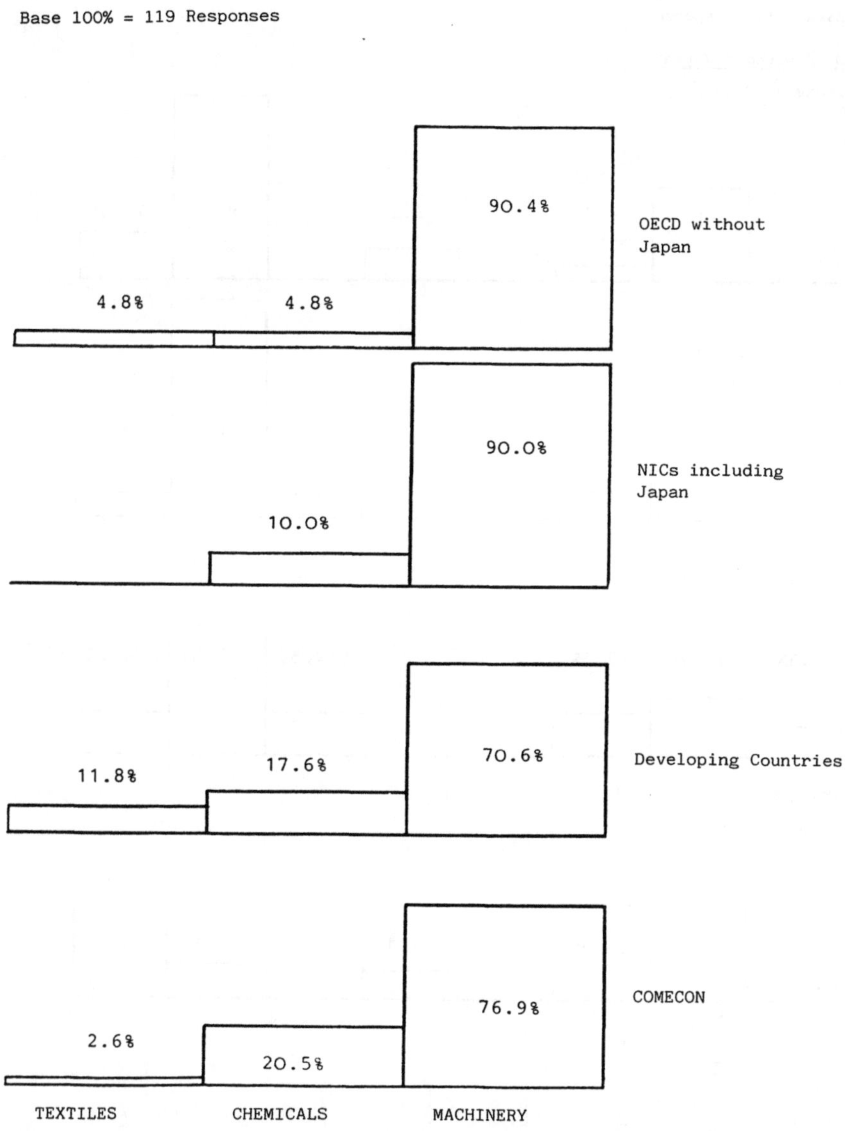

Fig. 14-1. New Forms of Export Financing: Geographical Distribution by Branch

- In the COMECON area, more than 80% of all items concern commercial compensation. This is due to the fact that technology transfer is excluded or minimized for security and/or safety reasons; there are political restrictions on technology transfer (e.g. COCOM). But also from the point of view of Swiss firms, transfer of know-how is not desirable since neither property rights nor contractual guarantees are, as a rule, considered to be sufficient for maintaining protective control.

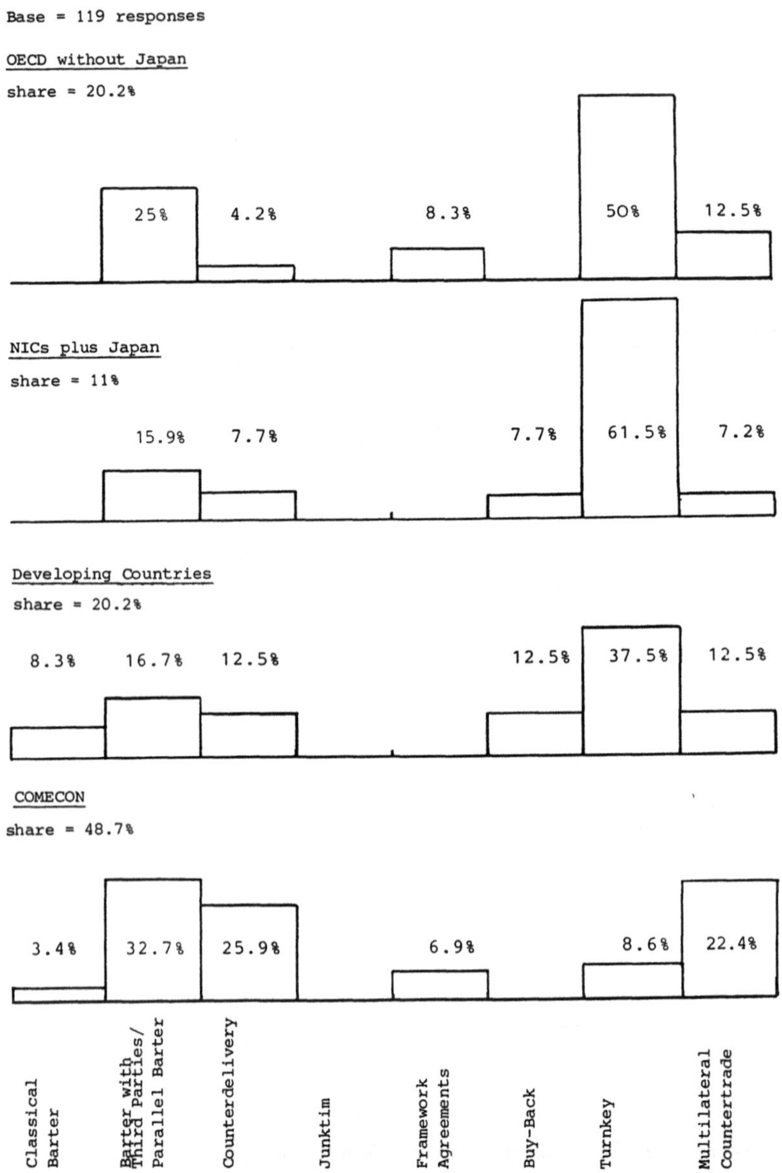

Fig. 14-2. Regional Distribution of Different Forms of Countertrade

- LDCs are involved in both categories, depending on the type of economic system and the country-specific locational advantages. This is illustrated by the role played by buy-back/turnkey agreements with low-cost and/or resource-rich LDCs or NICs.
- With a high share of industrial compensation the OECD countries and the NICs seem to be "partners of a higher order". The technological, socio-economic, and

political conditions in the OECD, Japan, and the NICs allow forms of countertrade which combine financing with technology transfer and thus establish qualitatively different, more permanent ties of cooperation.

14.4 Countertrade According to the Size of the Firm

Table 14-3 gives an overview of the survey responses according to size of firms. 57.5% of the firms employing New Forms of Export Financing were small and medium-sized firms, one third of the firms had more than 1,000 employees. Our evaluation of the survey responses concerning future plans indicates that this situation is most likely to remain stable in the near future. Further, firms with more than 500 employees accounted for 58% of commercial compensation agreements, small and middle-sized firms for only 30.2%. The smaller firms use industrial compensation to take advantage of market niches; they use countertrade framework-agreements, buy-back, and turnkey in about 55% of the cases. In general, these results supported our hypothesis that industrial compensation is primarily an instrument of internationalization employed by small and medium-sized companies in the marketing process in general and in the marketing of their core abilities in particular (cf. SCHLEMPER 1978, 1979).

Table 14-3. Frequency of New Forms of Export Financing According to Size of Firm

Number of Employees	Number of Occurrences (Base 100% = 119 Responses)
5- 50	11.5%
51- 500	46%
501-1000	12.6%
1000 and more	29.9%

14.5 Classical Exports Versus New Forms of Export Financing

One of our working hypotheses was that the defense and expansion of existing export markets or the opening up of new markets would be more successful among firms employing New Forms of Export Financing. To test this hypothesis we examined the yearly export quota for firms which had - or had not - employed innovative forms of countertrade. Figure 14-3 presents the results of this comparison. Indeed, the firms using countertrade showed a considerably (statistically significant) higher export quota. Our research indicates that a minimum of one-third of this difference can be considered to stem directly from the use of NFEF. Our data base did not permit us to estimate the quantity of exports indirectly induced by the employment of New Forms of Export Financing. Nonetheless, there are indications that the amount of exports indirectly induced is significant (cf. OKUN's contract-theory approach presented in Chapter 9).

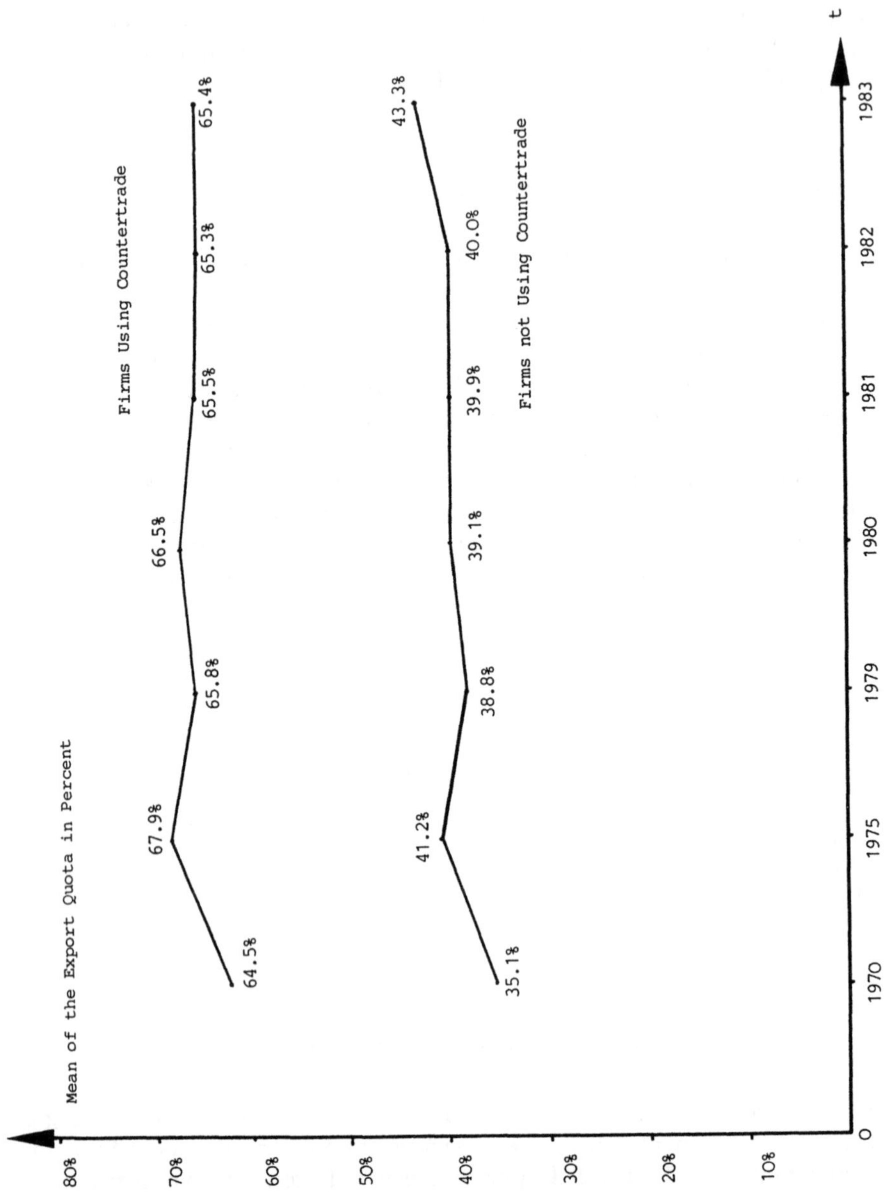

Fig. 14-3. Classical Exports vs. New Forms of Export Financing

Table 14-4 tabulates the relationship between the export quota of firms using various combinations of classical exports and New Forms of Internationalization, i.e., New Forms of International Investment and/or New Forms of Export Financing.

Table 14-4. Export Quotas as a Function of New Forms of Internationalization

Year	Export Quota: The Yearly Mean in Percent			
	Firms with NFEF and Classical Exports	Firms with NFEF and NFII and Classical Exports	Firms with NFII and Classical Exports	Firms with only Classical Exports
1970	64.5	56.7	49.5	45.3
1975	67.9	66.5	57.8	46.8
1979	65.8	59.9	52.7	46.2
1980	66.5	67.0	57.9	46.6
1981	65.5	60.0	52.6	46.8
1983	66.4	64.3	57.0	46.5

14.6 The Relative Importance of Countertrade in Export Activity

In our postal survey we asked firms to give the percentage of exports which were financed through any of the several forms of countertrade - as opposed to simple sale on the market. Twenty-nine firms responded to the this question - 21 small and mediumsized firms and 8 larger firms. 82% of the 29 firms were from the machinery branch, 13 from the chemical branch, and 5% from the textile branch. The results are presented in Table 14-5, whereby the percentages are based on an arithmetic average.

If we compare the results of Table 14-5 and the results presented in Figure 14-3 we note the following: From 1980 to 1983, the mean value of the export quota of firms employing countertrade was 28.75% higher than the figure for the remaining firms. At the same time Table 14-5 shows countertrade accounting for 9.74%. This means that a monocausal explanation accounts for at least 35% of the higher export volume. If one also takes indirectly induced exports into consideration, then we can accept our working hypothesis that New Forms of Export Financing do induce higher levels of exports within individual firms.

Table 14-5. The Relative Importance of Countertrade as a Percent of Export Volume

	1970	1975	1979	1980	1981	1982	1983
Number of Responses	10	18	20	20	21	20	23
Yearly Mean of Countertrade Activities as a % of Exports	6.45	6.41	6.45	7.31	9.32	9.84	10.07
Standard Deviation	8.99	8.86	10.73	15.24	14.3	16.11	15.73

14.7 Entrepreneurial Motivation for Export Activity

A question in the survey permitted the respondents to give a subjective weighting of concrete motives for changes in the firm's internationally oriented behaviour. The lack of responses written in the rubric 'other reasons' showed that our hypothesized reasons were the relevant ones.

14.7.1 The Motives Behind Export Expansion

195 or 84.8% of the 230 exporting firms plan to increase their export activities - either to increase or consolidate their sales. This includes 97.2% of the textile firms, 83.8% of the machinery firms, and 82.1% of the chemical companies. Above all, the firms see the OECD countries as important markets for future expansion: FRG (90 responses), USA (81), France (45), UK (33), Austria (30), Scandinavia (27), and the Benelux (12) were the most frequently mentioned. China (mentioned 15 times) and South Korea (7) are the only markets outside the OECD that seem to play a role in expansion strategies. The motives behind planned attempts to expand exports are

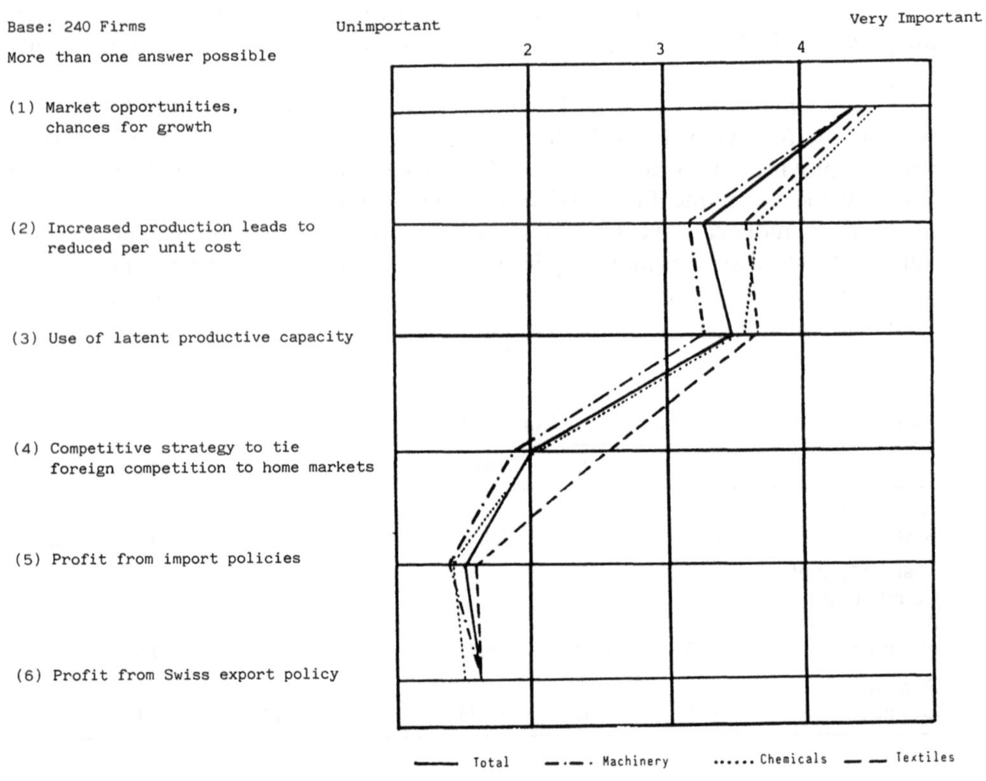

Fig. 14-4. Motives Behind Export Expansion

reported in Figure 14-4. Careful study of these results indicates that motives for expansion are based primarily on the perception of company-specific competitive advantages, rather than on general political or economic incentives. This implies that Swiss trade policy relies primarily on market forces. At the same time Swiss policy is unable to influence countervailing tendencies in the framework of the global economy. This is typical for a small open economy, like that of Switzerland.

14.7.2 The Motives Behind Export Contraction

The responses indicated that 13.5% of the 230 exporting firms participating in the survey are planning to reduce their export activities in some of their existing markets.[2] Countries in which firms plan a reduction of export activity include Argentina, Brazil, France, India, Irak, Iran, Italy, Yugoslavia, Libanon, Mexico, Nigeria, Poland, Turkey, Uruguay, and Venezuela. The motives for these planned reductions

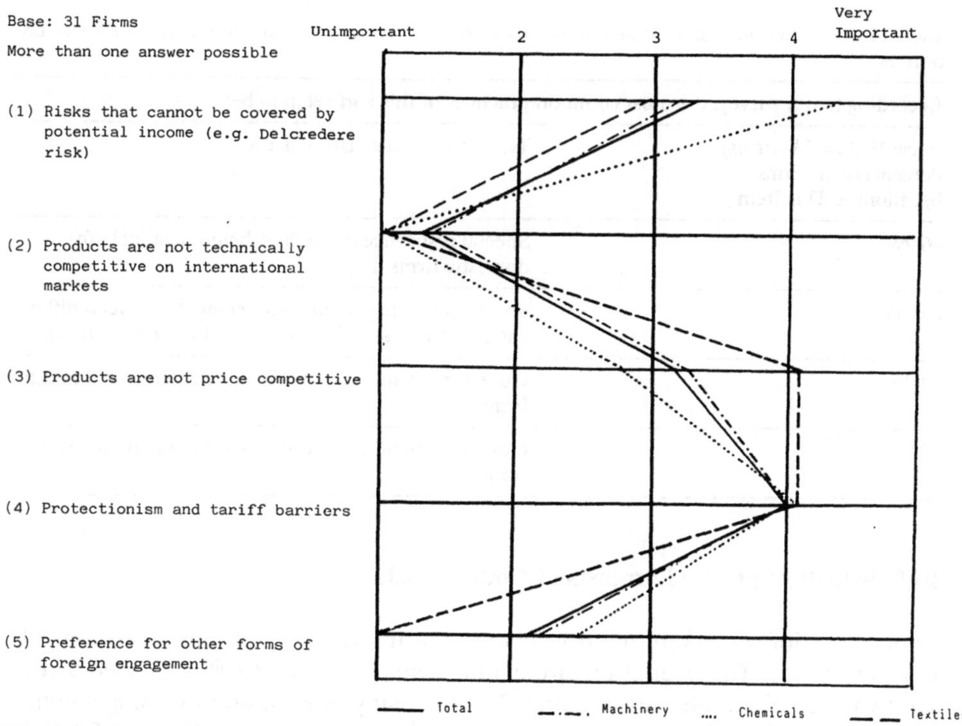

Fig. 14-5. Motives Behind Export Contraction

[2] Given that nearly 85% of the firms spoke of expansion, it seems inappropriate to speak of a significant threat to the Swiss export industry. Usually, questions on "main difficulties" in export markets produce more response, but no conclusions concerning real contractive forces can be drawn.

are given in Figure 14-5. The primary reasons have to do with conditions within the world market economy, that is, conditions exogenous to the individual firm. These conditions are only secondarily branch- or firm-specific.

14.8 Protectionist Distortions in Foreign Markets Due to Government Assistance of Foreign Competitors

In another question, we tried to gather some informations on those subtle and ingeniously hidden forms of government assistance practiced by many countries whose firms compete with Swiss suppliers on export markets. Are Swiss firms affected by this? If so, how much and in what ways? More than 50% of all exporters listed a grand total of 133 specific examples of such "new protectionism". The results in Table 14-6 show that all industries are more or less equally affected. Significant is the different impact on large and small firms. Since large firms are proportionately larger exporters, they are much more victimized by protectionist measures (68.1% of the large firms compared to 23.5% of the smaller firms).

Table 14-6. Protectionist Export Assistance by Foreign Governments to Competitors of Swiss Exporters

According to our survey, the most common practices of this sort seem to be:

(Base 100% = 133 firms) Percentage of Firms Mentioning This Item	Type of Protectionist Measure
66.9%	Special insurance or credit schemes available for domestic firms only
26.4%	Special advantages due to agreements between different countries assigning privileges to domestic firms
14.7%	Government-subsidized investment credits to domestic firms
12%	Government-subsidized R&D available to domestic firms

14.9 Industry-Specific Forecasts of Countertrade

In one question we asked the firms about their impression of future developments in countertrade. The overall picture is rather inconclusive: 30.9% expected a constant volume of countertrade, another 30.1% a rising or even rapidly rising volume. If we only consider those firms already engaged in countertrade activities, 55.4% are expecting higher turnovers in countertrade – and only 37% are anticipating stagnation. Most impressive is the sharp division along industry lines. The machinery and chemical industries mark the opposite extremes: 60% of the machinery producing firms expect countertrade to rise, whereas 63.6% of the chemical firms expect it to remain stagnant (cf. Figures 14-6 and 14-7 and Table 14-7).

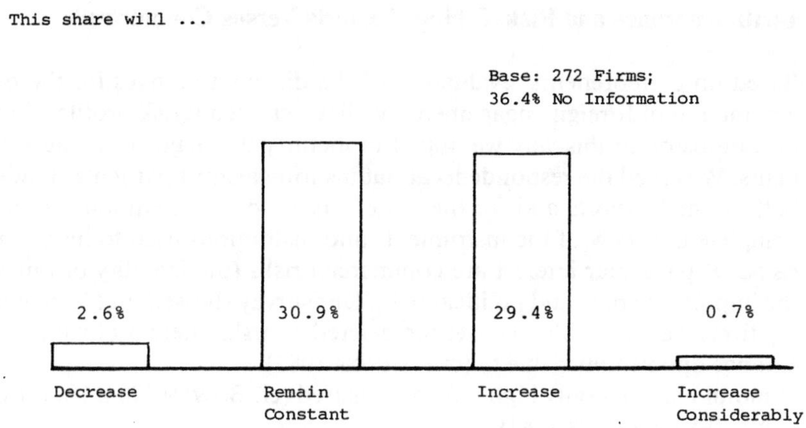

Fig. 14-6. Overall Forecast of Countertrade as a Share of Exports

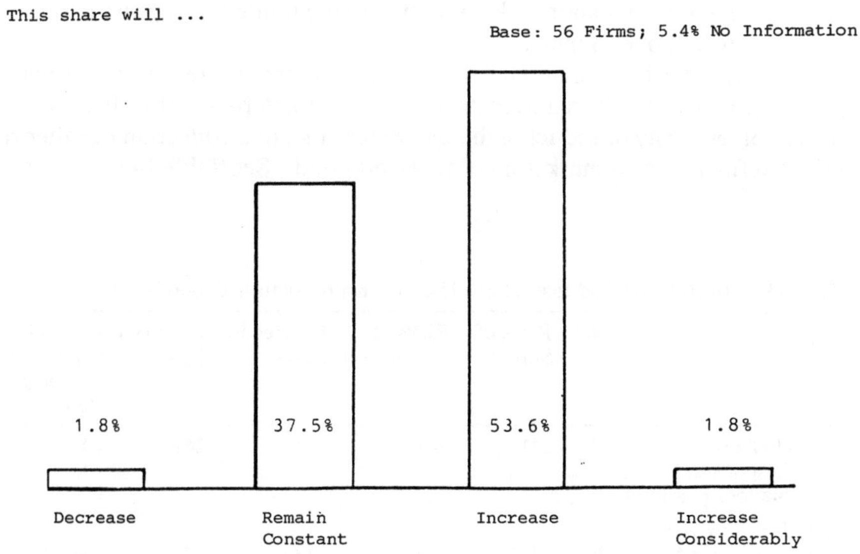

Fig. 14-7. Forecasts of Those Firms with Countertrade Experience Only

Table 14-7. Forecasts of Countertrade by Industry (Base 100% = 56 Countertraders)

	Total	Branches		
		Textiles	Chemicals	Machinery
Base 100%	56	4	11	40
The present share will				
- decrease	1.8%	0.0%	0.1%	0.0%
- remain constant	37.5%	25.0%	63.6%	32.5%
- increase	53.6%	50.0%	27.3%	60.0%
- increase considerably	1.8%	0.0%	0.0%	2.5%
- no information	5.4%	25.0%	0.0%	5.0%

14.10 Insurance and Risk-Taking: Exports Versus Countertrade

Based on entrepreneurs' evaluation of the different motives for the expansion or contraction of foreign engagement, we have created a risk profile of the Swiss export industry. In this way we hoped to identify the major risks faced by entrepreneurs. We asked the respondents about insuring against particular kinds of risks for both normal exports and for the various types of countertrade. Table 14-8 gives a complete overview of the instruments and institutions used to insure firms against risks. Of particular interest are commercial risks (the inability or unwillingness of the importer to pay) and political risks. Our survey showed that 12% of the responding firms were not able to cover the delcredere risk. There is obviously a lack of insurance opportunities due to (cf. VERNON 1983):

- moral hazard - only high risks are insured (cf. BOWEN 1984, HARVEY 1981, HERRIG 1983, HUGHES 1983)
- the coincidence of the evaluation of country risks by banks and private insurance companies (COLLINS 1981, CHEATLE 1983)
- the federal law on export risk guarantee being limited to supplying public bodies - eg. foreign governments.

In other words, commercial risks cannot be transferred onto the partner, nor, given the lack of markets and instruments, to a third party. Thus firms turn to compensation as a way of reducing the delcredere risk to a collection of other risks: political, refinance, and marketing of received goods. See Table 14-9:

Table 14-8. Instruments and Institutions Used to Insure Against Export Risks

		Total	Risks of Supply	Risks of Production	Delcredere Risks	Financial Risks	Risks of Changing Exchange Rates	Political Risks
Base (100% = 1427 Responses, combinations possible)		241	241	241	241	241	241	241
1. *Risk not Insured*								
risk unknown	ABS	104	41	47	13	50	31	23
	V-%	44.0	17.0	19.3	5.4	20.7	12.9	9.5
	H-%	100.0	38.7	44.3	12.3	47.2	29.2	21.7
we do not want to insure this risk	ABS	99	36	26	45	15	43	32
	V-%	41.1	14.9	10.8	18.7	4.2	17.8	13.3
	H-%	100.0	36.4	26.3	45.5	15.2	43.4	32.3
risk can not be insured	ABS	90	45	18	21	6	20	30
	V-%	37.3	18.7	7.5	8.7	2.5	8.3	12.4
	H-%	100.0	50.0	20.0	23.3	4.7	22.2	33.3
2. *Risk Insurance by Contract*								
risk contractually redeployed	ABS	61	26	8	5	0	40	2
	V-%	25.3	10.8	3.3	2.1	0.0	16.6	0.8
	H-%	100.0	42.6	13.1	8.2	0.0	65.6	3.3
advance payment	ABS	85	20	34	52	3	16	15
	V-%	35.3	8.3	14.1	21.4	1.2	6.6	4.2
	H-%	100.0	23.5	40.0	61.2	3.5	18.8	17.6

Table 14-8.

		Total	Risks of Supply	Risks of Production	Delcredere Risks	Financial Risks	Risks of Changing Exchange Rates	Political Risks
3. *Confirmed irrevocable credit*	ABS	122	29	29	101	3	10	27
	V-%	50.6	12.0	12.0	41.9	1.2	4.1	11.2
	H-%	100.0	23.8	23.8	82.8	2.5	8.2	22.1
forfeiting	ABS	14	1	3	7	3	4	4
	V-%	5.8	0.4	1.2	2.9	1.2	1.7	1.7
	H-%	100.0	7.1	21.4	50.0	21.4	28.6	28.6
factoring	ABS	4	2	1	0	2	1	0
	V-%	1.7	0.8	0.4	0.0	0.8	0.4	0.0
	H-%	100.0	50.0	25.0	0.0	50.0	25.0	0.0
4. *Insurance institutions*								
federal export risk guarantee	ABS	79	16	30	42	5	34	65
	V-%	32.8	6.6	12.4	17.4	2.1	14.9	26.6
	H-%	100.0	20.3	38.0	53.2	4.3	45.6	81.0
insurance by private insurance company	ABS	22	2	2	15	1	2	0
	V-%	9.1	0.8	0.8	6.2	0.4	0.8	0.0
	H-%	100.0	9.1	9.1	68.2	4.5	9.1	0.0
5. *Risk is taken over by a trading house*	ABS	16	4	4	8	2	2	1
	V-%	6.6	1.7	1.7	3.3	0.8	0.8	0.4
	H-%	100.0	25.0	25.0	50.0	12.5	12.5	6.3
6. *Other*	ABS	38	4	0	4	1	27	1
	V-%	15.8	1.7	0.0	1.7	0.4	11.2	0.4
	H-%	100.0	10.5	0.0	10.5	2.4	71.1	2.4
7. *No information*			103	111	86	165	98	103
	V-%		42.0	46.1	35.7	68.5	40.7	43.2

Legend: ABS: Absolute number of occurrences; V-%: Relative significance of the risk strategy to the respondents; H-%: Relative significance of an instrument in the risk strategy

Table 14-9. Distribution of Delcredere Risks (Base: 100% = 313 responses from 155 firms)

Banking instruments[a]	34.3%
Risk not insured	25.2%
Risk contractually redeployed	18.1%
Export risk guarantee	13.4%
Private insurance	4.7%
Miscellaneous	3.9%

[a] Confirmed irrevocable credit alone: 32.3% of the responses

The means by which firms insured themselves against political risk is summarized in Table 14-10:

Table 14-10. Insurance Against Political Risks (Base 100% = 199 responses from 137 firms)

Risk not insured	42.7%
Export risk guarantee	32.2%
Banking instruments	15.6%
Risk transferred to contractual partners	8.5%
Private insurance	1%

There are three major risks faced by firms engaged in the various forms of countertrade:
- the risk that the quality of the goods received in exchange is lower than contractually agreed upon
- risks against delays in delivery time (political risks)
- marketing risks for the goods received in exchange.

Depending on the form of countertrade employed, these risks can either occur individually or in addition to the various risks already faced by firms engaged in traditional export activity. The possibilities of covering these risks are listed in Table 14-11. Over three-fourths of the responses indicate that a risk did not exist, was passed on, or was consciously not insured against. Through the choice of countertrade forms, the selection of products received in exchange, the efficient use of banking instruments, the use of services from trading houses, etc., most countertraders seem to effectively redeploy their risks elsewhere. Only a fourth of the respondents checked the response "the risk cannot be insured against." (cf. MOUNTAIN 1984).

Table 14-11. Insurance for Types of Countertrade Risks

	Poor Quality of Goods Received	Time Delays	Marketing Risks
Base (100%) = 56 firms with 98 responses			
Risk does not exist	51%	56.3%	60.6%
Shifting of risk to contractual partner	9%	9.4%	3%
Risk not insured although possible	15%	12.5%	12%
Risk cannot be insured	24.2%	21.9%	24.2%

Chapter 15

Results of Surveys of Swiss Multinationals

15.1 Foreign Employment, FDI, and International Production by Swiss Multinationals

Switzerland is not only a country with an extremely high export share of 40% but also a very important home country of multinational corporations with very high levels of FDI. In blatant contrast to the extensive export activities carried out by all sizes and types of Swiss firms, Swiss Foreign Direct Investment consists almost entirely of the foreign operations of only about 50 multinational corporations whose headquarters are located inside Switzerland. With our first survey (1980) of the 15 largest Swiss industrial corporations - all with total sales in the billions of Swiss francs - at least 80% of Swiss industry's foreign personnel and production was accounted for.[1]

The results concerning employment of the 1980 survey are presented in Table 15-1. What strikes one immediatly is the extremely high level of employment outside Switzerland. Nine of the 15 multis employ more than two-thirds of their personnel outside Switzerland. Only Sulzer, ASUAG[2] and Von Roll have more employees in Switzerland than abroad. For the 15 companies taken as a whole, 75% of their total personnel worked abroad and a good fifth of these in developing countries. Thus the foreign employment of the 'top 15' - 483,000 - was equivalent to 70% of the total number of industrial jobs inside Switzerland.

Of the 100,000 employees in the Third World, almost 50,000 are to be found in the seven NICs: Brazil, Mexico, Argentina, Hong Kong, Taiwan, South Korea, and Singapore. The concentration on the three Latin American NICs, with their large attractive domestic markets, and on the dynamic Asian NICs is especially characteristic of the Third World activities of the 'smaller' machinery producers. Nestlé and the large chemical companies are represented in almost all developing countries.

It is interesting to note that the declining watch industry has hardly any employees abroad and none in the Third World - not even in Hong Kong. The design-oriented textile and garment industries in Switzerland are characterized by small companies producing inside Switzerland.

Table 15-2 shows changes in the level of personnel within the 15 largest Swiss MNEs for the period 1970-80. The table summarizes employment levels both for different size companies and for different groups of countries.

Inside Switzerland, the employment level of the 15 companies surveyed rose by

[1] For the complete reference see BORNER et al. (1985) BORNER/WEHRLE (1984 a), WEHRLE (1984).

[2] Today SMH (Schweizerische Gesellschaft für Mikroelektronik und Uhrenindustrie AG).

Table 15-1. The Geographical Distribution of Employment in the 15 Largest Swiss Industrial Multis (1980)

	Switzerland	Industrialized Countries	Developing Countries	Of which NICs	Total Abroad	Total Employment
Nestlé	7,400	99,600	46,000	20,100	145,000	153,000
Ciba-Geigy	22,900	45,770	12,520	6,830	58,290	81,190
BBC	21,760	74,640	8,900	5,500*	83,540	105,300
Alusuisse	8,650	32,720	3,710	2,000*	36,430	45,080
Roche	9,610	25,220	8,820	3,150	34,040	43,650
Sandoz	9,830	19,240	6,390	2,290	25,630	35,460
Largest 6	80,150	297,190	86,340	39,870	383,530	463,680
Oerlikon-Bührle	15,300	19,080	2,830	2,770	21,910	37,210
Sulzer	20,180	11,930	2.820	1,730	14,750	34,930
Holderbank	2,060	11,850	4,820	2,770	16,670	18,730
Georg Fischer	8,030	9,250	-	-	9,250	17,280
Schindler	6,010	12,660	2,990	2,310	15,650	21,660
Asuag**	12,830	2,740	-	-	2,740	15,570
Landis&Gyr	6,480	9,740	-	-	9,740	16,220
Von Roll	5,760	490	-	-	490	6,250
Hesta	3,840	8,040	570	570	8,610	12,450
Largest 15	160,640	382,970	100,370	50,020*	483,340	643,980

* Estimates. *Source:* Calculations by the authors.
** Today: SMH (Schweizerische Gesellschaft für Mikroelektronik und Uhrenindustrie AG)

Table 15-2. Change in the Level of Employment Abroad: Switzerland's 15 Largest Industrial Multis (1970-1980)

	The largest 6 firms		The 7th-15th largest firms		The largest 15 firms	
	Employment	%	Employment	%	Employment	%
In Switzerland	7,270	10.0	-4,200	-5.0	3,070	1.9
In Industrialized Countries	74,420	33.4	23,790	38.4	98,210	34.5
In Developing Countries	33,600	63.7	6,610	89.1	40,210	66.8
Total Abroad	108,020	39.2	30,400	43.8	138,420	40.1
Total Employment	115,290	33.1	26,200	17.0	141,490	28.2

Source: Calculations by the authors.

about 2% between 1970 and 1980. Taking account of mergers, one can speak of a stagnation of domestic employment. This domestic stagnation within the MNEs must be contrasted with the general reduction of Swiss industrial employment by nearly 240,000. The slump of the 1970s obviously affected the domestic employment of non-multinational industrial firms to a greater extent than that of the multinationals.

In other industrial countries the personnel of the 15 largest Swiss multis grew by more than 35% - almost 100,000 new jobs within ten years. In North America, acquisitions led above all to an increase of 55,000 employees - more than a doubling of employment within a decade. In Europe, where most Swiss multis have carried on production for many years, 44,000 jobs were added to the total - either through acquisition or through expansion. During the same time period, approximately 18,000 jobs were eliminated by five Swiss multis; activities were either reduced or sold to other firms. Thus, the net gain of employment for the Swiss multis was 26,000.

Levels of investment and investment growth for the 1970s are presented for the 15 largest Swiss multis in Table 15-3. With the necessary caution, a number of qualitative conclusions can be drawn. First and foremost, we note that domestic investment still accounts for about 33% of total investment, while domestic employment is only 25% of total employment. Yet investment in other industrialized countries was twice as high as in Switzerland during the 1970s. Only one-tenth of total investment went to the developing countries. Total European investment of the 15 largest Swiss multis reached (in 1980) the same volume as total investment in Switzerland. According to the data of individual firms, direct investments in the Federal Republic of Germany totalled 6.5 billion, in France 3.6 billion, and in North America 10.4 billion Swiss francs. Three billion of the five billion francs that went to the developing countries were invested in the seven NICs mentioned above.

Table 15-3. The Geographical Distribution of Investment of the 15 Largest Swiss Industrial Multis (1970*-1980)

	Switzerland		Industrialized Countries		Developing Countries		Total Abroad		Total Investment	
	Mio. Fr.	%	Mio. Fr.	%	Mio. Fr.	%	Mio. Fr.	%	Mio. Fr.	%
1970*	10,900	34.3	18,300	57.5	2,600	8.2	20,900	65.7	31,800	100.0
1980	17,800	32,4	32,200	58.5	5,000	9.1	37,200	67.6	55,000	100.0
1970-1980	+6,900	+63.6	+13,900	+76.0	+2,400	+92.3	+16,300	+78.0	+23,200	+73.0

* For 3 MNEs the data do not refer to 1970.

The concentration of investment among the six largest multis is even greater than the concentration of personnel: 81% of total investment - or 44 billion francs - is accounted for by the six largest companies. Investment estimates for 1985 are similar to those for employment. The most important exception is the development of domestic investment among the 15 largest multis. In contrast to a slight drop in domestic employment, investment has almost universally risen. Growth of investment abroad is expected to be concentrated, as is employment, in North America, the NICs, and, among the largest firms, in Japan. The level of investment in the developing countries is lagging behind the growth of employment in these countries. This reflects the fact that R&D and capital intensive activities lag behind in the Third World. In short, it seems that after a dynamic phase of foreign expansion in the 1970s, a more consolidated investment strategy is being carried out in the 1980s.

The planned expansion will be focussed on the dynamic economies of Latin America, Asia, and Africa. Unprofitable activities - especially in Latin America - will be sold, while new investments will be oriented to areas with growing markets. New foreign activities and growth in employment within the developing countries will take place for the most part in the East Asian NICs and in individual ASEAN member states (Malaysia, Indonesia). In other words, the concentrated presence in Latin America and the rather weak presence in Southeast and East Asia will balance out during the 1980s. Total sales of the 15 largest Swiss multis amounted to 82 billion francs in 1980. About three fourths or 61 billion francs stemmed from foreign operations. 80% of production abroad was located in the industrial countries, 20% in developing countries. The value of production in developing countries was equivalent to more than half the value of production inside Switzerland.

While expansion of production in the industrialized countries was usually coupled with a drop in the percentage of production in Switzerland, expansion in the developing countries was often the cause of a decline in the percentage of production in other industrialized countries. All in all, one cannot argue that there was a redeployment of production activities from Switzerland to foreign countries. Nonetheless, during the 1970s, Swiss industry expanded its productive capacity abroad rather than at home. Yet domestic activities clearly profited from this expansion - especially from a qualitative point of view.

The forecasts for corporate production in the various groups of countries have essentially been discussed in the paragraphs on employment and investment. The percentage of productive activities inside Switzerland can be expected to stagnate or decline slightly. The smaller multis in the machine industry, that is, companies with relatively few productive plants abroad, are counting on foreign expansion. The highest rates of growth are to be expected in the USA and in the NICs. None of the four firms which, at present, are not engaged in the developing countries is planning to take this step.

15.2 New Forms of International Investment by Swiss Multinationals

The year 1980 was a turning point in the history of foreign-based activities of Swiss industrial firms. After two decades of growth and market-share oriented strategy, more weight and attention is being given to the profit goal. This shift of emphasis hat yet to be recognized by the general public. The experience of the 1980s as well as the forecasts for the 1990s show only a low rate of expansion for FDI activities - for the most part in North America, Japan, and the NICs.

Given this background and given the results of our survey of small and medium-sized enterprises (cf. Chapter 13) it seemed particularily pertinent to investigate whether the Swiss MNEs were switching from FDI to NFII. This was an especially difficult endeavor since quantitative information on NFII is even harder to collect than information on FDI. Moreover, for some companies, the issues raised in the questionnaire were considered sensitive or even secret. Therefore, we must rely on responses of 11 of the 15 firms covered in the previous study on the one hand and on purely qualitative evidence on the other.

Table 15-4 confirms that NFII, as described in Chapter 5, are significant for the eleven firms participating in our survey.

Looking into the future, we can start from the following two premises:

(1) None of the various NFII will become less important for the strategies of Swiss multinational firms.

Table 15-4. Relative Importance of NFII in 1984

	Total: 11
Insignificant	0%
Of little significance	31%
Significant	69%
Highly significant	0%

Source: Calculations by the authors

(2) Some of the NFII will definitely become more important, especially licensing, joint ventures, and contractual cooperation.

An even better impression of what our Swiss MNEs expect for the future can be gained from examining the geographical distribution of NFII (cf. Table 15-6).

A summary of Tables 15-5 and 15-6 reveals the following:

- The highest potential for NFII is perceived for the USA on the one hand and for the NICs on the other.
- The most important correlations between forms and regions are
  - licensing with the USA, Japan, and the NICs
  - joint ventures with the USA and the NICs
  - sub-contracting with the NICs
  - contractual cooperation with European, US, and Japanese firms.

Table 15-5. Importance of NFII in the Future

	Significance
Licensing	0.5
Sub-Contracting	0.2
Management Consulting	0.1
Technical Consulting	0.3
Joint Ventures	0.4
Group Investment	0.3
Contractual Cooperation	0.5
Turnkey	0.1
Mean of all NFII	0.3

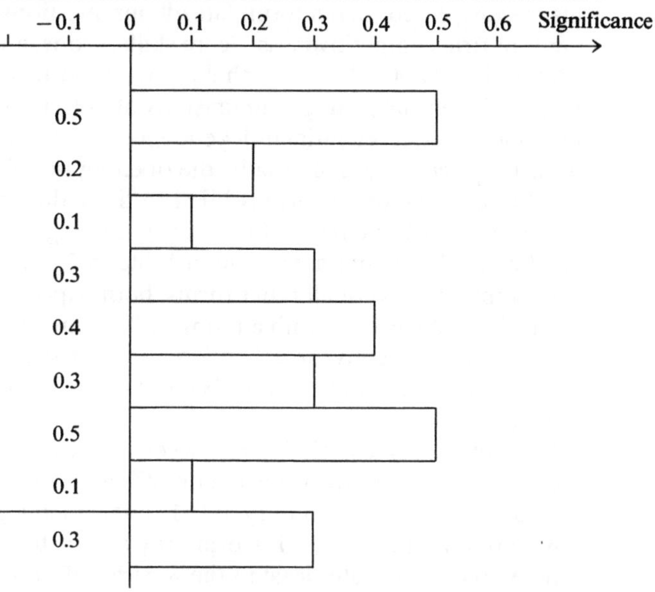

−1 = significance will decrease; 0 = significance will not change; 1 = significance will increase; 2 = significance will greatly increase

Table 15-6. Significance of NFII in the Future (Geographical Distribution)

	Industrial Countries				Delevoping Countries	NICs[b]	COME-CON	Mean
	Europe	USA/CAN	Japan	others[a]				
• Licensing	0.5	0.9	0.6	0.4	0.4	0.7	0.1	0.5
• Sub-Contracting	0.3	0.3	0.1	0.0	0.2	0.6	0.0	0.2
• Management Consulting	0.0	0.0	−0.1	0.0	0.3	0.3	0.2	0.1
• Technical Consulting	0.2	0.5	0.4	0.3	0.3	0.4	0.2	0.3
• Joint Ventures	0.3	0.7	0.5	0.3	0.5	0.6	0.2	0.4
• Group Investments	0.5	0.4	0.3	0.2	0.2	0.4	0.1	0.3
• Contractual Cooperations	0.8	0.9	0.6	0.3	0.3	0.4	0.2	0.5
• Turnkey	0.1	0.1	0.1	0.0	0.3	0.1	0.0	0.1
• Mean of all NFII	0.3	0.5	0.3	0.2	0.3	0.4	0.1	0.3

[a] Australia, New Zealand, etc.
[b] Hong Kong, Singapore, South Korea, Taiwan, Argentina, Brazil, Mexico

These findings seem to be compatible with our theoretical hypotheses, namely that NFII are primarily seen as a means to establish a foothold in new and dynamic markets and/or to promote technology transfers both into and out of Switzerland.

How do NFII influence the competitiveness of multinational firms? For obvious reasons, we could not formulate all our questions in terms of the conceptual elements of firm competitiveness - core skills, scope, and international profile - as developed in Chapter 10. Nevertheless, we tried to associate the different types of NFII with various strategic dimensions of entrepreneurial aims, such as return on investment, entrepreneurial independence, potential for innovation, security of jobs in the home country, and, finally, the opening-up of new markets.

The contribution of various NFII to these dimensions of microeconomic competitiveness could be marked on a scale ranging from 1 (insignificant) to 6 (highly significant). The results are shown in Table 15-7. The most interesting points are:

- In comparison with all other forms, both exports and FDI show the highest ratings (4.3, 3.8). NFII - with a rating of 2.5 - are clearly viewed as contributing less to overall competitiveness. Individual forms such as licensing with 3.3, and joint ventures with 2.8 come relatively close to the preferred classical forms of internationalization.
- Very interesting correlations between NFII and aspects of competitiveness become visible when we disaggregate. While exports rank highest with regard to job security in the home country, NFII engagements get top ratings in view of opening-up new markets. FDI is primarily associated with high returns. At the same time, FDI contributes least to the security of jobs in the home country and - not surprisingly - NFII seem most threatening to entrepreneurial independence. NFII are also perceived as threats to the security of jobs in the home country.

Table 15-7. Influence of NFII on Competitiveness

	Dimensions of Competitiveness					
	Return on Invest-ment	Entrepreneurial Independence	Potential for Innovation	Security of Jobs in the Home Country	Access to New Markets	Mean of all Dimensions
• Exports	4.4	3.2	4.2	5.1	4.7	4.3
• Licensing	3.6	3.0	3.3	2.8	3.9	3.3
• Sub-Contracting	2.6	2.2	2.1	1.8	2.6	2.3
• Management Consulting	2.2	1.9	1.9	1.6	2.2	2.0
• Technical Consulting	2.8	1.9	2.4	2.5	2.6	2.4
• Joint Ventures	2.8	2.5	2.8	2.4	3.7	2.8
• Group Investments	2.5	2.1	2.3	2.3	3.1	2.5
• Contractual Cooperations	2.3	2.4	2.3	2.0	3.2	2.4
• Turnkey	2.5	2.1	2.6	2.4	2.9	2.5
• FDI	4.6	4.0	3.4	2.9	4.3	3.8
• Mean of all NFII	2.7	2.3	2.5	2.2	3.0	2.5

Table 15-8. Influence of Exports, FDI, and NFII on Competitiveness

Forms / Dimensions	Exports		NFII		FDI	
	Grade Points	Rank	Grade Points	Rank	Grade Points	Rank
• Return on Investment	4.4	3	2.7	2	4.6	1
• Entrepreneurial Interdependence	3.2	5	2.3	4	4.0	3
• Potential of Innovation	4.2	4	2.5	3	3.4	4
• Security of Jobs in the Home Country	5.1	1	2.2	5	2.9	5
• Opening of New Markets	4.7	2	3.0	1	4.3	2

Table 15-8 summarizes these rankings in a more concise way by comparing the NFII aggregate with FDI and exports.

The information presented in Tables 15-7 and 15-8 fits quite nicely into our conceptual and theoretical framework. This is especially true for the association of all New Forms of International Investment (NFII) with the strategic goal of penetrating into new markets. With the exception of technical contracts, this aspect dominates very clearly. Other rather interesting and at the same time consistent findings are:

- the relatively high contribution of licensing and consulting activities to returns on investment

- the relatively high contribution of both joint ventures and licensing operations to innovation potential.

The first finding conforms to our view of the firm as a (multiple) seller of firm-specific "skills"; the latter demonstrates the importance of organizational aspects of "scope" for innovative activity.

The last section of the questionnaire deals with the consequences of NFII for (national) economic policy. Again the firms could mark the desirability of several policy measures on a scale of 1 through 6 (ranging from hardly desirable to extremely desirable).

The information in Table 15-9 speaks for itself and is consistent with other results. The clear preference for export insurance schemes is not surprising. Nevertheless, one result should be emphasized: firms definitely prefer bilateral instruments over multilateral initiatives (such as joining the UN) and over multilateral agreements and institutions. This is demonstrated in Table 15-10 and illustrates once more the neo-mercantilist sentiments of individual entrepreneurs, even of outward-looking Swiss business firms with global strategies.

Table 15-9. NFII and National Economic Policy

	Total: 11
Extension of Export Risk Insurance	4.8
Bilateral Contracts on a Governmental Level (Investment Protection, Research, etc.)	4.0
Joining Multilateral Agreements (e.g. Multifibre Agreement)	2.8
Joining the UN	1.8
Extension of Mixed Credits	4.3
Bilateral Trade Contracts	3.6
Building-up of Economic Aid to Developing Countries	2.4
Mean	3.4

Table 15-10. Bilateral Instruments and Multilateral Agreements

	Total: 11
Bilateral Instruments	4.0
Multilateral Agreements	2.3
Mean	3.4

Part V

Synthesis: Conclusions and Recommendations for Economic Policy and Business Strategy

Chapter 16

A Framework for the Evaluation of New Forms of Internationalization (NFI)

At this point of our analysis, we reach a crucial crossroads - if not a dark and blind alley. We should take the step from analysis to evaluation - and this poses very different but very difficult problems. The first is related to the question of perspective or point of view. From what perspective and with whose particular values and interests in mind do we evaluate NFI? A second major difficulty arises when we have to decide on the measuring rod for the efficiency and equity of NFI. What are the alternatives to NFII and NFEF in the world in which we are living?

A third major difficulty is simply our lack of understanding or, in other words, our high level of uncertainty concerning the causes and effects of the various strategies applied by business firms, as well as the various policies applied by national governments. A fourth problem is of a tactical or even philosophical nature. What should we advise economic actors to do: to resist and fight the neo-mercantilist forces or to adjust smoothly to them or even to circumvent the protectionist stumbling blocks by innovative modes of transactions? Will the latter not strengthen bureaucratic response as well as mercantilist sentiments? This leads us back to the first question. Problems look quite different to different actors - and so do remedies.

16.1 Perspectives and Interests of the Various Actors

In our project we have pursued our analytical goals along entrepreneurial tracks of thought. We have shown how - from the perspective of the isolated business firm - individual actors look at alternative ways of carrying on international business. Despite their weaknesses, our empirical findings clearly confirm that firms in fact are already using NFII and NFEF as alternatives to both exports and FDI. As long as we stick to the profit and/or growth objectives of the single firm, evaluation of NFI vis-à-vis exports or FDI is quite straightforward and not too difficult. Firms will apply those organizational or contractual modes of transfer which promise the greatest long-run, risk-adjusted profits. Unfortunately, the problems of uncertainty with respect to the exogenous factors on the one hand and the problems of finding an adequate model for causal predictions on the other turn even clear concepts into very fuzzy operational criteria for evaluation. Nevertheless, we shall present some conclusions and recommendations about internationalization strategies for business firms. Of course, these recommendations will have to be examined cautiously. Our primary aim is to stimulate business leaders and planners to think more in terms of alternative forms of internationalization and to utilize these forms in ways which harmonize with their exclusive skills and their scope of internalization.

International competitiveness is not only a microeconomic problem. In political terms, it has been discussed and evaluated mainly at the national level. This is not surprising since in any somewhat open (national) economy, lack or loss of international competitiveness of firms will add up to the evils of rising unemployment, lagging productivity, and sagging aggregate output. But there is a second, quite different, reason for national concern. Just as "what is good for General Motors is not necessarily good for the USA" it could also be that even if NFI are good for SMEs and/or MNEs they might not be good for either the home and/or host country. The relatively homogeneous nature of Swiss MNEs (research and know-how based skills) led us to identify their contribution to Swiss welfare as positive and substantive, with only minor qualifications regarding possible job losses.[1]

The main reason for this positive welfare balance sheet of the Swiss MNEs is quite simple. It is reasonable to assume that a large (measured absolutely and in relation to the size of the local market) MNE is able to grow world-wide - expanding both its size and its scope - without running into diminishing returns (cf. TEECE 1981:6). This was confirmed by our previous study: The more globally oriented and the faster world-wide expansion of a particular MNE, the more securely and faster the headquarters activities expand, including employment. Although Swiss MNEs can be expected to transfer rather above-average know-how (cf. WEHRLE 1984), the impact on host countries is another matter. "There are few circumstances where efficiency considerations would support the desirability of policies discriminating between indigenous and international firms." (TEECE 1981:15).

The complexity and diversity of NFI are far greater than in the case of FDI. Not only is the range of firms involved practically without limits; the variety of modes and objects of transaction are constantly changing, at a rate almost beyond comprehension. Our empirical research gave some spotty evidence for this phenomenon. Of course, it is also plausible that NFI are more likely to substitute for exports than for FDI. Given our research results, we postulate with some assurance that the greatly enlarged choice among forms of internalized or contractual cooperation will definitely improve the comparative institutional or organizational advantages of the firms involved. But will it improve the national comparative advantage of the home country? This is an intriguing question. NFI mobilize factors of production. Thus they increase both the microeconomic efficiency of the firm and the global allocation of resources. But what about the impact on the national economies and on national economic policies? This is an extremely difficult question. If practically all business firms become foot-loose, if practically all dimensions of competitive advantage can be bundled and unbundled at will, and if (in the end) anything leading to a comparative advantage becomes mobile either through internationalization or through contractual agreements, then no basis for national comparative advantage remains. Although this may seem to be an extreme position, it is conceptually no more extreme than either the perspective of free trade and immobile factors of production or the view of the MNE as a simple capital arbitrageur.

The sovereignty of the nation state is certainly further reduced by NFI, as the economy becomes more open - not only in regard to the intensity but even more so in regard to the quality of interdependence. STRANGE (1985) gives two reasons for

[1] BORNER/WEHRLE 1984a and BORNER et. al. 1985.

this "impoverishment" of national economic policies: "One, obviously, was the accelerated internationalization of markets, and the incorporation (...) of ever larger parts of national economies into a world market system." This, of course, undermined the assumptions of the KEYNESian middle ground about the power of government to equilibrate the flows of goods and money within the nation. According to STRANGE, the second major change was the overburdening of the public sector by mounting demands for "protection", not only against social evils in the narrow sense but against structural changes as such. The reach of economic policies is thus reduced, thereby reinforcing once more political pressures against structural changes, which seem to be imposed from "outside". One hypothesis to be developed more fully in Chapter 18 is that Switzerland has resolved this contradiction in a rather dialectical way: first by balancing the globally driven, market-dominated, ever-changing economy with a hyper-stable political system. Secondly, by countering the extraordinary openness in business matters with cultural provincialism and nationalism. This explains the paradoxical nature of Switzerland as a country. On the one hand it is (economically) extremely outward-looking and adjusts freely to global forces. On the other hand it is (politically) inward-looking and resists change to an almost pathological degree. KATZENSTEIN (1985:24) expresses this view very pointedly: "For the small European states, economic change is a fact of life. They have not chosen it; it was thrust upon them (...). They live with change by compensating for it."

But there is one more dimension in the complex of perspectives and interests of economic actors. Even before the publication of Adam SMITH's "Wealth of Nations" in 1776, economics as a science focussed on the nation.[2] Aggregate theories of income, wealth, and prices assume a closed economy, at least as the point of departure. International goods and financial markets are introduced later on in the analysis. Trade, FDI, and capital flows are thus integrated into national accounts. But the perspective remains one of a closed system, especially in view of (macroeconomic) fiscal and monetary policies. This tendency has been reinforced by two quite different influences. The first is that the USA, as the most powerful producer of both economic goods and economists, was until the 1970s "dominant", both with regard to the state of the world economy and the state of the art in economic science. The second is the change from a system of fixed to flexible exchange rates. This change was promoted by economists using precisely the argument that flexible rates helped nation states regain national autonomy over macroeconomic (and especially monetary) policies.

In the meantime, things have changed fundamentally. The USA has become a much more open economy, now vitally dependent on imports of goods and lately - to an extraordinary degree - even of capital. Flexible exchange rates have not reduced feedback from policy shocks in other countries. The economic arguments for this cannot be presented and discussed here in detail (see BUITER/MARSTON 1985). The decisive factor is clearly political in both its causes and effects. Flexibility of exchange rates has increased the variety of policy strategies and policy mixes. This variety is in turn based on widely diverging economic objectives and widely diverging views on economic theory. This has led to an almost experimental design of eco-

[2] In German "economics" is called „Nationalökonomie".

nomic strategies. France is fiscally expansionary and KEYNESian; the USA is fiscally expansionary and supply-side neo-classical; the British are wholly restrictive and supply-side monetarist; and the Germans are fiscally restrictive and KEYNESian.

For the detached observer and future historian, this may turn out to be an interesting experiment, but at this point it is clearly detrimental to the health of the world economy. By logical necessity the world economy is a closed system. The more the individual nations want to play the "open-economy-game", the more this unpleasant logical constraint imposes unexpected and unpleasant surprises. The result has inevitably been that although inflation rates have been converging and global demand rising, the recovery of the mid-1980s is the most unbalanced and fragile since World War II (MARRIS 1984). So again, we are confronted with the task of international policy coordination. The supersession of national policy sovereignty - especially relating to monetary, fiscal, trade, and regulatory policies - by supra-national institutions (such as IMF, GATT, etc.) has not taken place. And the rather naive hope that decentralized decision-making in the field of national economic policy would - under flexible exchange rates - be socially and globally optimal has been shattered by experience as well as by clear thinking. COOPER addresses this kind of "policy equilibrium" very distinctly with the following question: "(...) Does the collection of actions of interdependent nations settle down to an equilibrium as soon as the environment settles down?" (COOPER 1985:366).

COOPER's answer is negative and we fully agree with him. The first reason is purely economic. There are a series of nominal and real spillovers as well as international transmission routes for national policy shocks. But the second reason is political and looms much larger. The world economy is not made up of competitive, atomistic countries. Rather, it is dominated by a few "large countries" wielding strategic power. Consequently, we will have to reckon with national policy drives of the "beggarthy-neighbor" variety. The more open the economies are and the more divergent policy goals and styles become, the more we have to expect precisely this collectively damaging course of action. In the end, these efforts will be hampered or even thwarted by the constraints of a closed world economy. So we are back to rational international coordination as the only way out of the deadlock. But again, the prisoner's dilemma looms large, because "every negotiation is, at its core, a zero-sum game, even when there are substantial mutual gains to be had from it". (COOPER 1985:371). If there are no gains perceived, there is no interest in negotiating in the first place. But if a potential gain is perceived, it will immediately be taken for granted and negotiations will be limited to the distribution of gains. "Reciprocity, while ludicrous in an abstract economic sense, is the only way for governments which are genuinely interested in putting their economies on a more efficient footing through trade liberalization and in contributing to more harmonious international trade relationships, to do so and still remain in power ... The economist knows that what is seen as a cost is really the sole gain, but if reciprocity is needed as a marketing device, so be it." (CURZON/CURZON-PRICE 1984:7-8).

16.2 A Measuring Rod for the Efficiency and Equity of New Forms of Internationalization

In principle we have already encountered the problem of measuring the efficiency and equity of NFI in the context of MNEs and their FDI (see Chapter 7). The internalization paradigm can be the godfather either of market failure or efficiency explanations of FDI. Of course, we can always postulate a set of assumptions which lead to the conclusion that "trade" is the only efficient international transaction. Viewed from this perspective, FDI is at most a "second best" mode of international operations, and, consequently, NFI a "third best" route to internationalization. But all depends on the realism of these assumptions. Neoclassical economists have the paradoxical habit of either declaring anything but free trade as inefficient on a priori grounds or, on the contrary, of interpreting everything in existence to be efficient (otherwise it would not exist). Some authors jump back and forth between these two positions like PAVLOVian dogs - without even noticing the contradiction.

In our view, the evaluation of NFI really hinges on which restrictions on business strategies, national policies, and decisions of international institutions are exogenously imposed and which ones are endogenous and, therefore, part of the strategy, the policy, or the global regulations.

We encountered this problem again and again in interviews with representatives of SMEs and MNEs. Time and again we were told that firms would only consider NFI (not to speak of implementing them) when and if they were "forced" to do so. To the extent that neoclassical equilibrium economics is accepted, this is true for anything a firm does: the optimization rule leads to a deterministic outcome.[3] Only if firms possess some (dynamic) monopolistic and absolute advantages in the structure of their individual competitiveness, can they decide how to best exploit those advantages, that is, which route of internationalization to take. The borderline between the structural market failure and the efficiency interpretation of transaction costs and, therefore, of internalization and/or contractual cooperation strategies cannot be drawn analytically. On the one hand this depends on the particular situational characteristics of the firm (home and host country, size, type of industry, competitive environment) and on the other hand on subjective judgement. There are many similarities between the hiring and firing policies and the internationalization strategies of firms. Some firms have strong preferences for highly cooperative schemes, many for strongly hierarchical structures, and yet others for dealing at arm's length through markets. There are different corporate cultures based on different value systems as well as on different organizational philosophies.

A corporation committed to internal financing, hierarchical principles of organization, and centralized decision-making will most certainly have preferences for FDI, for 100 percent owned subsidiaries tightly knit into the global system. Yet another firm with a different corporate culture will welcome NFI as a way to establish long-term ties with flexible terms and differentiated sharing of costs, risks, and returns. In my view we encounter pretty much the same problems in the case of contractual forms with long-term mutual obligations as we do in the field of labor mar-

[3] Of course, we can avoid this by adopting a purely stochastic model. For the population of firms altogether, the outcome is still deterministic and the only strategic element is to hope for good luck.

kets or customer markets in general (cf. Chapter 9). Some economists explain the pervasiveness of such contracts as evidence for growing rigidity, social sclerosis, and other anti-market forces. Others explain this same phenomenon as evidence for the efficienc of contracts if uncertainties, complexities, and contingencies are properly taken into account. These contracts reduce information and transaction costs generally.

The same difficulties reappear at the national level. Do home and host countries have country-specific preferences for different forms of internationalization? They clearly do: but whether their motives are good or bad is hard to assess - unless we take a dogmatic position. Again, it is naive or outright hopeless to expect an analytical answer to the basic questions of national policy strategies. On the contrary, it should be obvious that different goals, different times, and different circumstances require quite different policy perspectives. India and China cannot simply follow the outward-oriented export strategy of Taiwan or Singapore. A development model for India cannot be found by multiplying some tiny country's variables by a factor of 100 or 1,000.

The main reason for this is again the fact that the world economy is a closed system, displaying a highly limited capacity for adjustment to disturbances and disruptions (see Chapter 1). Unfortunately, these zero-sum elements of the global economy make themselves felt more in hard times. This applies to "home countries" as well. A small open economy like Switzerland is not only politically rather insignificant, it is also not very visible. If Japan had the same percentage of exports and/or FDI relative to the size of its GNP as Switzerland, the public uproar in Europe and the US over Japanese "economic imperialism" would reach politically intolerable levels. The constraints of the zero-sum global economy are simply not so binding for small countries. At the same time, small countries have extremely narrow local markets so that only a few industries with natural or political protection (such as construction, agriculture, or telecommunication) can develop strategies which do not focus on the world market. Furthermore, Switzerland has never really been a technological leader in the sense that basic innovations originated from Swiss companies. We lived (well) by being a faster, better, more reliable, and - thanks to an undervalued currency during the late 1960s and early 1970s - also a cheaper "second" compared to the innovative "first".

Alongside the lack of natural resources and therefore the nonexistence of resource-based MNEs, these factors explain why Swiss firms in general are less hostile to NFI than US firms. Nevertheless, our policy stance could still cause headaches. For Swiss entrepreneurs a prospering, stable, and open global economy is the best we as a nation can hope for or work toward. But such hopes are stronger than the possibilities of realizing them. For Switzerland, most global forces are indeed exogenous. Yet, our firms have to survive or even grow in an environment which makes their preferred strategies of exports and FDI more and more difficult. So firms naturally adjust - because they are "forced to", as they tell us time and time again. From a normative perspective, government policy recommendations are much more controversial. Should we as a nation continue to pursue a free trade and investment strategy and let our firms adjust to all respective restrictions? Or should we encourage, support, subsidize, etc., NFI operations through our foreign (economic) policy?

16.3 The Main Elements of a Framework for Evaluation

Our basic premises for drawing our policy conclusions are the following:

- Competitiveness is, analytically, a microeconomic concept applicable to firms trying to establish, defend, and extend absolute competitive advantages over other firms.
- The quantity/quality of skills, the organizational scope, and the international profile determine the depth and the reach of this competitive advantage.
- Knowledge and skills are also decisive factors for economic development in an environment characterized by international competition among different types of firms in global markets.
- Just as geographically unevenly distributed immobile resources lead to international trade, the uneven geographical and organizational distribution of internalized skills will lead to international transactions among firms with different locations, with different skill levels or qualities, and with different scopes of internalization.
- From all this, a variety of international transaction possibilities result. However, they can and will be realized "only if institutional modes are established to provide the appropriate linkage mechanisms and governance structures to surround and protect transactions." (TEECE 1981: 8).

But what determines these "linkage mechanisms" and "governance structures"? There are clearly two main groups of forces. One refers to the strategic potential for organizational scope and international profile; the other stems from the rules and regulations of policy frameworks. From a normative point of view the crucial questions are (1) the issue of market failure versus monopolistic, anticompetitive behavior of firms with strategic potential and (2) which rules and regulations are both fair and effective for the transfer of technological and/or managerial know-how in the light of the existence of sovereign nations and seriously impaired markets.

We are utterly unable to give definite answers. But at the same time - and for the same reasons - we fundamentally question certain orthodoxies with respect to trade and MNEs. There are a number of transactional difficulties - within both a framework of open markets and the scope of a hierarchical firm - which call for other modes of transactions and consequently for other policy rules and regulations. Whether the former are monopolistic and thus anti-competitive or efficient and thus optimal is extremely difficult to determine. The same is, of course, true for policy regimes. When do they restrain trade and decrease consumer welfare and when do they achieve the opposite?

In the two final chapters we will suggest some answers and evaluate them in the light of business strategy (Chapter 17) and in the light of the national policy of a small open economy, such as Switzerland (Chapter 18).

Chapter 17

Recommendations for Private Business Strategies

17.1 New Forms of Internationalization: the Link Between Global Disintegration and the International Operations of Firms

Our main theme has been the disintegration of global structures and worldwide institutions, primarily at the political level. But the other side of the coin is the multidimensionally increasing internationalization of MNE and SME business operations. At various points in our report we pointed out how internationally operating firms display innovative and efficient modes of organization, modes of organization capable of transferring technological knowledge and firm-specific ownership and internalization advantages abroad - despite the rising barriers to classical trade and investment. The constituent elements of a corresponding NFI strategy are summarized under the following four headings:

- Transactors: Enterprises of various characters and sizes, equipped with specific skills and trying to create value via a multitude of activities/functions.
- Object of transfer: Complex bundle of goods, assets, rights, financial capital, and human capabilities.
- Form of transaction: Spot exchange on open markets (export sales), transfer of capital and technology within property-controlled MNE (FDI), and/or contractual forms of sharing firm-specific competitive advantages (NFI).
- Strategic options: The basis of firm-specific competitive advantages (core skills), their functional and geographical internalization within a structure of market relations, hierarchies, contractual ligatures (scope), and modes of effecting value-creating (profit-maximizing) transactions within and without the managerial organization (form).

In the next paragraphs we will explore this concept of competitiveness in the light of these inter-related levels of strategic behavior.

MNEs and SMEs are confronted with the same global forces of "protectionism" in the broadest sense of the word. Both "free trade" and "free investment" are complemented or superseded by bilateral, restricted, regulated trade on the one hand and constraints, regulations, and even prohibition of foreign ownership on the other. Thus, exporters and MNEs must learn to operate differently. They must innovate their modes of international transactions. Actors on both ends of the spectrum of international operations (exports, FDI) have a wide range of strategic options to choose from, partly because regulations and restrictions are never complete or final. Therefore, administrative discretion in implementing all these constraints provides leeway for negotiating specific terms of agreement. This is especially true for MNEs which can try to get exemptions from minority ownership requirements if they are able to convince host governments that they fulfill the aims behind these restrictions. The chances of success for such a strategy rise as local R & D expenditure rises, as export shares grow, or as the technology import of the foreign subsidiary increases. But even here, contractual arrangements will at least supplement FDI operations. New forms are emerging alongside FDI.

This will usually happen when existing FDI are threatened by new regulations. In instances where new foreign operations are at stake, firms will be less constrained by existing FDI and correspondingly high sunk costs. The range of options widens. Consequently, many MNEs have experienced a gradual change of mind. Impediments can be turned into new possibilities, restrictions into new opportunities, and local regulations into more durable cooperative relationships. But this often requires changes in management perspectives at headquarters, namely:

- the realization that management control over core skills is more important than ownership control
- the reduction of risks of nationalization or transfer restrictions through dilution of equity ownership and/or geographical spread of operations
- the decentralization of managerial decisions by greater reliance on foreign subsidiary managers and/or local partners, especially in the case of negotiations with local governments.

Again, we stress the importance of entrepreneurial structures and cultures. And it is here where country-specific factors take on particular significance. As will be argued in Chapter 18, companies from small European countries will be more internationally oriented than US firms. The latter are almost always deeply rooted in the US market, with exports or FDI being at most subsidiary elements in their overall strategy. A typical Swiss MNE, such as Nestlé or the pharmaceuticals from Bâle, is simply married to the global economy. Such firms have no possibility of divorcing themselves from global markets and retreating to the home market. Due to the small size of the local market Swiss exporters are in a similar position. The high export shares (see Chapter 13) demonstrate that SMEs oriented toward export have had at least a long-term and intense exposure to foreign conditions. Together with the high proportion of investment goods in Swiss exports, opportunities for NFI arrangements on the basis of mutually advantageous know-how transfer and cooperation seem numerous and growing.

17.2 A Strategic Concept for New Forms of Internationalization

As was demonstrated in Chapter 10, the transaction cost approach to international operations is a very fruitful and promising one. It provides a synthesis capable of explaining exports, FDI, and NFI within the same analytical framework. In our view this is not only an improvement over the separate theories of trade and multinationals, but it is also a basis for a new strategic concept at the microeconomic level. Let us approach this concept from the extremes. Traditional international trade will occur

- if competitive advantages are exclusively country-specific and relatively immobile (endowment-based trade such as mining)
- if consumer preferences are primarily nationally differentiated so that product

differentiation by firms with similar endowments and types of know-how is viable (intra-industry trade)
- if political transaction costs do not inhibit international exchange, that is, if there are no political barriers to trade (free trade with all transaction costs being "natural").

On the other hand, firms will definitely choose FDI under the following conditions:
- if firm-specific competitive advantages can be combined with country-specific factors in the host country
- if the firm-specific core skills which determine competitive advantage are ownership-specific, that is, if control over know-how is only possible through ownership
- if political transaction costs for fully internalized intrafirm exchanges do not inhibit FDI, that is, if there are no barriers to free international investment (free international investment with all internalization costs being "natural").

Synthesizing the characteristics of the extremes, we arrive at the general framework for NFI. The conditions will have to be reformulated as follows. NFI will be the predominant mode of international transactions
- if firm-specific ownership and internalization advantages can be combined to the mutual benefit of both firms
- if the firm-specific core skills can be controlled and exchanged with contractual agreements and not only by internalization through ownership
- if the "natural transaction costs" associated with either full internalization (FDI) or full externalization (free trade) are raised by government interference (protectionism in the broadest sense) to such a degree that NFI contractual arrangements become more efficient.

These conditions are very general and very abstract. The theoretical model does not, therefore, lend itself to concrete or specific strategic advice to individual firms. All it does is to provide a conceptual framework for strategy formulation. Our empirical material has shown the enormous complexity of real world transactions and their determinants. Our own research strategy is thus one of radical abstraction and simplification with respect to the strategic concept of international competitiveness. Its structure is supported by three cornerstones:

1) Core Skills of the Firm

Core-skills define the nature of absolute, firm-specific advantage. What do we as firm X know or what can we do better than our competitors? Core-skills can be rooted in technological, managerial, intellectual, or marketing know-how. They can be embodied in tangible or intangible assets for which property rights are either present or absent.

2) Scope of the Firm

Scope defines the "size of the firm", yet not in absolute terms (employment, capital, market share, etc.) but in view of the boundaries between transactions at arm's length (markets) and transactions under managerial control (degree and type of internalization). Analoguous to the economies of scale of the "one-product-firm" so commonly found in textbooks, the economies of scope are the name of the game of the know-how based, multi-product firm in the real world. How do we bundle our core skills to form a firm-specific package of competitive advantage, and how do we exchange the package as a whole, or parts thereof, in order to protect it from imitation and in order to achieve cumulative know-how development.

3) International Profile of the Firm

International profile defines the space dimensions and the routes of international exchange. Given our core skills and our scope of internal control, how do we best exploit our competitive advantage in different places, i. e. locations characterized by different endowments, different development stages, and above all different policy regimes? What the firm optimizes here is the mode of its international transactions - either by choosing one mode or by combining market exchanges, investments, and a whole array of contractual arrangements of the NFI-type.

One final word of caution is absolutely necessary. These three aspects of microeconomic competitiveness are not hierarchical levels with "skills" being the foundation, scope the structure, and profile the outward connections. These three elements are fully interdependent. Strategy means precisely treating these dimensions as mutually dependent.

Of course, successful strategies maximize positively reinforcing elements in a dynamic setting. And in this setting, key features of the national institutional home-country economy play a central role. We will analyze these links in the final chapter.

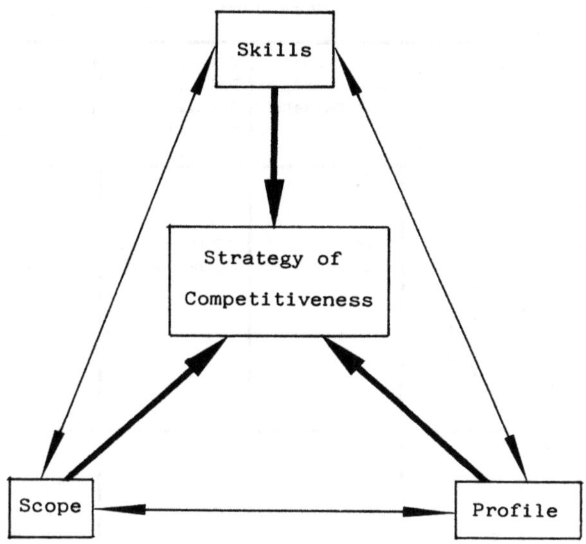

Fig. 17-1. Skills, Scope, and Profile: The Three Interdependent Elements of Firm Strategy of Competitiveness

17.3 The Choice between Exports, New Forms of Export Financing, and New Forms of International Investment

In the previous section, we developed a conceptual framework for international competitiveness on the level of the firm in the light of a NFI-perspective. In the following paragraphs, the specific choice between NFEF and exports on the one hand and NFII and FDI on the other will be outlined in more detail. From a pragmatic viewpoint, we accept the various New Forms of Export Financing (countertrade) as "one of the rules of the game". At this point, we restrict ourselves to the task of assessing the use of NFEF as opposed to classical trade forms from the point of view of the firm. In Chapter 18, we will come back to the question of what a small open economy like Switzerland can and should do to either promote or restrict NFEF operations.

In a bilateral situation, we can capture the essence of transaction modes since they depend on the foreign trade-policy regimes in the home and host countries. For simplicity's sake, we assume that the contracts under consideration fulfill the condition of double coincidence of wants. By this we mean that the trade-restrictions present in the home and/or host country apply to the goods of a potential exchange (cf. Figure 17-2).

When a complete transaction failure occurs in a bilateral situation, a multilateral countertrade operation might still permit contractual exchange. In these instances a

Host Country (Importer B) \ Home Country (Exporter A)	Free Trade Policy and Open Markets	Free Trade Policy and Regulated International Markets	Trade Restrictions (Protectionism) for B-Goods	High Political Risks of Exports to B	Prohibition of Exports to B (COCOM)
Free Trade Policy for A-Goods	Free Trade	NFEF (Commercial Compensation)	Free Trade	NFEF (Commercial Compensation)	Complete Transaction Failure
Bilateral Countertrade Requirements for A-Goods	NFEF (Commercial and/or Industrial Compensation)	NFEF (Commercial and/or Industrial Compensation)	Bilateral Transaction Failure	NFEF (Commercial and/or Industrial Compensation)	Complete Transaction Failure

Fig. 17-2. Entrepreneurial Strategies of Exchange under Different Foreign-Trade Regimes

third party from a third country represents a new market through which the failure of the bilateral transaction may be avoided.

The entries in the squares of the matrix represent first-best options from the point of view of the firms. In other words, these are efficient modes of transactions if the foreign economic policy regimes are treated as exogenously given. The social (national and global) efficiency, however, must be interpreted quite differently. Keeping in mind the closed nature of the world economy, global welfare will diminish if all trading partners switch from a multilateral (free) trading system to bilateral countertrade strategies. Under such circumstances, the entries in the matrix would clearly be "second-best". The exception would be those cases where, as a consequence of internationally regulated markets (such as international cartels), countertrade occurs despite free trade regimes.

Parallel to the previous section where we analyzed the determinants of alternatives to classical exports, this section is devoted to developing a framework for comparing FDI to NFII. As our previous discussions on the choice of organizational modes of transactions showed, the determinants for the relative frequency of NFII vis-à-vis traditional FDI are threefold:

- the position of policy regimes in regard to international operations of MNEs in both home and host countries (cf. VACCA/RULLANI 1983)
- the macroeconomic growth dynamics of industrial restructuring (cf. KOJIMA 1978, 1982; OZAWA 1979, OZAWA/KOJIMA 1984)
- the firm-level strategies for globally exploiting internalization and ownership advantages (cf. DUNNING 1981, 1982b; BUCKLEY/CASSON 1976).

OZAWA (1985) has attempted a thought-provoking synthesis of these three levels. For this purpose he developed a very simple but ingenious two-by-two grid in the form of an interaction matrix, positioning home country variables and firm-level characteristics against host country variables. This grid is reproduced below with some adjustments in terminology and a stronger orientation toward a small open economy like Switzerland's. Thus we eliminate the variables regarding the adjustment policies of the home country, which are in any case relatively liberal (no discrimination against foreign firms and no specific policies toward these foreign firms in order to achieve industrial restructuring).

The so-called Japanese school led by KOJIMA and OZAWA argues that internationalization by home country firms in young industries with comparative advantages (from the national perspective) and high levels of technological skills will be rather trade-averse unless FDI or NFI are absorbed in sectors of host countries with comparative advantages (quadrants II and III). In the opposite cases, a more complementary interdependence will result. At the same time, NFI have a higher frequency than FDI. Here, the growth environment of the host country is crucial "... otherwise they (home countries) would turn inward and protectionistic." (OZAWA 1985:11). Again we see that the real alternative to NFI in a situation like II or III is not free trade but simply protectionism.

The main difference between high and low tech firms can be explained by firm-specific ownership advantages, thus implying different internalization and thereby internationalization strategies. "... The low technology MNEs are, indeed prone to use new forms of investment ... First of all, unlike the high-technology firms which are microeconomically motivated to go overseas ..., the low-technology firms are

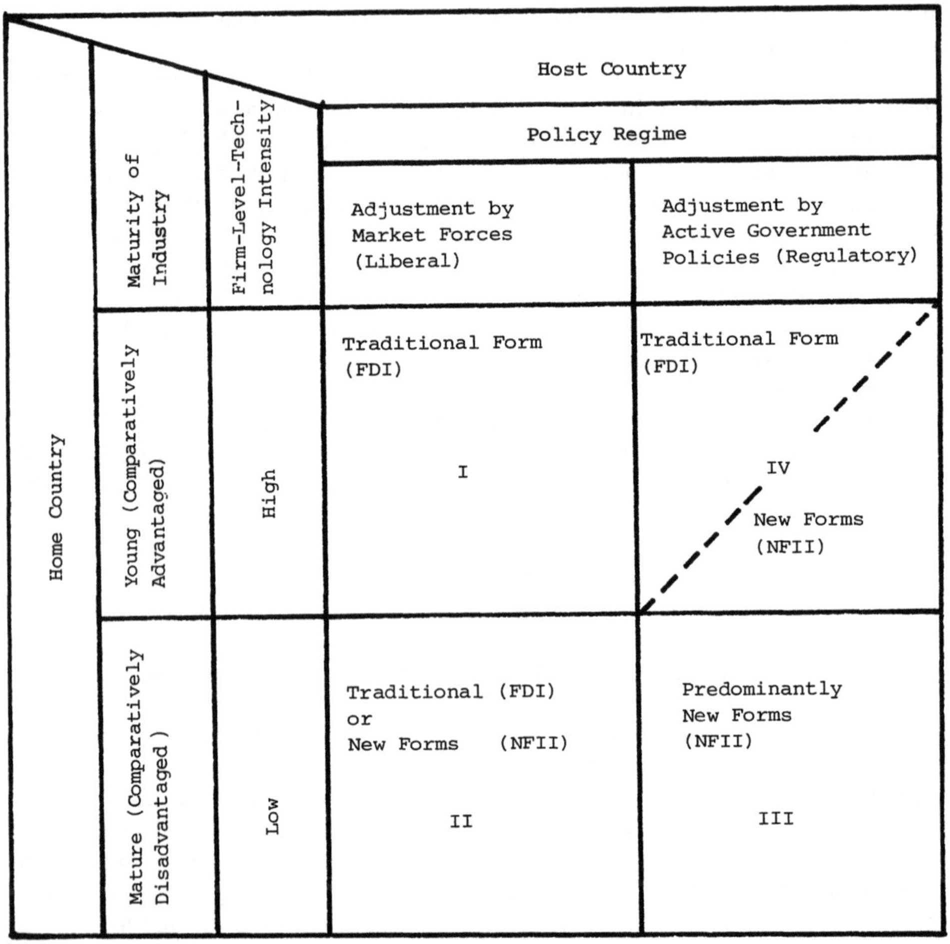

Fig. 17-3. Determinants of Forms of Investment: An Interaction Matrix

compelled to seek a more suitable factor-endowment condition than at home ..." (OZAWA 1985:13). At the same time, most low-tech firms are small and medium-sized and therefore lacking the capital and management capacity necessary for traditional FDI.

The host country variables are quite self-evident. Highly industrialized countries will be of the liberal type, whereas in LDCs and COMECON countries regulations of all types will be present. Just as in the case of the trade matrix (Figure 17-2), quadrant I characterizes a situation where FDI clearly dominates. In quadrant IV two dominant groups (high-tech MNEs and policy active host countries) confront each other. "Whichever form, traditional or new, is adopted, some sort of corrective maneuvering is apt to be initiated, overtly or covertly ..." (OZAWA 1985:17). In quadrant II the outcome is similarily uncertain, yet for different reasons. In the absence of active policy priorities, the absorption and assimilation capacity of local firms will determine the form of investment together with the strategic possibilities of the home country firm. Quadrant IV again leads to a rather clear-cut solution, since conflicts between all relevant actors are in general absent "... the tripartite relationships among low-technology MNEs, their home countries, and the host countries ... are essentially harmonious and cooperative, since their interests are mutually complementary and supportive." (OZAWA 1985: 18).

The KOJIMA/OZAWA model naturally has severe limitations with regard to the underlying assumptions. Nevertheless, it synthesizes the relevant factors on the micro and macro levels. Furthermore, it clearly shows that a general judgement of NFI is impossible, just as it is impossible in the case of FDI. NFIs offer more options and therefore, on the whole, more promise for mutually benefitting forms of cooperation among all actors involved. It is up to national policy-makers and firms to exploit this potential. We will take this question up in the next chapter.

Chapter 18

Recommendations for Economic Policies at the National and International Levels

18.1 Internationalization of Industry and the Sovereignty of the Nation State

Internationalization is a complex phenomenon with cultural, geographic, technological, social, political, and economic dimensions. English is becoming the global language; western mass media represent (and even create) the global tastes of consumers; modern technology produces global products (such as cars), as well as global threats to the natural environment and to world peace. In this concluding chapter only the social and political consequences of the internationalization of firms will be analyzed.

In this respect, two fundamental issues have to be faced: the first has to do with the tension arising from increasing internationalization of business and decreasing national sovereignty. In the case of a small open economy, this conflict can reduce the room for maneuvering national macroeconomic policy to its extreme - to none at all. This situation calls for cultural and/or political compensation at the least. The second basic issue is the growing divergence between the magnitude of Gross Domestic Product and Gross National Product. In other words, the process of internationalization via FDI and NFI widens this gap by increasing the net capital income earned from "human", financial, and real capital invested abroad. This "foreign dividend" has to be distributed domestically, just as the "growth dividend" of the past had to be socially redistributed by the welfare state.

Let us begin with the first question.

In the domain of economic internationalization we can differentiate four dimensions.

a) The Exchange of Goods and Services

As a country with scarce natural resources, Switzerland must depend primarily on the import of raw materials and intermediate products. Swiss exports are characterized by high-quality industrial finishing processes for both investment and consumer goods.

Foreign trade of immaterial goods means the buying and selling of services. Conceptually, services are dealt with in the same way as material goods.

The internationalization of a national economy through the exchange of goods and services is measured by the export quota (exports over Gross National Product) and the import quota. Exports and imports can also be compared historically on a per capita basis, whereby the rate of inflation must be taken into account.

b) Capital Transfers and Returns to Capital
Direct investments and portfolio investments by foreign companies in Switzerland and in Swiss firms operating abroad are the second dimension of the internationalization process. Investigation of this dimension of internationalization was neglected for a long time. But recent research (cf. BORNER/WEHRLE 1984) has revealed the importance of this type of activity for Switzerland.

The extent of capital transfers, and the interconnections thereby implied, can be measured via the relationship between the level of return on industrial and finance capital and exports or the current account surplus.

c) Wages and the Migration of "Human Capital"
The migration of labour from foreign countries into Switzerland and from Switzerland to other countries was and is of great significance for our country's economic well-being. The productivity of the Swiss economy makes the employment of foreign workers necessary; Switzerland's low rate of unemployment, even during periods of recession, is the other side of the coin.

The expansion of the Swiss economy abroad and the fact that important areas of know-how are not available in Switzerland explain why such a large number of Swiss citizens live and work abroad.

These dimensions of internationalization can be measured by migration patterns, by the wages earned by foreigners working in Switzerland, and by the earnings of Swiss citizens working abroad.

d) Technology Transfer
The first three dimensions all include an element of technology transfer. Technologies can be transferred through exchange of goods and services, through direct investments, and also through various forms of cooperation, such as joint ventures or migration of "human capital". But the returns to "human capital exports" are reflected incompletely by the labour income earned abroad. Moreover the significance of the technology outflow from a particular country can only be estimated inadequately by net returns on the sale of know-how (royalties on licenses and patent contracts). It could be argued that technology transfers include "economies of scope" generated by international cooperation schemes. This interpretation would imply returns of international organization by way of contractual cooperation.

Each alteration in the pattern of interaction and the pattern of partner choice and concentration in each of these four dimensions produces macro-economic effects in terms of employment, production, and the price level. There is hardly another country which is, in this sense, so vulnerable to foreign influences as Switzerland. How is it possible for Switzerland to deal with the dialectical relationship between the extreme internationalization of its economy and its tradition of socio-cultural stability?

Before we analyze specific national and international policies and economic measures, we want to take a brief look at the relationship between economic activity and other human - especially societal - values. Specifically, we want to examine the question: what aims and purposes does economic activity serve in the first place? We do not accept the premise of many economists that production and consumption of commodities is the "be-all and end-all" of human existence or that the state is merely an economic puppet. We have repeatedly referred to the fact that Switzerland is a small open economy, subject to the forces of the global economy. And, as we have stressed, this is true - but only for industrial activity. If we look at markets for goods and services other than industrial commodities, even Switzerland has quite a remarkable record of protectionism. Why is this so?

Naturally, it would be a great advantage to Switzerland's banking and insurance industries if they could operate freely abroad, if consulting and engineering firms could accept contracts wherever work is available. Even the Swiss multis would be happy to see investment restrictions in host countries disappear. That is, it seems that Switzerland would profit from a fully and consequently implemented regime of free trade. At the same time, however, completely free trade implies that Swiss labour markets would no longer be subject to national "import controls", that national postal services - the PTT - would be subject to competition from technically more advanced countries, and that freeways and railroads might be built more efficiently by brigades of Korean engineers and technical workers. Perhaps the most dramatic changes would occur if Switzerland were to eliminate import restrictions on foodstuffs and cancel all subsidies to Swiss farmers. Without doubt, Switzerland would soon be a country without any agriculture, perhaps a country with a majority of inexpensive English and Indian physicans, a country with a private telephone service under the control of an American multi, etc. In short, Switzerland does not practice free trade - except in the rather narrow range of industrially manufactured goods. This is, of course, our political right as a nation state. But we must be careful not to judge the economic practices of other nations as if we were defenders of free trade at all costs. BHAGWATI warns about the dangers of hypocrisy, while at the same time recognizing the role of national governments to care for and protect their citizens: "That fairness in trade implies that the members of a society should not profit from cheaper imports if that means that the workers in the import-competing industries are seriously hurt ... is rather a sense of 'social contract' which says that if efficiency improvement comes to an outside factor, such as lower import prices, that should not be accepted if it hurts someone badly; whereas if it comes from an inside factor, such as technical change, it is kosher" (BHAGWATI in CLINE 1983:732).

Swiss citizens are simply not willing to eliminate agriculture from Swiss economic life and from the Swiss countryside. This decision stems from long-standing social, ecological, cultural, and military considerations. For other countries import restrictions and government subsidies are used in the same way - but often to protect other activities - industrial production, the urban and rural landscape, and/or cultural life. DIAZ-ALEJANDRO (in CLINE 1983:307) makes this point poignantly: "Factor payments are generated by stock of machines and people living among foreigners, a process that historically has been accompanied by asymmetrical intrusiveness and noneconomic side effects, not all desirable either from a national or a cosmopolitical perspective.... Reopening these issues in 1982 seems singularly bizarre and dangerous, particularly when done in an imperial style that appears to regard other countries' sovereignty and culture as nontariff barriers."

More and more economists and economic policy-makers are going to have to come to the logical conclusion that the world economy results from the way in which nations and their citizens allow economic life to take place. Access to markets must be regarded as a privilege to be politically granted by nations on the basis of the individual and social values of their citizens. That is, trade regulations are not in the end a subject for abstract GATT-type agreements. They are first and foremost an opportunity, the rights to which are distributed according to national societal criteria, criteria which may have little to do with economic efficiency and material gain.

18.2 The Choice of a National Strategy

In the previous section, we reminded the reader that even in an extremely open economy with highly and fully internationalized business enterprises, the issue of "national sovereignty" looms large. Many, and even important, sectors of the economy are declared and protected as "reservations" for endangered species. Furthermore, private cartels and public regulation often go hand in hand in many domestically oriented industries, such as construction and various types of small-scale business and industry. The most important effect of these corporatist arrangements is "protectionism" by non-tariff barriers, some of the barriers even being induced by private action (cartelization). A good example is safety norms for electical appliances. Developed by private organizations of producers and dealers, these norms are later adopted and enforced by regulatory government agencies - and the trade barrier is created.

The first reaction to internationalization is, therefore, the active promotion or passive tolerance of "national reservations" where influences from foreign competition are kept out by various and ingenious measures. The second strategy is "social and political compensation" of current and potential losers in the course of structural changes dictated by global forces. Viewed from such a perspective, the overall policy options of a small open economy such as Switzerland are quite limited. Global market forces on the one hand and the strategies of larger countries on the other substantially narrow down the room for policy-maneuvering in the sense of macroeconomic adjustment policies.

KATZENSTEIN (1985) distinguishes three main groups of policies, which mirror respectively the ways national elites are attempting to meet structural change in the world economy. The first group includes "liberal economies such as the United States (which) rely on macroeconomic policies and market solutions" (KATZENSTEIN 1985: 23). Lacking a political mandate, as well as concrete instruments in the field of active adjustment policy, the US will typically resort to ad hoc protectionist policies when market forces appear to fail or seem to place an intolerably high political price on market adjustment. Selective intervention in extraordinary situations is thus reserved for foreign economic policy. Selective intervention serves the double purpose of, first, creating temporary "breathing space" for producer groups or regions under too much pressure from international competition, and second, shifting the burden of adjustment back to where it apparently came from, back to the trading partners.

The second so-called "statist strategy" is exemplified by Japan. Here, the national government is armed with both the necessary means and the appropriate institutions for facing structural change directly. The main goal is to "preempt the cost of change through policies that pursue the structural transformation of these economies. Because they seek to meet structural changes in the world economy head on, their strategy often requires systematically protectionist policies, at least in the short and medium term" (KATZENSTEIN 1985:23).

Exporting (the liberal policy) or preempting the cost of structural adjustment (the statist strategy) are two extreme strategies available only to those (few) countries which are large enough either to exert control over the international environment or to consciously shape long-term developments within their societies. The common denominator in both cases, however, is 'protectionism'.

Small internationally exposed and dependent economies have neither the power to export adjustment costs nor to achieve long-term sectoral planning. They are just too dependent on world markets and, consequently, too vulnerable to political disciplining by the large countries, as well as to global market forces. Thus, living with the costs of adjustment by somehow compensating for them is the third strategy or policy. Maybe it would be more realistic to view this option as a matter of necessity rather than of social choice. Nevertheless, despite this necessity to adapt, different forms of compensating for the costs of adjustment remain. And just as in case of protectionism of either the "liberal" or the "statist" type, compensation for externally necessitated structural adjustment can simply be a failure to adjust at all. "Compensating too little for adverse economic changes can be detrimental to the political consensus on coping with change; compensating too much can impair economic efficiency. In assessing the success or the failure of adjustment, we need to take into account both its economic and political costs and benefits" (KATZENSTEIN 1985:30).

There can certainly be no quantitative answer to this optimization problem between economic adjustment to global forces and political compensation by the national structures of the corporatist state. Even qualitative reasoning is highly speculative. But judging from Swiss experience, in comparison to let's say Austrian, Belgian or Danish experience, the following conclusions seem to be defensible.

First of all, the traditional instruments of macroeconomic policy cannot be effectively used in a small open economy. This leads to a sense of frustration and helplessness on the part of the government (MALMGREN, 1983:191). The worst outcome of this unhappy state is outright and cumulative neo-mercantilism. But the other extreme, a total liberalization of all four routes to internationalization (described in section 18.1) will most probably imply political costs which are even higher than the efficiency loss of protectionism.

In the case of Switzerland, political stability and social peace, the two crucial national competitive advantages, would be at stake. Foreign labour, structural displacement in agriculture, and the resistance to change of Swiss cartels in many branches of industry and services are highly sensitive sources of social unrest and political instability. The traditional consensus which characterizes the Swiss government is shared by all major parties, but it only works on the executive and (partially) on the legislative level. If the issues and problems discussed above get out of hand, the electorate will resort to radical solutions at the polls: not in elections but in referenda covering single topics, such as foreign workers, agricultural support, competition in retail trade, etc.

Between these extremes of outright resistance to structural change (as practiced for some time by Austria) or total and unconditional capitalism (such as practiced in Hong Kong) there remains a wide middle-ground for flexible responses. Some sectors and groups will always have to be protected. What has to be avoided, however, is the self-induced spread of this protection to other sectors, industries, interest groups, and so on. The best weapon to fight this war of the "protected reservations" against the welfare of the nation as a whole is the lobby of consumers and importers, a lobby which, however, is often weaker than its opponents.

The weak members of society and those who suffer from structural change need protection and compensation. Again, this is a question of degree – and of targeting social policies. The more a society is politically united and socially integrated, the more social policies can be restricted to reducing the risks of individuals and to targeting transfers to specific groups. Switzerland has gone a long way in this direction; its welfare systems look impressive in quantitative terms. With regard to economic incentives and structural flexibility this rather classical policy of redistribution at the level of personal income and wealth has not yet proved too dangerous! Compare the Swiss situation to the strategies of other countries which focus on avoiding unemployment by granting extensive rights to work (to existing workers) or by imposing barriers to exit of all sorts. These protective and compensatory actions may not cause budgetary outlays for the government but they demand a high price in terms of economic efficiency.

18.3 Foreign Trade Policy and New Forms of Internationalization

Small open economies with highly internationalized firms view the demand side of their markets as part of the exogenous environment and not as a task of national economic policy. Demand management by way of international policy coordination is, of course, of decisive importance – but out of reach of both the policy-maker in the (small) home country and the entrepreneurial strategist. Neither business leaders nor political elites develop a demand for a national macro perspective with regard to economic policies. What dominates political as well as entrepreneurial thinking is microeconomic integration into the international division of labour. Naturally, there are some minimal requirements for national macro policies, especially with regard to a stable and steady monetary policy. On the supply side, policy issues include incentives with respect to taxes, regulations, etc.

But the focus of economic policy is always international. This implies that the question of international competitiveness is primarily one of adjustment, adaptation, innovation, and specialization of business enterprises. The replacement of a narrow trade perspective by the "internationalization paradigm" allows us to view this structural adjustment in all dimensions of international transactions: trade, factor income, FDI, technology transfer, countertrade, etc. National strategies to improve international competitiveness must therefore focus on all possible comparative (national) advantages and all absolute (entrepreneurial) advantages resulting from all possible types of international operations.

But this goal can and usually will clash with internal, national policies of guaranteeing welfare standards, of insuring all sorts of risks (including the risks of world-wide and/or technological changes), of redistributing income vertically and regionally, of protecting locational and/or size structures of certain industries, etc. (cf. Hesse et al. 1985: 137–139).

The main conclusions to be drawn is that, once more, it is analytically impossible to distinguish between economic and political aspects of adjustment. They are logically interdependent. The more that economic forces, working through global markets, disrupt political structures, the more these forces will mobilize counterforces working through political interest groups. And these in turn will, as OLSON (1982) has so convincingly argued, finally lead - via bureaucratization and interest-group haggling - to social sclerosis. Thus, any rational discussion of costs and benefits of adjustment policies must necessarily encompass the interdependencies between economic and political criteria of success and failure. Despite these limitations, the economic cost of government interventions intended to defend or even to extend the reach of national policies is associated with two different kinds of economic costs. The first kind obviously refers to the direct costs associated with "closing" the economy. The second type results from indirect effects. Not only is international instability increased by uncoordinated national policies (cf. Chapter 16), adjustment problems will also be shifted from one group to another within an individual country. International trade and global allocation are, therefore, two quite different things (cf. HESSE et al. 1985: 141-142).

If access to world markets is sought by a greater and greater variety of strategies, designed and chosen by internationalized firms, and if this access is increasingly regarded as a privilege to be granted (or not) according to national(istic) preferences, then rules of trade alone will no longer suffice. Trade rules will not do justice either to the complex nature of international interdependence or to the interdependence among national policies - regional policy, social policy, educational policy, R&D policy, industrial policy, etc. Again, we are confronted with the problem of international policy coordination either in the form of global rules about fair and unfair practices in all these fields or in the form of functional (rather than territorial) authorities which would take over clearly defined (functional) sovereignty rights (cf. HESSE et al. 1985: 141). As we have argued before, neither is likely to happen. Since all these dimensions of economic policy are relevant for establishing comparative advantage at the national level, as well as for the absolute competitive advantage of individual firms, it is difficult indeed to draw a sharp line between foreign and domestic policy or between market-conform and interventionist measures. As foreign governments set up whole arsenals to fight imports, to regulate FDI, and to profit from NFI, the home country government is bombarded with the following kinds of demands:

- The first is the demand to make competition fair, that is, to compensate the disadvantaged home country firms. This is the "equally long speer" argument, especially popular among Swiss industrial lobbies. The argument allows those asking for subsidies, or other indirect regulations which represent an implicit subsidy, not to lose their straight liberal faces. Industry would, they argue, fight it out without any government assistance, but since other national governments are helping their firms, a fair chance in international competition means government aid. The argument does not really hold water. If governments or taxpayers in other countries choose to subsidize their exports, then they pay part of the cost of our imports as well as the cost of inefficiency.
- The second demand arises from the policy distortion affecting different home country firms with different core skills, different scope, and varying international

profiles. This problem arises in the context of export risk insurance or other forms of export promotion. If these insurance schemes are subsidized by tax money or if promotion expenses one-sidely benefit classical export activities in comparison to FDI or NFI, then distortions occur. Again, it is extremely difficult to draw a dividing line between efficient compensation for exporters, who are mostly SMEs, more vulnerable to protectionism and often creating more value-added and employment than NFI operations, on the one hand, and just plain old export subsidies on the other. We could produce a lengthy list of reasons for and against any specific home country policy in favour of NFI. On analytical grounds, there is no compelling case for or against NFII or NFEF promotion policies (cf. BÜRGIN 1985).

As our empirical research has demonstrated, Switzerland is still a very good home country for firms specializing in various forms of internationalization. Orientation toward open world markets for final and intermediate goods, for the flow of capital and know-how, and for a set of general rules representing a collective good will remain the first best foreign policy option for Switzerland. Whenever and wherever these ideal conditions are violated, Swiss firms will, by themselves, try to find ways and means around the obstacles. Downhill and slalom are too different alpine sports. But gifted skiers will perform well in both of them - if we let them practice and experiment. Swiss industrial firms, be they large or small, do not expect active government assistance for restructuring. They themselves view the adjustment problem mainly as a strategic challenge at the level of the firm. The firms will be more than pleased if the features of an institutional economy can be maintained in the future: "An entrepreneurial drive in industry strengthened by bank credits at favorable terms, dealing with cooperative labor leaders, and unencumbered by government interventions" (KATZENSTEIN 1985:74).

The more traditional exports are replaced and/or complemented by all kinds of NFI, the more Gross Domestic Product and Gross National Income will diverge. More and more of the components of foreign income will no longer mirror current production but rather the income from previously transferred assets: real capital in the case of FDI, "human capital" in the case of technology and know-how sales, and "returns to scope" in the case of cooperation among independent firms.

18.4 Democratic Corporatism and Swiss Domestic Policy

According to KATZENSTEIN (1985), democratic corporatism, as a label for a small country's socio-economic order, is characterized by three main traits:

- An ideology or at least a fundamental consensus of social partnership expressed at the national level. This excludes class conflicts or other sharp divisions by including all significantly large groups of economic and political actors in the political process.
- A relatively centralized and concentrated system of organized interest groups. This ensures not only collective self-regulation but also a kind of federalism in bargaining among interest groups. Together, these two processes explain why uniform national policies are subsidiary to interest group negotiations.
- Voluntary and informal coordination of conflicting objectives through continu-

ous political bargaining between interest groups, state bureaucracies, and political parties. In the case of Switzerland the so-called "sovereign" (referendum by the people) is very important. This produces social accomodation rather than resistance to structural changes due primarly to market forces.

The upshot of this view is that socio-economic adjustment is neither headed toward conflict and final collapse in a Marxist sense nor toward revitalization of international market competition in a neo-conservative sense. The direction is toward "accomodation" by multi-dimensional compensation between winners and losers, by constant bargaining between shifting coalitions, and by various forms of cooperation among agencies from the private and public sector.

The strengths of this strategy have been acknowledged by and American student (KATZENSTEIN 1984 and 1985). It is the task of the local observer to point out weaknesses and to make a few suggestions about how to oppose the negative aspects of democratic corporatism of the Swiss type. What are these dangerous features?

The first danger is that this social contract, or the notion of fairness on which it is based, is stretched too far. This tendency is clearly visible in the case of Switzerland. Especially those efficiency improvements coming from outside (imports of cheaper labour and or commodities, etc.) meet resistance as soon as organized groups get hurt by them. Contrary to large and liberal economies, this will not lead to protectionism in the narrow sense, but it will call for compensation either by subsidies or regulations. In the end, the efficiency loss is the same or may be even greater than that resulting from outright protectionism.

The second danger is that society turns from being achievement-orientied toward being insurance-oriented. Society, in becoming a gigantic machine for redistribution and insurance, runs the risk of becoming too inflexible to absorb the variety of individuals - especially the creative individuals - which it encompasses.

Based on these general ideas, three lines of attack are recommended on the national policy level for Switzerland's small open economy.

1) Stable Conditions as the Central Country-Specific Comparative Advantage

In contrast to stereotype demands for "improving conditions for doing business" we emphasize that the stability of these conditions, or at least the ability to predict changes, may be more important. Even if particular conditions are improved, such piecemeal improvement might worsen the entire situation by increasing the frequency and the unpredictability of change. Maintaining stable conditions for doing business means that more attention must be paid to the social and political dimensions and fewer ad hoc changes must be made.

A great deal of political stability within a democratic state is a central factor for entrepreneurial success; but this is not without risk. The risks lie above all in an increasing inconsistency in regulatory measures as these become subject to manipulation by interest group egoism. In addition, political structures may be evaded altogether by splinter groups carrying out direct actions. It becomes dangerous if more and more interest group coalitions receive special privileges and are granted advantages to the detriment of the general welfare.

2) Support for New Business and Innovation

Experience indicates that the establishment of new firms by governments shows minimal chances for success. This does not mean that economic and social policy is insignificant for influencing the quantity and quality of new industries. Progressive patent laws, generous amortization regulations, profit and loss considerations in taw law, and high levels of general education and research have always played an important role. Finding sources for financing in a land as rich in capital and with such low interest rates as is the case in Switzerland should not be a problem. The biggest danger here lies in the restructuring of savings activity to favour the collective task of financing pension funds and caring for the aged, thereby promoting security-oriented investment regulations. In addition, the one-sided concentration of wealth among older people and the high level of profits earned through real estate speculation during the growth era of the 1960s and 1970s led to very conservative and non-innovative financial practices. Has the system of education not also kept many creative young people with unconventional ideas and strong interests in alternative life styles from participating in the high technology branches of the Swiss economy?

In the future we will have to rediscover the economy as an ideal "playground" for autonomous structuring of our private lives. The revitalization of flea markets, street music, and abandoned alpine farms by members of the younger generation is a positive entrepreneurial response but not in regard to increasing the international competitiveness of the Swiss productive apparatus.

3) The Revitalization of Older Firms and Mature Industries

Vitality and old age are not just problems for individuals. Analagous to the shrinking forces of achievement and regeneration which go hand in hand with the increased age of individuals, an aging process also goes on in industries. Here the problem is a continued narrowing of the production function and processing techniques. The world record for the marathon according to age category begins to decrease after age 30. This is our biological fate. But at the same time the differences between the physically fit and the flabby become greater and greater as people get older. In contrast to people, enterprises are not subject to biological laws. The best conditions to keep fit are open markets and the fresh air of competition. Entrepreneurial revitalization is primarly carried out by eliminating the hurdles to innovation - not necessarily in the form of an active government innovation policy which implies burdens for successful companies, which creates new market distortions, and which reduces competition. The regulation of single elements of the competitive environment - via subsidies, import protection, or cartelization - bring about a drop in the general level of conditions favorable to business. It is bad enough that our agricultural policy finds itself in such a situation. A similar policy for Swiss industry would certainly cripple our economy.

The most important conclusion which can be drawn from our research is the recognition that a highly internationalized country like Switzerland is not heading for collapse as a result of insoluable socio-economic conflicts. At the same time, however, Switzerland is not headed toward a renaissance of free competition on open world markets.

The direction which we anticipate is a modified continuation of the strategy of the past: an intensification of internationalization through innovative economic behaviour coupled with a policy of compensating those who lose from structural change. Such a policy can only be carried out in a political climate of consensus and cooperation.

References

ABERNATHY WJ, CLARK KB, KANTROW M
Industrial Renaissance. Producing a Competitive Future for America. Basic Books Publishers, New York 1983

ACECO (Association pour la Compensation des Echanges Commerciaux)
Le Guide pratique de la Compensation. Paris 1983

AGMON T, KINDLEBERGER ChP (eds)
Multinationals from Small Countries. MIT Press, Cambridge (Mass.) 1977

AKERLOF GA
The Market for Lemmons: Quality, Uncertainty and the Market Mecanism. Quartely Journal of Economics, August 1970

ALIBER RZ
Money, Multinationals, and Sovereigns. In: Kindleberger/Audretsch, 1983

ALTMANN F, CLEMENT H
Die Kompensation im Ost-West-Handel. Gutachten im Auftrag des Bundesministers für Wirtschaft. München 1979

AMIN S, ARRIGHI G, FRANK AG, WALLERSTEIN I (eds)
Dynamics of Global Crisis. MacMillan, London 1982

ARNDT H
Markt und Macht. J.C.B. Mohr, Tübingen 1973

ARRIGHI G
A Crisis of Hegemony. In: Amin et al. (eds.), 1982

AYRES RU
The Next Industrial Revolution. Reviving Industry through Innovation. Ballinger Publishing Company, Cambridge (Mass.) 1984

BANKS G
The Economics of Countertrade. The World Economy, June 1983

BANKS G
Constrained Markets, 'Surplus' Commodities and International Barter. Kyklos, 2/1985

BAUMOL W, PANZAR J, WILLIG R
Contestable Markets and the Theory of Industry Structure. Harcourt Brace Janovich, New York 1982

BELTRAMO MN
The Future of Military Offsets. Countertrade and Barter Quarterly, May/June 1985

BERGER M, UHLMANN L
Kleine und mittlere Unternehmen und Auslandsinvestitionen. ifo-Institut, München, December 1983

BHAGWATI J (ed)
The New International Economic Order. MIT Press, Cambridge (Mass.) 1977

BHAGWATI J
Toward a Policy Synthesis: Panel Discussion. In: Cline (ed.), 1983

BHAGWATI J
Weltwirtschaftliche Spannungsfelder der 90er Jahre - Impulse für eine neue Zusammenarbeit. In: Borner (ed.), 1981

BLUM G
Die Finanzierung von Schwellenländergeschäften unter erschwerten Bedingungen. Vortrag, gehalten an der HSG-Weiterbildungsstufe, 3.11. 1983

BORNER S
Die Internationalisierung der Industrie. Kyklos 1/1981

BORNER S (ed)
Sachzwänge und Gestaltungsräume des Unternehmens von morgen. Verlag Birkhäuser, Basel 1981

BORNER S
Die Wettbewerbsfähigkeit im internationalen Markt: Theoretische Verknüpfung von Weltwirtschafts- und Unternehmungsebene. Diskussionspapier der beiden Basler sozialwissenschaftlichen Institute. Basel 87/1983

BORNER S
Drei Grundperspektiven zur Interpretation des weltwirtschaftlichen Strukturwandels. Außenwirtschaft, III/1984a

BORNER S
Internationale Wettbewerbsfähigkeit - Fragmente zu einer Theorie internationaler Unternehmenstätigkeit. Weltwirtschaftliches Archiv 3/1984b

BORNER S, SIMMA B
Unternehmungsführung im Strukturwandel. In: Die Orientierung (ed. Schweizerische Volksbank), 82/1984

BORNER S, WEHRLE F
Die Sechste Schweiz. Überleben auf dem Weltmarkt. Orell Füssli Verlag, Zürich, 1984a

BORNER S, WEHRLE F
Weltwirtschaftlicher Strukturwandel und internationale Wettbewerbsfähigkeit von Industrieunternehmen. Hamburger Jahrbuch für Wirtschafts- und Gesellschaftspolitik 1984b

BORNER S
Protectionism in the Developing Countries: A Need for Reestablished Rules. In: EFTA, 1985

BORNER S
Wettbewerbsfähigkeit in der internationalen Industrie. In: Zielsetzung Partner, Dokumente zum Malenter Symposium 1984, Verlag Bonn Aktuell, Stuttgart 1985

BORNER S, BURGENER, B, STUCKEY B, WEHRLE F
Global Structural Change and International Competition Among Industrial Firms: The Case of Switzerland. Kyklos 1/1985

BORNSCHIER V
Wachstum, Konzentration und Multinationalisierung von Industrieunternehmen. Huber, Frauenfeld 1976

BOWEN D
Private Insurers Chivvy the National Agencies. Euromoney, May 1984

BRADA JC
Markets, Property Rights, and the Economics of Joint Ventures in Socialist Countries. Journal of Comparative Economics 1/1977

BRADA JC
Technology Transfer by Means of Industrial Cooperation: A Theoretical Appraisal. In: Marer/Tabaczynski (eds), 1981

BUCKLEY PJ, CASSON M
The Future of the Multinational Enterprise. MacMillan, London 1976

BUCKLEY PJ, DAVIES H
The Place of Licensing in the Theory and Practice of Foreign Operations. University of Reading Discussion Paper, 47/1979

BUCKLEY PJ
A Critical Review of Theories of the Multinational Enterprise. Außenwirtschaft, 36/1981

BUCKLEY PJ
New Forms of International Industrial Cooperation: A Survey of the Literature with Special Reference to North-South Technology Transfer. Außenwirtschaft, II/1983 a

BUCKLEY PJ
Macroeconomic Versus International Business Approach to Direct Foreign Investment: A Comment on Professor Kojima's Interpretation. Hitotsubashi Journal of Economics, 24/1983 b

BUITER WH, MARSTON RC (eds)
International Economic Policy Coordination. Cambridge University Press, Cambridge 1985

BÜRGIN R
Multifunktionaler Countertrade als Internationalisierungsinstrument der Schweizer Industrie: Ausprägungen, Determinanten, Bedeutung und außenpolitische Beurteilung. Diss., Basel 1986

BURGENER B
Zur Wettbewerbsfähigkeit schweizerischer Unternehmungen: Bedrohungslage und Handlungsspielraum. Diskussionspapier der beiden Basler sozialwissenschaftlichen Institute, Basel 88/1983 a

BURGENER B
Strukturwandel und Unternehmungsstrategien: Fallstudien kleiner und mittlerer Unternehmungen. Diskussionspapier der beiden Basler sozialwissenschaftlichen Institute, Basel 89/1983 b

Business International
Current Countertrade Policies and Practicies in East-West Trade. A Group Research Study, Geneva 1976

Business International
Countertrade with Developing Countries. Geneva 1983

Business International
Doing Business with Eastern Europe. (Part VI: Countertrade and Buy-Back-Transactions), Geneva 1984 a

Business International
Exploring Countertrade Opportunities in Africa, Geneva 1984b

Business International
Threats and Opportunities of Global Countertrade. Marketing, Financing and Organizational Implications. BIC, New York 1984c

Business Research International
Effective Countertrade Strategies. London 1984

CANTWELL JA
The Relevance of the Classical Economists to the Theory of International Production. University of Reading Discussion Paper, 79/1984

CANTWELL JA, DUNNING JH
The "New Forms" of International Involvement - British Firms in the Third World (mimeo). OECD Development Center, Paris, June 1984

CARLSON S
How Foreign Is Foreign Trade. Acta Universitatis Upsaliensis, Uppsala 1975

CASSON M
Alternatives to the Multinational Enteprise. MacMillan, London 1979

CASSON M
Foreward. In: Rugman, 1981

CASSON M
The Entrepreneur. Robertson, Oxford 1982a

CASSON M
Transaction Cost and the Theory of the Multinational Enterprise. In: Rugman (ed.), 1982 (Casson 1982b)

CASSON M (ed)
The Growth of International Business. Allen & Unwin, London 1983

CASSON M
Foreign Divestment and International Rationalisation in the Motor Industry: The Sale of Chrysler (UK) to Peugeot. University of Reading Discussion Paper, 86/1985

CAVES E
International Corporations: The Industrial Economics of Foreign Investment. Economica, 38/1971

CAVES RE
The Economics of Reciprocity: Theory and Evidence on Bilateral Trading Arrangements. In: Sellekaerts (ed), 1975

CAVES RE
Multinational Enterprise and Economic Analysis. Cambridge University Press, Cambridge 1982

CHANDLER AD, DAEMS H (eds)
Managerial Hierarchies, Comparative Perspectives on the Rise of the Modern Industrial Enterprise. Harvard University Press, Cambridge (Mass.) 1980

CHEATLE J
Why the banks have to barter. Euromoney, Trade Finance Report, May 1983

CLIFTON J G
Competition and the Evolution of the Capitalist Mode of Production. Cambridge Journal of Economics, 1/1977

CLINE W R (ed)
Trade Policy in the 1980s. Institut for International Economics, Washington D. C. 1983

CLINE W R
International Debt: Systemic Risk and Policy Response. MIT Press, Cambridge 1984

CLINE W R
International Debt: From Crisis to Recovery? The American Economic Review, May 1985

COASE R H
The Nature of the Firm. Economia IV/1937

CODDINGTON A
Re-Thinking Economic Policy. Political Quartely, 4/1974

COLLINS St H
Green Light for US Banks to Barter? Euromoney, November 1981

COOPER R N
Panel Discussion: The Prospects for International Economic Policy Coordination. In: Buiter/Marston (eds) 1985

COTTIS P
Legal Aspects of Countertrade. Business Research International, 1984

CURZON G, CURZON PRICE V
Negotiations Between Developed and Developing Countries on Trade Restrictions. Conference: Participation of Developing Countries in the International Trading System. Wiston House, October 1984

COUGHLIN C C
The Relationship Between Foreign Ownership and Technology Transfer. Journal of Comparative Economics, 7/1983

DE MIRAMON J
Countertrade: A Modernized Barter System. In: OECD Observer 114/1982

DE MIRAMON J
Countertrade: An Illusory Solution. OECD Observer, 134/1985

DIAZ-ALEJANDRO C F, HELLEINER G K
Handmaiden in Distress: World Trade in the 1980s. The North-South Institute, Washington/London 1982

DIZARD J W
The Explosion of International Barter. Fortune, 7.2. 1983

DORNBUSCH R
On the Consequences of Muddling Through the Debt Crisis. The World Economy 2/1984

DORNBUSCH R, FISCHER S
The World Debt Problem. Report to the Group of Twenty-Four. Studies of International Monetary and Financial Issues for the Developing Countries, UNCTAD 1984

DUNNING J H
Trade, Location of Economic Activity and the MNE: A Search for an Eclectic Approach. In: Ohlin et al. (eds), 1977

DUNNING J H
International Production and the Multinational Enterprise. Allan and Unwin, London 1981

DUNNING J H
International Business in a Changing World Environment. Banca Nazionale del Lavoro Quarterly, 143/1982a

DUNNING J H
Non-Equity Forms of Foreign Economic Involvement and the Theory of International Production. University of Reading Discussion Paper, 59/1982b

DUNNING JH, CANTWELL J A
Joint Ventures and non-equity Foreign Invovement by British Firms with Particular Reference to Developing Countries: An Exploratory Study. University of Reading Discussion Paper, 68/1982

DUNNING J H, MC QUEEN
The Eclectic Theory of the Multinational Enterprise and the International Hotel Industry. In: Rugman (ed), 1982

DUNNING J H, RUGMAN A M
The Influence of Hymer's Dissertation on the Theory of Foreign Direct Investment. The American Economic Review, May 1985

Economic Commission for Europe
Countertrade Pratices in the ECE Region. Trade/R.385, Geneva 9.11. 1979

Economic Commission for Europe
Reciprocal Trading Arrangements at the Western Enterprise Level with Special Reference for East-West-Trade. United Nations Trade AC. 18/R.2, Geneva 9.9. 1981

Economic Commission for Europe
Compensation Trade in the ECE Region: A Survey of Quantitative Estimates. Trade/AC, 19/R.1, Geneva 1983

EFTA (European Free Trade Association)
Protection and Growth. Geneva 1985

EHRENFELD H
Außenhandel, Direktinvestitionen und Lizenzen. Peter Lang, Frankfurt 1985

EMMENEGGER A
Patente und Technologietransfer nach Entwicklungsländern. Diss. Basel 1978

ENGELHARDT W, SCHUSTER F
Kompensationsgeschäfte - Erscheinungsformen und Marketing-Probleme. Zeitschrift für Betriebswirtschaft, 32/1980

FISHER S, HARTE K M (eds)
Barter in the World Economy. Praeger, New York 1985

FONTAINE M
Aspects juridiques des contracts de compensation. In: 'Aspects juridiques des contracts de compensation' der 'Fondation pour l'etude du droit et des usages du commerce international', Paris 1982

FREY B S
Die Politische Ökonomie des Protektionismus. Außenwirtschaft 39/1984a

FREY B S
The public choice view to international political economy. International Organization, Winter 1984b

GADBAW R M
The Implications of Countertrade under the General Agreement on Tariffs and Trade. Journal of Comparative Business and Capital Market Law, 5/1983

GATT (General Agreement on Trade and Tariffs)
International Trade. Geneva, various volumes

GERMIDIS D (ed)
International Subcontracting - A New Form of Investment. OECD, Development Center Studies, Paris 1980

GERSTER R
Patentierte Profite. Z-Verlag, Basel 1980

GIDDY I H, YOUNG S
Conventional Theory and Unconventional Multinationals: Do New Forms of Multinational Enterprise Require New Theories? In: Rugman (ed.), 1982

GLOVER D J
Contract Farming and the Transnationals. University Microfilms, Ann Arbor (Michigan) 1983

GOLDSCHEIDER R
1982 Technology Management Handbook, Clark Boardman, New York 1982

GORDON R J, PELKMANS J
Challenges to Interdependent Economies. The Industrial West in the Coming Decade. Council of Foreign Relations, New York 1979

GMÜR Ch
Barter, Compensation and Cooperation. Exportfinancing Part IV, SKA-Schriftenreihe 47/1980

HAGER W
Protectionism and Autonomy. How to Preserve Free Trade in Europe. International Affairs, Summer 1982

HÄMISSEGGER K
Neue Formen des Auslandengagements - Erhöhte Interdependenz in einer fragmentierten Weltwirtschaft. Diss., Basel 1986

HARRIS N
Of Bread and Guns. Penguin Books, Harmondsworth 1983

HARVEY Ch
On reducing the risks in finance - for both parties. IDS-Discussion Paper, 167/1981

HAUSER H
Joint Ventures: Sonderlösungen für Einzelfälle oder allgemein verwendbare Instrumente der internationalen Kooperation? Außenwirtschaft, 2/1981

HELLEINER G K
International Economic Disorder. Essays in North-South-Relations. MacMillan, London 1980

HERRIG RJ (ed)
Managing International Risk. Cambridge University Press, London 1983

HESSE H, KEPPLER H, PREUSSE HG
Internationale Interdependenzen im weltwirtschaftlichen Entwicklungsprozeß. Verlag Otto Schwartz, Göttingen 1985

HIRSCHMAN AO
The Political Economy of Import-Substituting. Industrialization in Latin America. Quarterly Journal of Economics 1/1968

HUG P
Was sind Lizenzverträge? In: ZfU, 1983

HUGHES H
The Risks of Lending to Developing Countries. In: Herring (ed), 1983

HUNZIKER E
Auslandsmarktstrategien. Verlag Industrielle Organisation, Zürich 1983

HYMER SH
Die Internationalisierung des Kapitals. In: Kreye (ed), 1974

HYMER SH
The International Operations of National Firms: A Study of Direct Foreign Investment. MIT Press, Cambridge (1960) 1976

JACKSON JH
World Trade and the Law of GATT. New York 1969

JONES S
North/South Countertrade: Barter and Reciprocal Trade with Developing Countries. The Economist Intelligence Limited, London 1984

JUCKER E
Patents and Pharmaceuticals. Selbstverlag, Basel 1980

KAIKATI JG
The Reincarnation of Barter Trade as a Marketing Tool. Journal of Marketing, 40/1976

KAIKATI JG
The International Barter Boom: Perspectives and Challenges. International Marketing, 1/1981

KATZENSTEIN PJ
Corporatism and Change. Austria, Switzerland, and the Politics of Industry. Cornell University Press, London 1984

KATZENSTEIN PJ
Small States in World Markets. Industrial Policy in Europe. Cornell University Press, London 1985

KAY NM
Multinational Enterprise: A Review Article. Scottish Journal of Political Economy, 3/1983

KINDLEBERGER CP
Government and International Trade. Princeton University Essays in International Finance, 129/1978

KINDLEBERGER Ch P
Debt Situation of the Developing Countries in Historical Perspective (1800-1945). Außenwirtschaft IV/1981

KINDLEBERGER Ch P, AUDRETSCH D B (eds)
The Multinational Corporation in the 1980s. MIT Press, Cambridge (Mass.), 1983

KINDLEBERGER Ch P
Multinational Excursions. MIT Press, Cambridge (Mass.) 1984

KNESCHAUREK F, MEIER P
Der sektorale Strukturwandel in der Schweiz von 1960 bis 1980. Verlag Ruegger, Diessenhofen 1983

KOJIMA K
Direct Foreign Investment. Croom Helm, London 1978

KOJIMA K, OZAWA T
Micro- and Macro-Economic Models of Direct Foreign Investment: Toward a Synthesis. Hitotsubashi Journal of Economics 25/1984

KRÄGENAU H
Internationale Direktinvestitionen 1950-1973. Weltarchiv, Hamburg 1975

KREYE O (ed)
Multinationale Konzerne. Entwicklungstendenzen im kapitalistischen System. Carl Hauser, Munich 1974

KRUEGER A O
Protectionism and Growth. In: EFTA, 1985

KUHN T S
The Structure of Scientific Revolutions. The University of Chicago Press, Chicago 1962

KYUNG M H
Warentauschgeschäfte: Handel ohne Geld? Finanzierung & Entwicklung 12/1983

LAWRENCE R Z
Can America Compete? The Brookings Institution, Washington 1984

LES (Licensing Executives Society)

Licensing and Marketing. Konferenzunterlagen, Brüssel 1984

LEVER H
Begin Now to Write Down World Debt. Wall Street Journal, 7.6. 1984

LINDBECK A
Industrial Policy as an Issue in the Economic Environment. The World Economy 4/1981

LIST F
Der internationale Handel, die Handelspolitik und der Deutsche Zollverein. Stuttgart 1841

LIST F
Das internationale System der politischen Ökonomie. Kyklos-Verlag, Basel 1959

MACAULAY S
Non-Contractual Relations in Business. American Sociological Review, 1/1963

MADDISON A
Phases of Capitalist Development. Oxford University Press, Oxford/New York 1982

MAGEE S P
Information and the Multinational Corporation: An Appropriability Theory of Foreign Direct Investment. In: Bhagwati (ed), 1977

MALMGREN H B
Threats to the Multinational System. In: Cline (ed), 1983

MARER P
Import Protectionism in the US and Poland's Manufacturers Exports. In: Marer/Tabaczynski (eds), 1981

MARER P, TABACZYNSKI E (eds)
Polish-US Industrial Cooperation in the 1980s. Indiana University Press, Bloomington 1981

MARRIS S
Managing the World Economy: Will We Ever Learn? Princeton Essays in International Finance, 155/1984

McVEY T
Countertrade and Barter. Alternative Trade Financing by Third World Nations. International Trade Law Journal, 6/1980/81

McVEY T
Policy Issues in Countertrade. In: Fisher/Harte (eds), 1985

MEADE J E
Trade and Welfare: A Numerical and Geometrical Representation of Some Barter Deals. Oxford University Press, London 1955

MOMIGLIANO F, BALCET G
New Trends in Internationalization: Processes and Theories. Diversified Patterns of Multinational Enterprise and Old and New Forms of Foreign Involvement of the Firm. Economic Notes 3/1983

MOUNTAIN G
What Comfort for Countertraders? The private underwriting market will insure some of the risks of countertrade - even though national agencies will not touch them. Euromoney, November 1984

MURRELL P
Product Quality, Market Signaling and the Development of East-West-Trade. Economic Inquiry, XX/1982

NELSON P
Advertising as Information. Journal of Political Economy, July 1974

NIEHANS J
Benefits of Multinational Firms for a Small Parent Economy: The Case of Switzerland. In: Agmon/Kindleberger (eds) 1977

NIEHANS J
Theorie des Geldes: Synthese der monetären Mikro- und Makroökonomik. Haupt, Bern/Stuttgart 1980

OECD
East-West-Trade. Recent Developments in Countertrade, Paris 1981

OECD
Positive Adjustment Policies. Managing Structural Change. Paris 1983

OHLIN B, HESSELBORN P-O, WIJKMAN P-M (eds)
The International Allocation of Economic Activity. Holmes & Meier, New York 1977

OKUN AM
Prices and Quantities. A Macroeconomic Analysis. The Brookings Institution, Washington 1981

OLSON M Jr
The Rise and Decide of Nation. Yale University Press, Yale 1982

OMAN Ch
New Forms of International Investment in Developing Countries. OECD, Development Center Studies, Paris 1984

OUTTERS-JAEGER I
The Development Impact of Barter in Developing Countries. OECD, Paris 1979

OZAWA T
Multinationalism, Japanese Style. The Political Economy of Outward Dependency. Princeton University Press, Princeton (New Jersey) 1979

OZAWA T
On New Trends in Internationalization. A Synthesis Toward a General Model. Economic Notes, 1/1985

PELKMANS J
Economic Cooperation among Western Countries. In: Gordon/Pelkmans (eds), 1979

PETERS TJ, WATERMAN RH
In Search of Excellence. Harper and Row, New York 1981

POLEY WL
Know-how Vergabe: Gewußt wie. Absatzwirtschaft 12/1978

POLLAK C
Neue Formen internationaler Unternehmenszusammenarbeit ohne Kapitalbeteiligung. Weltforum Verlag, München 1982

POLLAK RA
A Transaction Cost Approach to Families and Households. Journal of Economic Literature, June 1985

PORTER ME
Competitive Strategy: Techniques for Analyzing Industries and Competitors. The Free Press, New York 1980

PORTER ME
Competitive Advantage: Creating and Sustaining Superior Performance. The Free Press, New York 1985

PÖTZ T
Bilaterismus. In: Handwörterbuch der Sozialwissenschaften, Gustav Fischer Verlag, Stuttgart 1959

PÜMPIN C
Redimensionen oder neuer Pioniergeist? Wirtschaftspolitische Mitteilungen 5/1985

RAMANADHAM VV (ed)
Joint Ventures and Public Enterprises in Developing Countries. ICPE, Ljublijana 1980

RICHARDSON GB
The Organisation of Industry. Economic Journal, September 1972

ROBINSON J
Preface. In: Eichner A. S., A Guide to Post-Keynesian Economics. MacMillan, London 1979

ROBINSON R D
Major Issues in Joint Ventures Between Developed and Developing Countries. In: Ramanadham (ed), 1980

ROBINSON R D
Background Concepts and Philosophy of International Business. From World War II to the Present. Journal of International Business Studies, Spring/Summer 1981

ROHL C
Technologietransfer durch Industrielizenzen. E. Schmidt Verlag, Berlin 1980

RUGMAN A M
Internalization as a General Theory of Foreign Direct Investment: A Reappraisal of the Literature. Weltwirtschaftliches Archiv, 116/1980

RUGMAN A M
Inside the Multinations: The Economics of Internal Markets. Columbia University Press, New York 1981

RUGMAN A M (ed)
New Theories of the Multinational Enterprise. Croom Helm, London 1982

SACHS J
LDC Debt in the 1980s. Risk and Reform. NBER Working Papers, Cambridge (Mass.) 896/1982

SCHÄRER K
Die bilateralen Investitionsschutz-Abkommen der Schweiz. Der Schweizer Treuhänder, 8/1979

SCHAFFNER H
Die Wettbewerbsfähigkeit der schweizerischen Textilindustrie. Rüegger, Diessenhofen 1982

SCHAUB R P
Der Engineeringvertrag. Schulthess, Zürich 1979

SHARPSTON M
International Sub-Contracting. Oxford Economic Papers, March 1975

SCHLEMPER A
Die Bedeutung des Warenverkehrs mit der DDR für Klein- und Mittelbetriebe. East-West Cooperation, Essen, 6. 12. 1978

SCHLEMPER A
Gegengeschäfte: Wiedergeburt eines Absatzinstrumentes oder Rückfall in veraltete Handelsformen? Eine theoretische Analyse unter besonderer Berücksichtigung kleiner und mittlerer Unternehmen. In: Festschrift für Matthias E. Kampf. Perspektiven der Mittelstandspolitik und Mittelstandsforschung. Göttingen 1979

SCHMOLL G A, GOLDBERGER E
Schweizer Exporthandbuch. Kooperationsgemeinschaft SWISSEXPORT, Geneva 1983

SCHNEIDER F, FREY B S
Economic and Political Determinants of Foreign Direct Investment. World Development, 13/1985

SCHUMPETER J A
Capitalism, Socialism, and Democracy. (3rd. edition) Harper and Row, New York 1962

SCHUSTER F
Barter Arrangements with Money: The Modern Form of Compensation Trading. Columbia Journal of World Business, 1980

SCHWENK M H
North-South Barter Trade. In: Fisher/Harte (eds) 1985

SELLEKAERTS W (ed)
Essays in Honour of Jan Tinbergen. MacMillan, London 1975

SENGHAAS D
Abkopplung als entwicklungspolitische Devise. In: Entwicklungspolitik im Umbruch. NZZ Schriften zur Zeit Nr. 41, Buchverlag NZZ, Zürich 1979

SHARPSTON M
International Sub-Contracting. Oxford Economic Papers, März 1975

SIMONSEN M
The Developing Country Debt Problem. Unpublished manuscript, Fundacao Getulio Vargas, 1984

SOLOW R M
Economic History and Economics. The American Economic Review, May 1985

SOMBART W
Der moderne Kapitalismus. Duncker & Humblot, München and Leipzig (1919) 1927

SPENCE A M
Market Signaling: Informational Transfer in Hiring and Related Screening Prozess. Harvard University, Cambridge 1974

STANFIELD J R
Social Reform and Economic Policy. Journal of Economic Issues, 1/1984

STRANGE S
Interpretations of a Decade. In: Tsoukalis (ed), 1985

STRAUSS M J
Barter Accounts for about 8% of World Trade, GATT Says. Wall Street Journal, 17.4. 1984 and 19.4. 1984

SULZER P G
Marketing: ein Schlagwort von heute? Sulzer Horizonte, 7/8/1984

TEECE D J
Technology Transfer by Multinational Firms: The Resource Cost of Transferring Technological Know-How. The Economic Journal, June 1977

TEECE D J
Economies of Scope and the Scope of the Enterprise. Journal of Economic Behavior and Organization, 1/1980

TEECE D J
The Multinational Enterprise: Market Failure and Market Power Considerations. Sloan Management Review, September 1981

TEECE D J
A Transaction Cost Theory of the Multinational Enterprise. University of Reading Discussion Paper, 66/1982

TEECE DJ
Technological and Organizational Factors in the Theory of Multinational Enterprise. In: Casson (ed), 1983

TEECE DJ
Multinational Enterprise, Internal Governance, and Industrial Organization. American Economic Review, May 1985

TERPSTRA V
International Marketing. Dryden Press, Chicago 1983

TROLLER A
Der rechtliche Schutz des Know-how. Referat: Informationstagung Know-how-Vertrag, Geneva 1981

TRUMPY T
Contractual Arrangements in International Joint Ventures. Conference: International Center of New England, Boston 1984a

TRUMPY T
Non-Licensing Technology Transfers. Conference: Licensing Executives Society, Brussels 1984b

TSOUKALIS L (ed)
The Political Economy of International Money. In Search of a New Order. Sage Publications, London 1985

UNCTC (United Nations Centre on Transnational Corporations)
Transnational Corporations in World Development (Third Survey). United Nations, New York 1983

UNECE (United Nations Economic Commission for Europe)
Industrial Cooperation. Geneva 1982

UNIDO (United Nations Industrial Development Organization)
Sub-Contracting for Modernizing Economies. United Nations, New York 1975

United States International Trade Commission
Analysis of Recent Trends in U.S. Countertrade. Report on Investigation. No 382-125, U.S.I.T. Publication 1237, Washington, March 1982

VACCA S, RULLANI E
Oltre il modello classico di impresa multinazionale: nuovi ruoli e nuovi compartamenti nel processo di internazionalizzazione delle imprese. Finanza, Marketing, Produzione 1/2/3:1983

VAUPEL JW, CURHAN JP
The World's Multinational Enterprises. Geneva 1974

VERNON R
International Investment and International Trade in the Product Cycle. Quarterly Journal of Economics, May 1966

VERNON R
Sovereignty at Bay: The Multinational Spread of U.S. Enterprises. Basic Books, New York 1971

VERNON R
Storm over the Multinationals: The Real Issue. Harvard University Press, Cambridge (MA.) 1977

VERNON R
Organizational and Institutional Responses to International Risk. In: Herring (ed), 1983

WALMSLEY J
Handbook of International Joint Ventures. Graham & Trotman, London 1982

WEHRLE F
Veränderung der weltwirtschaftlichen Rahmenbedingungen und die Internationalisierung der Schweizer Industrie. Diskussionspapier der beiden Basler sozialwissenschaftlichen Institute, Basel 84/1983 a

WEHRLE F
Der exportorientierte Industrialisierungsprozeß in den Schwellenländern Asiens und Lateinamerikas und Japans Aufstieg zur Wirtschaftsgroßmacht - Betrachtungen aus einer schweizerischen Perspektive. Diskussionspapier der beiden Basler sozialwissenschaftlichen Institute, Basel 85/1983 b

WEHRLE F
Perspektiven der Entfaltung und Erlahmung der wirtschaftlichen Dynamik in den neuen und alten Industrieländern auf dem Hintergrund machtpolitischer Verschiebungen. Diskussionspapier der beiden Basler sozialwissenschaftlichen Institute, Basel 86/1983 c

WEHRLE F
Die Sechste Schweiz. Bestandsaufnahme und Analyse der Dritt-Welt-Aktivitäten der Schweizer Industriemultis. In: Jahrbuch Schweiz-Dritte Welt, Institut universitaire d'etudes du developpement, Geneva 1984

WEIGAND R
Barters and Buy-Backs: Let Western Firms Beware! Business Horizons, June 1980

WELLS LT
Third World Multinationals. MIT Press, Cambridge (Mass.) 1983

WELT L
Countertrade as a Tool for ETC's. In: Beyond the Debt Crisis: New Direction in World Trade, Washington D.C., 24.1. 1984

WIDMER S
Erfolg und Lizenzen. Verlag Industrielle Kooperation, Zürich 1980

WILLIAMSON J
The Theorists and the Real World. In: Tsoukalis (ed), 1985

WILLIAMSON O E
Markets and Hierarchies: Analysis and Antitrust Implications: A Study of the Economies of Internal Organizations. Free Press, New York 1975

WILLIAMSON O E
Emergence of the Visible Hand: Implications for Industrial Organization. In: Chandler/Daems (eds), 1980 (Williamson 1980 a)

WILLIAMSON O E
The Organization of Work - A Comparative Institutional Assessment. Journal of Economic Behavior and Organization, 1/1980 b

WILLIAMSON O E
The Modern Corporation: Origins, Evolution, Attributes. Journal of Economic Literature, December 1981

YOFFIE D B
Power and Protectionism. Columbia U. P., New York 1983

ZfU (Zentrum für Unternehmungsführung)
Management Seminar Lizenzen. Kilchberg-Zürich 1983

ZWEIFEL P, PEDRONI G
Innovation und Imitation. Pharma Information, Basel 1985

ZYSMAN J, TYSON L (eds)
American Industry in International Competition. Cornell University Press, Ithaca/London, 1983

MIX
Papier aus verantwortungsvollen Quellen
Paper from responsible sources
FSC® C105338

If you have any concerns about our products,
you can contact us on
ProductSafety@springernature.com

In case Publisher is established outside the EU,
the EU authorized representative is:
Springer Nature Customer Service Center GmbH
Europaplatz 3, 69115 Heidelberg, Germany

Printed by Libri Plureos GmbH
in Hamburg, Germany